Schleiermacher the Theologian

SCHLEIERMACHER THE THEOLOGIAN

The Construction of the Doctrine of God

ROBERT R. WILLIAMS

FORTRESS PRESS   PHILADELPHIA

Library of Congress Cataloging in Publication Data

Williams, Robert R.
  Schleiermacher the theologian.

  Includes bibliographical references and index.
    1. God—History of doctrines.   2. Schleiermacher,
Friedrich Ernst Daniel, 1768–1834.   I. Title.
BT101.S144W54   231   77–78650
ISBN 0-8006-0513-6

6448J77   Printed in the United States of America   1-513

For Irma,
who thought it might never end

Contents

Preface

The recent reappearance in print of Schleiermacher's *The Christian Faith,* together with frequent journal articles on Schleiermacher, suggests a continuation of interest in his thought. At the same time, however, there is an absence of consensus concerning his meaning and significance. Most will agree that Schleiermacher is a seminal figure, perhaps the founder of modern theology; on the other hand he has few followers, for his theology is allegedly beset with internal flaws and failures. No doubt this odd situation is due to the fact that it has been Karl Barth who, more than anyone else, kept Schleiermacher's name before the theological public. However, Schleiermacher's visibility has been notorious, owing to Barth's making him his foil and whipping boy. Schleiermacher has thus come to epitomize virtually all that can go wrong theologically: from a theological method vitiated by Romantic subjectivism and preoccupation with private experience, to an utterly disastrous reduction of theology to anthropology.

To be sure, there have been some challenges to Barth's one-sided interpretation of Schleiermacher. Tillich complained that Barth, following Hegel and Feuerbach, had misrepresented Schleiermacher to the point of caricature. Richard Niebuhr suspects that Barth's polemics against Schleiermacher serve mainly to conceal the extent of Barth's dependence on and borrowing from Schleiermacher. However, the absence of a full-scale treatment of Schleiermacher's thought, which alone could counter the dominance of the Hegel-Feuerbach-Barth interpretation, tends to make such defenses appear halfhearted and to confirm the impression that Hegel, Barth, et al. are right after all.

A personal statement may explain the background of this study. For several years I accepted the Hegel-Barth interpretation of Schleiermacher. Then I became acquainted with the thought of Edmund Husserl, particularly his critique of psychologism, his thesis of the intentionality of consciousness, and his development of phenomenological method. I also became interested in the application of phenomenology to the study of human being, as exhibited in Husserl's *Ideen II,* and in Paul Ricoeur's massive multivolume *Philosophy of the Will.* Professor Edward Farley also convinced me of the relevance of phenomenology for theological method; his recent book, *Ecclesial Man,* demonstrates this relevance and is an outstanding contribution to phenomenological theology. I suspected that phenomenology might serve as a valuable research and interpretive tool for Schleiermacher's thought, serving to correct and restate Schleiermacher's account of religious consciousness. I proceeded to explore this suggestion in my Ph.D. thesis.

However, I was not prepared for what I subsequently discovered, namely, that Schleiermacher himself was already utilizing a kind of phenomenological method in his major work, *The Christian Faith.* The novelty of Schleiermacher's thought is that he seeks to describe God as the pregiven intentional correlate of religious consciousness. One of the basic axioms of his theology is that theological predication and language about God cannot be understood without a prior understanding of religious experience through which God is given to consciousness in an original way. Furthermore, I discovered that Schleiermacher, like Paul Ricoeur, was employing a two-step procedure of exposition, beginning first with a theological eidetics which brackets existence and focuses on the meaning, that is, the essential structures of religious consciousness. Second, Schleiermacher removes the brackets of the initial abstraction and considers the eidetic structures of theology as they are concretely modified and rendered determinate in actual religious experience.

I became convinced that this two-step procedure is so fundamental and essential to Schleiermacher's theological method and argument that the latter cannot be sufficiently understood without understanding the former. In short, if we did not have Husserlian phenomenology, we should have to invent or create something very much like it in order to appreciate and understand Schleiermacher! The recognition that Schleiermacher practices phenomenology as an initial moment in his theological method prepares the way for a fresh reading and new interpretation of Schleiermacher. There is virtually no disputed point in Schleiermacher interpretation that is not affected and illumined by this insight. Some of these disputed questions that have been confronted by this study are: (1) Schleiermacher's so-called subjectivism, (2) the relation between his philosophy and theology, namely, whether he derives his theology from a prior speculative scheme or natural theology, (3) whether his theology is dominated by classical, monopolar theism, (4) whether his doctrine of God and divine attributes forms an internally consistent whole, and (5) whether he holds a Sabellian view of trinity.

To anticipate some of the results of this study, I have been led to reject virtually all of Barth's adverse judgements on Schleiermacher. Barth's reading and interpretation of Schleiermacher is sloppy, fragmentary, and piecemeal. Barth either misses or simply ignores Schleiermacher's major methodological moves and thus fails to understand sufficiently Schleiermacher's substantive theological argument. In sum, Barth-Hegel et al. fail to come to terms with Schleiermacher, and thus fail as responsible criticism.

I should add that I am not claiming that the recognition that Schleiermacher utilizes phenomenology solves all interpretive or theological problems. If only that were so! It does however make possible a much more accurate understanding of Schleiermacher, and therefore better understanding of his theological problems. I am not claiming that Schleiermacher is beyond criticism, but only that worthwhile criticism presupposes an accurate understanding of what is being criticized. In view of the foregoing discovery, I do not believe that this minimal condition has yet been fulfilled in Schleiermacher interpretation and criticism. This study is offered in the hope that it will bring Schleiermacher's acknowledged genius more clearly into focus and allow us to address the real problems raised by his thought.

One such problem is that of the concept of God. It will be argued that Schleiermacher breaks with classical monopolar theology, and that his concept of God resembles that of Nikolaus Cusanus, namely, God is a coincidence of opposites. This concept of God is bipolar, and presents a metaphysical alternative to the traditional concept of *actus purus;* in the former, God does not cease to be God in his relation to the world. Moreover, Schleiermacher's theological argument concerning developmental or two-stage creation has significant implications for the concept of divine immutability. Specifically, Schleiermacher anticipates the brilliant essay of I.A. Dorner on divine immutability. The latter is really an extension of Schleiermacher's own argument. This contention places Schleiermacher in a favorable relation to contemporary process theology.

I should like to take this opportunity to acknowledge my gratitude to Northland College for a sabbatical leave during which substantial progress was made on the manuscript, to the National Endowment for the Humanities for fellowship support during the period of revision, and to

Hiram College for support during the stages of final editing and completion. In addition, there are several people who have contributed towards making the manuscript a better one. I have already indicated my considerable indebtedness to Edward Farley of Vanderbilt University. Claude Welch and the late Cyril C. Richardson made valuable criticisms and suggestions for chapter 6. Robert F. Brown of the University of Delaware helped me to see the independence of Schleiermacher from Schelling, and to clarify the argument of the final chapter. My colleagues Eugene H. Peters of Hiram College and John B. Bennett of Northland College have increased my appreciation of process theology. Naturally, none of these persons should be blamed for any mistakes, errors, or theological and philosophical naïveté that the manuscript may exhibit. Finally I owe a special word of thanks to Peter C. Hodgson of Vanderbilt University, without whose special efforts and encouragement this study might not have been set before the public.

Abbreviations

Cusanus, *ET*   Nikolaus Cusanus, *Of Learned Ignorance,* trans. Germain Heron, with an introduction by D.J.B. Hawkins (London: Routledge & Kegan Paul, 1954).

Dial. (J)   Friedrich Schleiermacher, *Dialektik,* ed. Ludwig Jonas (*Saemmtliche Werke* III/5 [Berlin: G. Reimer, 1835]).

Dial. (O)   Rudolf Odebrecht, *Friedrich Schleiermachers Dialektik* (Leipzig: J.C. Hinrichs, 1942).

EM   Edward Farley, *Ecclesial Man: A Social Phenomenology of Faith and Reality* (Philadelphia: Fortress Press, 1975).

Gl   Friedrich Schleiermacher, *Der Christliche Glaube.*

PTS   Nikolaus Cusanus, *Philosophische-Theologische Schriften,* ed. Leo Gabriel, trans. and with a commentary by Dietlind and Wilhelm Dupre (Vienna: Herder Verlag, 1964).

Schleiermacher the Theologian

Introduction: Towards a Reappraisal of Schleiermacher

Few will deny that Schleiermacher is one of the most important figures in philosophy of religion and theology in the last two centuries. His penetrating grasp of important issues and his innovations in method make him the founder of modern religious and theological thought. There is scarcely a topic in the field not touched by Schleiermacher or indebted to his treatment. However, few would suppose that Schleiermacher's innovative predominance and influence extend to the doctrine of God. His doctrine of God, including divine attributes and trinity, is widely considered to be Schleiermacher's Achilles' heel. It is alleged that his so-called subjectivism, that is, his contention that doctrines are accounts of religious affections, dissolves the objective basis of theology and reduces theology to anthropology. Feuerbach is held to be Schleiermacher's nemesis; consequently Schleiermacher's doctrine of God is something of an embarrassment, if not outright disaster. The apparent lack of an objective, unifying basis of religious experience is also supposedly reflected in his treatment of the doctrine of God. For example, the divine attributes are not treated as a unity, or unified as a theological locus, but are parceled out over the course of the *Glaubenslehre* and so widely separated from each other that the unity and coherence of the doctrine of God are allegedly lost. And there are doubts whether Schleiermacher's haphazard account of the divine attributes is internally consistent: Is divine love compatible with divine omnipotence? Some would deny that it is, but this denial presupposes that Schleiermacher reflects classical theology. This is a presupposition which, together with the entire foregoing interpretation of Schleiermacher, we shall challenge and reject.

We are not the first to challenge this interpretation of Schleiermacher. In opposition to the prevailing consensus concerning Schleiermacher's doctrine of God, Gerhard Ebeling has written: "No theologian in the modern age can compare with Schleiermacher in his attempt to refashion the doctrine of God. He subjected the dubious aspects of its traditional formulation to a penetrating criticism, but thought through the abiding elements of the doctrine of divine attributes with a systematic power which puts all previous models in the shade."[1] If Ebeling is correct, then nearly two-hundred years of Schleiermacher interpretation from Hegel to Barth are fundamentally wrong and mistaken. In our view, Ebeling is correct, both in the above statement and in his further contention that the doctrine of God is the central, objective, and unifying element in the overall argument of the *Glaubenslehre*. However, Ebeling's essay is only a beginning and falls short of a full-scale inquiry into Schleiermacher's doctrine of God. It is astonishing that, despite all the controversy over Schleiermacher and his significance, neither his defenders nor his critics have made a comprehensive study of his doctrine of God to support their interpretations and contentions.[2] This omission reflects the consensus: there can be no doctrine of God on Schleiermacher's principles.

THE POST-CRITICAL SITUATION IN
THEOLOGY AND CULTURE

Historically speaking, Schleiermacher's is one of the first theological responses to Kant's critical philosophy. There are two elements of Kant's philosophy against which he reacts: the dualism between theoretical and practical reason and the resulting noncognitive interpretation of theology; metaphysics and theology deal with objects transcendent to sensible experience, and which can be merely thought, but not known. Kant is a major contributor to the dualism pervading Western culture, between the cognitive and noncognitive, between reality and nonreality. Reality has virtually come to mean that which is researched and experimented with in the natural sciences, and knowledge is patterned after the experimental methods of the physical sciences. Anything not an object in the physical sense is not real. Examples of such "unrealities" include the humanities, man as an ethicoreligious being, the transcendent, and paradoxically, even the critical philosophy itself![3] Kant's determination of the limits of knowledge is not itself knowledge as established by his *Critique of Pure Reason*. Kant provides no account of the epistemological status of the

Critique itself, which surely has epistemological significance. Yet his determination of the limits of knowledge tends to precipitate the crisis of Western culture:

> The reality of human being means what is researched, experimented with, and known acccording to the procedures of natural science. The human being is acknowledged as a reality only in the sense of a naturalized, mathematized object. The consequence is that Western man has no way of interpreting himself. His entire life and life-world, the world of concrete decisions, values, aesthetic objects, history, evil, hopes, and dreams, all fall outside of "reality."[4]

Philosophy and theology are not insulated from the crisis of culture, but reflect it. Kant attacks traditional natural and rational theology; his attack on the proofs for God applies and illustrates his prior analyses and decisions concerning the nature, conditions, and limits of knowledge. The traditional proofs for God do not fit the model of knowledge derived from the physical sciences; metaphysics and natural theology are rejected as noncognitive, their objects falling outside of "reality." From this aspect of Kant's thought derives a host of antimetaphysical theologies which follow Kant in rejecting natural theology and in seeking to base theology on something else.

In his second *Critique* Kant reintroduces the concept of God, but only as a postulate of reason in its practical employment. God is postulated as the ultimate guarantor of the connection between virtue and happiness, that is, the guarantor of the intelligibility of morality and ethics. Although such postulation of God is crucial for practical reason, it does not enlarge our knowledge of reality. Although as a postulate God is constitutive and immanent rather than transcendent and regulative (as Idea of reason), Kant refuses to allow that such "access" to God as constitutive of morality is cognitive. Theoretically God is and remains, for Kant, a regulative Idea, transcendent to experience. Thus Kant in effect seems to be saying that practically God exists, but theoretically God is unknown. He appears to retain the classical conception of deity as abstract and transcendent to the world and experience. As a postulate, God is just as transcendent and unrelated to the world as is Aristotle's concept of God as pure thought contemplating itself. In neither case is God capable of manifesting himself in or relating himself to the world. Man is related to God (qua postulate of practical reason) but God is not related to man or the world. As Hegel observed, this is tantamount to asserting that God has no reality beyond or apart from the ethicoreligious postulations.[5] This implies that God has no reality beyond or independent of ethicoreligious consciousness, and if so, that God is merely a projection of such consciousness. It is a short step from Hegel's critique of Kant to Feuerbach's interpretation of theology as anthropology.

SCHLEIERMACHER'S RESPONSE: A GENERAL OVERVIEW

Schleiermacher is sharply critical of the dualism of the critical philosophy and the apparent metaphysical favoritism that Kant bestows on practical reason. There is no dualism for Schleiermacher, because religion—a modification of feeling—is the underlying foundation and unity of both knowing and doing. Schleiermacher's disagreement with Kant centers on two important points: the account of consciousness and the account of the relation between God and experience. According to Schleiermacher, feeling is neither knowing nor doing, but immediate consciousness; as such it is not simply noncognitive as in Kant, but rather it is the original, pretheoretical consciousness of reality. Knowing and doing are more determinate, circumscribed, and mediated modes of consciousness, which presuppose feeling or immediate self-consciousness. Like Husserl and Kant, Schleiermacher thinks that theoretical cognition presupposes and is limited by practical, pretheoretical acts. However, unlike Kant and with Husserl, Schleiermacher believes that theoretical cognition is logically founded upon pretheoretical intersubjective consciousness and its life-world. The latter cannot be dismissed as noncognitive, for if the life-world praxis is noncognitive and invalid, so is theoretical cognition.

Schleiermacher contends that religious belief in God is pretheoretical: it is not the result of proofs and demonstrations, but is conditioned solely by the religious modification of feeling, namely, the feeling of utter dependence. Belief in God is not acquired through intellectual acts of which the traditional proofs for God are examples, but rather from the thing itself, the "object" of religious experience. If, as Schleiermacher says, God is given to feeling in an original way, this means that the feeling of utter dependence is in some sense an apprehension of divine being and reality. This is not meant as a Barthian fideism or appeal to revelation, but rather as a theological eidetics or religious a priori. The feeling of utter dependence is structured by a correlation with its Whence; this theological correlation is presupposed by and immanent in historically determinate religious experience, including historical revelation. At the heart of this theological eidetics is Schleiermacher's Platonic and ontological approach to the question of God. With Plato, Schleiermacher believes that it belongs to the divine being and perfection to relate itself to and disclose itself in the world. In short, God is not jealous, incommunicable, and unknowable, but rather a self-communicating, self-disclosing being. With Anselm, Schleiermacher believes that God's self-disclosure and communication are based in God himself. He accepts the ontological principle that God is the presupposition of the idea of God, and believes that the idea can be identified with nothing less than the transcendent, nonmundane Whence of utter dependence. These considerations will be developed in subsequent chapters; as we shall see, Schleiermacher presents a pretheoretical, reflexive version of the ontological argument. For the present it is sufficient to note that on such assumptions God is more than and is independent of religious consciousness, and that it is at least plausible to construct a doctrine of God, in contrast to a mere postulation or projection of God in the Kantian and Feuerbachian senses.

Such Platonic and Anselmian assumptions and principles help to fund an experiential theology in which God is originally given and is accessible to consciousness as the Whence of utter dependence. Schleiermacher's theology is phenomenological in that he approaches the question of God and the entire doctrine of God through a reflective analysis of religious consciousness and its object. All determinations of the sense of the word "god," such as occur in the doctrine of God and divine attributes, must be developed from and traceable to the various modifications of the feeling of utter dependence. Given the pretheoretical correlation between utter dependence and God, the fundamental thesis of Schleiermacher's phenomenological theology can be formulated thus: Understanding theological assertions concerning God and divine attributes presupposes a prior understanding of religious consciousness and the religious states of mind from which such assertions derive and which they are meant to express. Traditional theology, whether based primarily in "reason" or in scriptural revelation, bypassed this existential relation and correlation. Its speculative philosophical elaboration led to the adoption and formulation of an abstract, metaphysical theology which spoke of God in separation from his actual manifestation and self-disclosure, and thus violated the ontological principle by separating God's being from his act. Schleiermacher's method is a corrective to that abstract mode of treatment in the tradition; the doctrine of God must be set forth step by step with the exposition of human existence qualified by redemption. It is complete only together with the completion of the analyses of creation, sin, and grace.

SCHLEIERMACHER AND PHENOMENOLOGICAL METHOD

WHAT IS PHENOMENOLOGY?

One hundred years before Husserl made phenomenology an explicit self-conscious philosophical method, Schleiermacher was practicing something very much like it. However, since phenomenology never acquired a precise meaning, and since it has recently become faddish, some words of explanation are necessary to clarify this contention. Following Edward Farley,[6] I find it helpful to distinguish phenomenological philosophy, phenomenological method, and phenomenological attitude. The phenomenological attitude is characterized by openness towards and careful attention to a phenomenon in order to allow the subject matter to generate its own categories, method(s) of inquiry, and criteria of interpretation. The opposite of the phenomenological attitude is the dogmatic or reductive attitude, in which foreign and external interpretive schemes and categories are imposed on a subject. Important and widespread as the phenomenological attitude is, it falls short of the distinctive method for achieving nonreductive interpretations as set forth by Husserl.

It is misleading to offer any simple characterization of "the phenomenological method," especially in view of Husserl's continually changing program which is reflected in his repeated efforts at introduction to phenomenology, and his regressive mode of inquiry. The picture is further clouded by various and diverse developments and application of the method by Husserl's students and associates. Despite such obstacles, there is a central core, at least for Husserl, which can be set forth in a preliminary way. Husserl's method is rooted in and a counterpart of his description of consciousness as essentially intentional, as consciousness of ——.[7] The starting point of phenomenological method is human being in its pretheoretical, prereflective intentionality. The method of phenomenology can in part be characterized as intentional analysis. Such analysis proceeds by distinguishing and investigating the object intended (*noema*) and the consciousness-act through which the object is given and intended (*noesis*). The basic principle of intentional analysis is that the treatment of the consciousness-act and its intentional object must follow the kind of act-object under concrete consideration. This is the reason why "the phenomenological method" looks different when it is applied to different subject matters, for example, perception, willing, religion. Such divergence is an intrinsic requirement of the method itself. Moreover, any consciousness-act and its intentional object can be studied and investigated by means of this method. The method is therefore exportable beyond phenomenology per se into psychology, religion, and so forth.

A second, closely related facet of phenomenological method is the reduction or epoché. The reduction is employed to facilitate the basic principle that investigation must follow the kind of act-object under consideration. The reduction is a suspension of judgment, a holding in abeyance of any theory or anticipatory scheme transcendent to the act-object correlation. To practice the reduction is not to doubt or reject all transcendent presuppositions and schemes, but rather to suspend them and make no use of them in the initial, phenomenological inquiry and clarification. The phenomenologist takes no position, affirmative or negative, with respect to them. This is what is meant by attempting to philosophize without presuppositions or prejudgments. The reduction serves the ancient philosophic quest for a radically open, unprejudiced inquiry into what is the case whose results are not determined in advance by prejudgments—especially methodological prejudices—naïvely or dogmatically held. As Husserl repeatedly indicates, he is after the things themselves as they give themselves, prior to all theory and anticipations.[8]

Finally phenomenological philosophy consists in a philosophical account of the phenomenological method and its implications. Since the method is a regressive inquiry into the conditions of possibility of various regions of being and experience, culminating in the transcendentally constituted, intersubjective life-world, Husserl's philosophy is transcendental and moves towards a transcendental idealism. Whatever this means, Husserl's idealism is not that of Fichte, positing an absolute ego as the causal or explanatory principle of all being. Husserl's is a methodological idealism rather than an ontological and metaphysical idealism. His late elaboration of the intersubjective life-world stands in tension with any traditional, purely idealist philosophy.

SCHLEIERMACHER'S USE
OF PHENOMENOLOGICAL METHOD

Given this threefold distinction between phenomenological attitude, method(s), and philosophy, our thesis is that Schleiermacher is a phenomenologist in the first and second senses, but not the third. He stands in relation to Husserl much as Merleau-Ponty and Alfred Schutz. His analyses of the essence of Christianity and the doctrine of God make use of the scheme of act-object correlation. His account of the essence of

Christianity, whatever else it may involve, consists in a kind of intentional analysis of consciousness and redemption. There is an essential correlation between anthropological and christological features; Schleiermacher's determination of the limits of variation of that correlation is a morphology of Christian consciousness and existence, together with its intentional object. The natural heresies of Christianity involve a violation of the ideal, morphological limits, and result in falsifications of the fundamental intentionality of Christian consciousness.

Moreover, Schleiermacher's proposal concerning the three forms of proposition serves a function similar to the phenomenological reduction. Specifically, his contention that the first form of reflection is the fundamental dogmatic form is clearly meant to exclude anticipatory theoretical schemes from prejudicing and distorting the inquiry. Like Husserl, Schleiermacher is after the things themselves prior to and independent of abstract theory:

> If we compare these three possible forms [of reflection] with each other, it is clear that descriptions of this content of human states of mind [namely, the correlation between God and utter dependence qualified by redemption] can be derived only from the sphere of inner experience, and that therefore *in this form nothing alien can insinuate itself in the Glaubenslehre*. In contrast, assertions concerning the constitution of the world may belong to natural science, and concepts of divine modes of action may be purely metaphysical. Both types of concepts are produced by science [*Wissenschaft*] and thus belong to the objective consciousness and its fundamental conditions. As such, they are independent of that inner experience.[9]

The first form of proposition is a description of Christian religious experience prior to theoretical and metaphysical interpretations of its meaning and implications. Such a phenomenological description is prior to and neutral to any particular metaphysical-theoretical account and reconstruction of religious experience and its object; this moment of phenomenological elucidation and clarification precedes the work of theoretical and speculative disciplines such as anthropology, cosmology, and philosophical theology. As theoretical and speculative, the latter disciplines make use of theoretical constructions, abstract idealizations, and concepts which go beyond lived experience. Hence they are independent of lived experience. Common to the theoretical disciplines is an objectifying language, which is used primarily to portray and explain events in space and time. When consciousness itself and religious consciousness in particular are set forth in such objectifying language, distortions occur because consciousness and its objects are portrayed as if they were external, mundane, spatiotemporal entities. This is what Husserl calls the naturalization of consciousness, or "naturalistic miscontructions." Such naturalization is rooted in the naïve prejudices of ordinary experience, and is further refined and built upon by the sciences of the natural standpoint. Schleiermacher's point in seeking to base his theology on the first form of reflection is to correct such distorting, objectifying prejudices in theology. Such prejudices represent the encroachment of objectifying speculative thought upon original religious experience. Traditional philosophy and theology have objectified man and God and have produced misleading accounts of God, human being, and redemption.

However, while Schleiermacher's *Glaubenslehre* is meant to be an antireductive, antiformalist corrective to traditional theology, it is not an antimetaphysical theology, nor does it involve a wholesale rejection of metaphysics as such. Schleiermacher knows full well that a rejection of metaphysics is itself a strange and inconsistent form of metaphysics. Besides, Christian religious consciousness has metaphysical presuppositions and implications, and requires metaphysical analysis and conceptual formulation. Although systematic theology is based on experience, it remains an essentially intellectual, reflective enterprise; as such it cannot dispense with concepts and metaphysical language. Such language must be borrowed from other disciplines and adapted to the special requirements of expressing the distinctively Christian religious experience. This constitutes the methodological task of theology: the task is not to eliminate metaphysical concepts and language, but to control them. If the peculiarity of scientific, theoretical language is that it translates what is particular into formal and universal terms and thus goes beyond experience, theological control over such formal and abstract language will be exerted by deriving the explicitly theoretical forms of theological propositions (namely, the second and third forms) from the first or *Grundform:*

> Thus these two forms (the first of which includes, of course, all propositions of a generally anthropological content) do not in and of themselves yield any guarantee that all propositions so conceived are genuinely dogmatic. Therefore, we must declare the description of human states to be the fundamental dogmatic form, while propositions of the second and third form are admissible only to the extent that they can be developed out of propositions of the first form. For only on this condition can they be authenticated as expressions of religious emotions.[10]

Such is Schleiermacher's version of the method of correlation: Christian religious experience is both clarified by and modifies the abstract concepts used to articulate and express it. It is only through such correlation and modification that objectifying theoretical discourse receives its theological

justification. All such language must be revised and interpreted to signify
the distinctive content of actual religious experience; in short, it must be
traceable to and derived from religious experience. Schleiermacher considers the second and third forms of propositions as more abstract than the
first form, which is a phenomenological description of actual religious
experience itself. For this reason, the second and third forms of proposition
are less directly expressive of Christian faith-certainty than is the first, and
so are derivative, conceptually mediated, and even dispensable. However,
this does *not* mean that Schleiermacher considers it possible, much less
desirable, to detheologize the *Glaubenslehre*. It is true that the doctrine of
divine attributes comprises the third form of proposition, but this definitely
does not mean that God is introduced into systematic theology only at a
secondary and derived level. Schleiermacher's point is that religious experience is already theologically constituted; God therefore is part of the
given to be elucidated phenomenologically in the first form of proposition.
Schleiermacher makes this point clearly in the first edition of the
Glaubenslehre: "The description of the [religious] self-consciousness in the
first form of proposition will contain expressions of the relation of God to
the world."[11]

The task of phenomenological theology is to describe the actual
correlation between God and world as immediately given in religious
consciousness. This distinguishes the *Glaubenslehre* from speculative
natural theology; for the latter, owing to the universalizing formalism
inherent in conceptualization, involves an abstract separation between
God's being (abstractly conceived in universal terms) and God's act
(concretely experienced). It is precisely this abstract formalism and
separation which Schleiermacher is determined to avoid and whose per-
nicious influence in theology he seeks to overcome. Schleiermacher points
out that the second and third forms of proposition, as objectifying, involve
a consideration of God alone and of the world alone. Such separate consideration is necessary for purposes of conceptualization, but it is an abstraction from the actual correlation between God and world given in
religious consciousness. The possible distortion in such abstraction is
minimized by deriving the second and third forms of proposition from the
first. Schleiermacher's insistence on this derivation is an attempt to overcome the abstract separation between God's being and act at the level of
actual theological procedure and method. Consequently, when he says that
the doctrine of divine attributes constitutes the third (or second) form of
proposition, he does not mean that God is herein being introduced into the
discussion of religious consciousness for the first time, as if it were a

dispensable, superfluous afterthought. Rather what this stage of reflection introduces are metaphysical concepts and considerations of God and divine attributes, that is, a philosophical theology. To portray the *Glaubenslehre* as essentially an anthropology with a doctrine of God illicitly smuggled in from speculative natural theology and tacked on for purposes of giving it historical continuity with previous Christian theology is an irresponsible caricature.[12]

PURE DESCRIPTION AND THE PRINCIPLE OF POSITIVITY

Schleiermacher's project in his *Glaubenslehre* also resembles methodologically Paul Ricoeur's multivolume philosophy of the will. In the first volume, Ricoeur says that his procedure is pure description, which is similar to what Husserl calls the eidetic reduction, that is, a bracketing of fact and an elaboration of meaning.[13] Through such pure description or eidetic reduction, Ricoeur seeks to isolate the general structures of the will; an abstraction from factual, contingent expressions of willing is necessary in order to grasp its essential structures.

In the first half of his *Glaubenslehre,* Schleiermacher is doing something very similar. His account of the general correlation between God and world constitutive of religious consciousness is a theological-anthropological eidetics. Schleiermacher's account of utter dependence abstracts from the historically determinate Christian consciousness qualified by redemption, and sets forth a regional ontology of religious consciousness. This is Schleiermacher's version of the religious a priori. However, the regional ontology of God, man, and world, which is the transcendental condition of possibility of religious consciousness, is indeterminate and abstract.[14] It is abstracted from its concrete actualization in the consciousness of sin on the one hand, and the consciousness of grace or redemption on the other.[15] Schleiermacher calls attention to the indeterminate results of pure description in the first half of the *Glaubenslehre,* especially in his doctrine of God.

The second volume of Ricoeur's philosophy of the will removes the brackets of factual and temporal determinacy practiced in the first.[16] This is done to introduce a new set of considerations not accessible to pure description, namely, the consciousness of fault or fallibility. Ricoeur observes that "to take away the abstraction or to remove the parenthesis is not to draw the consequences or apply the conclusions of pure description. It is to disclose a new thematic structure which calls for new working hypotheses and a new method of approach."[17] In the second half of the *Glaubenslehre*

Schleiermacher likewise removes the brackets, opening up new inquiries into sin and grace which are not simply derivable from pure description. Man is essentially free, but concretely he exists in bondage to sin, or is liberated from such bondage through redemption. Sin and grace presuppose and modify (to be sure, in different ways) the general ontology of God, man, and world.

There is an important principle which presides over and unifies these two stages of eidetic and existential analysis, namely, the concrete does not derive from the abstract. Rather the concrete and actual is always more than the merely abstract. This empirical principle of positivity implies that the actualization of abstract eidetic structures involves modification. Temporal actualizations of generic structures are more than mere instantiations which leave the former unmodified and unchanged. In such actualizations the eidetic structures themselves undergo modification and determination. Consequently the way in which the a priori generic structures come to concrete expression determines and shapes their full meaning. Edward Farley has stated this principle of positivity in somewhat more systematic form:

> The structures described in various "regional ontologies" such as nature, man, history, and society, are not simply in correlation with theological realities, and are not simply the occasions in which faith acts occur, but are actually modified in the determinate modes of a faith community. This axiom is itself a derivation of a more general and philosophical one, according to which the features isolated in regional ontologies do not reappear unchanged in their state of actualization.[18]

The concrete is more than the merely abstract, and cannot be derived or deduced from the merely abstract. Schleiermacher embraces this principle when he writes that while the same generic features are present in all religions, they are differently determined, that is, concretely modified, in each.[19] Consequently the essence of any religious faith-community is always a synthesis of generic eidetic features or pure descriptions, with specific, historically determinate modifying features which render the former concrete and determinate: "Each particular form of communal piety is a unity, constituted outwardly by an historical factor stemming from a definite beginning, and constituted inwardly by a distinctive modification of everything which is common to and occurs in all developed modes of faith of the same type and level."[20] This principle of positivity and synthesis of generic with historical elements is the clue to the arrangement and argument of Schleiermacher's *Glaubenslehre,* including the doctrine of God.

THE CRITICAL ISSUE: GENERIC FORMALISM

Such a two-step phenomenological and existential procedure raises questions concerning the extent to which the generic structures are modified in their concrete actualization. If the essence of a religion is identified with the generic features alone, or if the historically determinate features are regarded merely as instantiations of the generic, universal structures which leaves them unmodified, the result is generic formalism. Generic formalism means that the "essential or distinguishing features of an entity are 'abstracted' from generic features. The result is that the generic features alone are set forth, simply replacing distinctive features, or distinctive features are retained, but are not allowed to transform the generic features. This means a loss of concreteness. . . in the sense that the distinguishing features which express concreteness are omitted."[21] Thus the methodological task is to show not only that the generic features have concrete realization and instantiation, but that they undergo modification in such actualization. Stated in other terms, the method of correlation between consciousness-act and intentional object must not suspend, but respect the principle of positivity.

It is important to observe that the issue of generic formalism is not external, but is raised by Schleiermacher's own procedure. It is a question which can and must be pursued over the entire argument of the *Glaubenslehre;* in other words, the *Glaubenslehre* cannot be read piecemeal, at least not critically. If the concrete is more than and modifies the abstract, then the full meaning of the doctrine of God, including the generic divine attributes, cannot be fully understood until the consciousness of sin and the consciousness of redemption have been set forth and the divine attributes constitutive of that concreteness have been attended to. This is the reason why Schleiermacher insists that understanding divine attributes presupposes a prior understanding of religious states of mind, and that the doctrine of God can be completed only simultaneously with the analysis of the totality of the states of mind comprising Christian consciousness. Only in this way can the full, concrete God-consciousness be taken into account. We shall return to the question of generic formalism in the final chapter.

THE PLATONIC BACKGROUND
OF SCHLEIERMACHER'S THOUGHT

An historical dimension in our inquiry is necessary, not only because Schleiermacher spoke the language of his day, but because it is necessary to understand the specific type of theological thought that Schleiermacher represents. It is frequently alleged that Schleiermacher's doctrine of God is under the domination of classical theology (for example, Thomas Aquinas) and continues its questionable conceptions of divine aseity, monopolarity, and immutability. This contention is refuted by our investigation. Although Schleiermacher undoubtedly was influenced by classical theology, he was more directly influenced by and sympathetic to German idealism on the one hand and by Plato on the other. It should not be forgotten that Schleiermacher was the translator of Plato, and that he regarded Plato's philosophy sympathetically as an ideal to which he himself sought to approximate. However, the *kind* of Platonism Schleiermacher represents has not received much attention, despite a general recognition of a Platonic background and even Platonic elements in his thought, for example, dialectics.[22] This consideration is important in view of the tendency of some writers to think of Platonism as a seamless cloth and to regard it as merely another version of classical theology.

Our thesis is that Schleiermacher embodies a type of Platonic theological thought similar to Nikolaus Cusanus.[23] The significance of Nikolaus' type of theology is that it represents a significant departure from the monopolar Platonic tradition stemming from Plato's *Republic* and from Plotinus' synthesis of Plato and Aristotle. Cusanus' main idea is that God is coincidence of opposites, which is a bipolar rather than monopolar theological concept. Note that our contention is not that Schleiermacher actually read or was directly influenced by Cusanus, but only that he represents and embodies a similar *type* of theological thought. It is possible, indeed even probable that Schleiermacher reached his position independently. However, it is not a mere historical accident that there is intellectual kinship between Schleiermacher and Cusanus, for Cusanus is a seminal thinker in the German philosophical and theological tradition in which Schleiermacher stands. On the philosophical side, Lewis White Beck situates Cusanus at the beginning of his *History of Early German Philosophy,* and traces themes and motifs from Cusanus to Kant; Copleston continues the story by noting parallels between Cusanus and German idealism, notably Schelling and Hegel.[24]

In our view, Schleiermacher is Cusanus' true heir in nineteenth century German philosophy and theology, not only because he has a concept of God as bipolar coincidence of opposites, but chiefly because he continues, in a way that the idealists do not, Cusanus' thesis that theology is learned ignorance. Cusanus and Schleiermacher occupy a position midway between Kant and Hegel, or midway between Kierkegaard and Hegel.[25] On the theological side, Cusanus originates the contrast between God hidden and God revealed (*Deus absconditus et Deus revelatus*) which influenced Luther and which Luther developed. This same contrast is also central in Schleiermacher's doctrine of God. It is no exaggeration to say that in Schleiermacher the divergent philosophical and theological themes and motifs of Cusanus' thought once again converge.

Viewed against this background, Schleiermacher's thought appears in a much different light than usual. It is not simply another instance of classical theology. It offers an alternative conception of the relation between God and world to both classical theology and to process theology. As coincidence of opposites, God is both living and bipolar—a break with monopolar classical theology. Moreover, coincidence of opposites serves to distinguish Cusanus and Schleiermacher from process theology's version of bipolar theology. If we are correct in the identification of the genuine background of Schleiermacher's thought, this interpretation should clarify whether his doctrine of God forms a coherent whole or is flawed by internal inconsistency and contradiction. Is divine love compatible with divine omnipotence? Certainly the answer in part depends on what is meant by love and what is meant by omnipotence. Our thesis is that Schleiermacher does reconstruct the notion of divine omnipotence as an ethically ordered and motivated power, and that this revision is an attempt to blunt, if not avoid the contradiction between love and aseity, love and omnipotence in classical theology.

PLAN AND OVERVIEW OF THE STUDY

Following our above distinction between pure eidetic description and existential description and analysis, and following Schleiermacher's actual procedure, the study is divided into two parts. The first part deals with the generic scheme of philosophy and theology—including the relation between God and world—comprising the religious a priori. We focus on Schleiermacher's phenomenology of feeling or immediate consciousness, and his account of religious consciousness. We seek to show that he presents a pretheoretical, existential version of the ontological argument, finding divine reality at the heart of human freedom. We show how this account leads to a scheme of the relation of God and world similar to Cusanus, and sketch some of the important aspects of Cusanus' thought.

The second part of the study is devoted to Schleiermacher's doctrine of God, including divine attributes and trinity. Abstract, formal analysis is continued in chapter 3, in which the generic divine attributes are set forth as an indeterminate theological schematism and not as a complete or explicit doctrine of God. Chapter 4 presents Schleiermacher's account of the essence of Christianity and its natural heresies. The implications of Christian historical positivity are explored in respect to their modifications of the formal generic scheme presented in part one. Pure description is now supplemented with existential analysis. Chapter 5 examines the divine attributes constitutive of the consciousness of sin and the consciousness of redemption. Chapter 6 reexamines Schleiermacher's account of trinity in relation to the fundamental concepts of God as coincidence of opposites and the contrast between God hidden and God revealed. We reject the contention that Schleiermacher presents a merely economic version of trinity and argue that he is very close to orthodoxy's ontological trinity. Chapter 7 is an assessment of Schleiermacher's accomplishment. It is argued that he avoids a reductive interpretation of Christian faith (generic formalism) and presents an alternative to classical theology in respect to divine immutability, love, and power.

NOTES

1. Gerhard Ebeling, "Schleiermacher's Doctrine of the Divine Attributes," *Schleiermacher as Contemporary* ([*Journal for Theology and Church,* no.7, ed. Robert W. Funk], New York: Herder & Herder, 1970), p. 127; cf. also Ebeling's citation of Emmanuel Hirsch, p. 128.

2. I did not have available to me the most recent work on Schleiermacher's doctrine of God when this manuscript was being written. I have just obtained a copy of Friedrich Beisser's *Schleiermachers Lehre von Gott* (Göttingen: Vandenhoeck & Ruprecht, 1970). This study, which is more detailed and longer than mine, is marred by two important defects: First, Beisser interprets the two sets of divine attributes (the generic and the attributes derived from sin and grace) by means of the alien idealist categories of *Wesen und Erscheinung,* or essence and appearance. This is precisely the issue at stake in Schleiermacher interpretation, as this study will show. I think that such an interpretation results in a fundamental distortion of Schleiermacher's thought for it implies that the second set of attributes derived from redemption are merely *Erscheinungsformen,* or particular instantiations of the generic attributes (cf. ibid., 62 ff.; 179 ff., 227-28). This violates Schleiermacher's basic axiom and principle of positivity that the concrete is always more than and cannot be derived from the abstract. Second, Beisser assumes throughout a sharp separation between philosophy and theology which implies their incompatibility. He appears to prefer an antimetaphysical, biblical theology and proceeds to play off the "New Testament concept of God" against Schleiermacher's critical, hermeneutical program in a most unfortunate way, as if the two were mutually exclusive (ibid., 108 ff.; 253). The issues are not fruitfully joined: the biblical "lord" is wholly other than and has nothing to do with a "transcendent ground of being." Beisser's study, which has a wealth of information, winds up repeating a standard Barthian criticism: Schleiermacher speaks only of man, and not of God (242 f.). A detailed reply is not possible here; I can only refer the reader to this study, especially those rebuttals of Barth and Feuerbach.

3. See Hans-Georg Gadamer, *Truth and Method* (New York: Seabury Press, 1975) pp. 38 ff.; and John E. Smith, *Reason and God,* chap. 1 (New Haven: Yale University Press, 1961). See also Smith's *Experience and God* (New York: Oxford University Press, 1968), especially his excellent comments and observations on the transformation of the dialogue between philosophy and theology when philosophy ceases to put forth comprehensive in-

terpretations of the world and experience and is identified with a second-order, critical apparatus (pp. 6 ff.).

4. *EM*, p. 31. Despite its misleading title, this book is the best investigation of Husserl's phenomenology and its potential significance for philosophy of religion and theology available in English. The present study of Schleiermacher is indebted to it; conversely, Farley's book could aptly be subtitled *Schleiermacher redivibus*.

5. G.W.F. Hegel, "Lectures on the Proofs for the Existence of God" in *Lectures on the Philosophy of Religion*, trans. E.B. Speirs and J.B. Sanderson (New York: Humanities Press, 1962), 3:192 ff.

6. *EM*, pp. 24 ff.

7. See Eugen Fink, "The Phenomenological Philosophy of Husserl and Contemporary Criticism," in *The Phenomenology of Husserl*, ed., trans., and with an introduction by R.O. Elveton (Chicago: Quadrangle Books, 1970); see also Gaston Berger, *The Cogito in Husserl's Philosophy*, trans. Kathleen McLaughlin (Evanston: Northwestern University Press, 1972), pp. 9 f., 70 ff.

8. Edmund Husserl, *Ideas: A General Introduction to Pure Phenomenology*, trans. W.R. Boyce Gibson (New York: Collier-Macmillan, 1962), § 30, 43. See also Berger, *Husserl's Philosophy*, pp. 7 ff.

9. *G1*, § 30.2. Hereafter, when the first (Reutlingen: J.J. Mächen, 1928) edition of the *Glaubenslehre* is cited, it will be identified as *G1*, 1st ed. When no particular edition is specified the reference is to the second (1830) edition. All citations of this second edition are from the best modern critical edition of it, namely, *Der Christliche Glaube*, ed. Martin Redeker (Berlin: Walter de Gruyter & Co., 1960). All translations are my own, although I have made use of the H.R. Mackintosh translation, *The Christian Faith* (Edinburgh: T & T Clark, 1928; reprint ed., Philadelphia: Fortress Press, 1976).

10. *G1*, § 30.2.

11. *G1*, 1st ed., § 42. Schleiermacher adds the following explanation: "On the one hand the world is included in our self-consciousness as we feel ourselves dependent; and on the other hand, we feel both ourselves and the world dependent on the highest being coposited in our self-consciousness. Consequently, in this state of mind the relation between God and world is itself expressed. *God can be described only if this relation is described.* Moreover, since . . . reflection can be directed upon God alone and the world alone, there can also be descriptions of that element in God which conditions the world, and descriptions of that element in the world conditioned by God" (italics by R.R.W.). The latter descriptions of God alone and the world alone are abstractions from the full concrete reality, the relation of God and world given directly in feeling, and constitute the second and third forms of proposition. See *G1*, § 35.

12. The chief purveyor of this caricature is Karl Barth. Barth is one of the few theologians who actually read Schleiermacher, and who should have known better. Nevertheless, he offered this caricature of the three forms of proposition not once, but twice! See his *Theology and Church*, trans. Louise Pettibone Smith (New York: Harper & Row, 1962), pp. 163–65; and *From Rousseau to Ritschl*, trans. Brian Cozzens (London: SCM Press, 1959), pp. 336–38. Barth's caricature has been highly influential.

Another interpreter who repeats Barth's caricature is Gerhard Spiegler, *The Eternal Covenant* (New York: Harper & Row, 1967), p. 69. Spiegler also follows a version of the critique of classical theology from the perspective of process theology: Schleiermacher's concept of God is self-contradictory. On the one hand, God is conceived as a metaphysical absolute which exists in separation from the world. On the other hand, this metaphysical absolute is also claimed to be related to the world. In Spiegler's view, Schleiermacher never succeeds in relating these two elements, or in purging his thought of the metaphysical absolute. Spiegler fails to appreciate the Platonic background of Schleiermacher's thought, specifically, that it belongs to God to reveal himself (*G1*, § 54.4), that is, God is not jealous. But then Spiegler completely ignores Schleiermacher's doctrine of God in the *Glaubenslehre*. Moreover,

Spiegler conveys the false impression that process theology has somehow dispensed with God as a metaphysical absolute, as if it had suddenly ceased to be concerned with divine immutability and absoluteness. We shall have more to say about this issue in chapter 7.

13. Paul Ricoeur, *Freedom and Nature: The Voluntary and the Involuntary,* trans. Erazim V. Kohak (Evanston: Northwestern University Press, 1966), introduction.

14. *Gl*, § 62. Schleiermacher's version of the religious a priori is not reducible to a Kantian transcendental deduction of the categories of the understanding. Following Nygren, the Scandinavian school of Schleiermacher interpretation tries to interpret Schleiermacher in this way. For example, Regin Prenter treats Schleiermacher's analysis of the feeling of utter dependence as a transcendental deduction of the religious category (See his *Creation and Redemption,* trans. Theodor I. Jensen [Philadelphia: Fortress Press, 1967], pp. 20 ff.) If this interpretation were correct, religion would be a merely anthropological phenomenon. But surely this is the very point at issue! This interpretation fails to note that not even Kant attempted a transcendental deduction of the Ideas of reason, and that Kant himself would not be happy with a merely phenomenalist interpretation of the idea of God. Schleiermacher's version of the religious a priori goes beyond Kant, for it includes a version of the ontological argument. We shall return to this issue in the next chapter. For a similar criticism of Nygren's interpretation of Schleiermacher, see William A. Johnson, *On Religion: A Study of Theological Method in Schleiermacher and Nygren* (Leiden, Holland: E.J. Brill, 1964).

15. This presupposes that not every transcendent account of the act-object correlation of religious consciousness is reductive in a distorting sense. However, all such accounts, whether adequate or reductive, presuppose the possibility of getting at the things themselves prior to theoretical anticipations and schemes. And this in turn requires and presupposes the phenomenological epoche, that is, suspension of theoretical prejudgments whether correct or reductive.

16. Paul Ricoeur, *Fallible Man,* trans. Charles Kelbley (Chicago: Henry Regnery, 1965).

17. Ibid., p. xvii.

18. Edward Farley, "Can Revelation be Formally Described?" *Journal of the American Academy of Religion* 37(September 1969): 270 ff.

19. *Gl*, § 10.2.

20. *Gl*, § 10.

21. Farley, "Can Revelation be Formally Described?" p. 270.

22. Hans-Georg Gadamer, "Schleiermacher als Platoniker," *Kleine Schriften* (Tübingen: J.C.B. Mohr, 1972). Perhaps the best article is Werner Schulz, "Das griechische Ethos in Schleiermachers *Reden* und *Monologen," Neue Zeitschrift fur systematische Theologie und Religionsphilosophie* 10(1968): 261–88. Schulz discusses the problems Schleiermacher faced in appropriating Platonic thought for Christian faith, but his discussion is limited only to the *Reden* and *Monologen*.

23. After I had reached this conclusion and written chapter 2, I discovered Wolfgang Sommer's interesting article, "Cusanus und Schleiermacher," *Neue Zeitschrift fur systematische Theologie und Religionsphilosophie* 12(1970): 85–102. Sommer also contends that there is an intellectual kinship between Schleiermacher and Cusanus which extends into common interests and themes, including the relation between God and world, God and discursive understanding, and the positive status of individuality (see pp. 100 f.). The fundamental conceptions are similar, even though Sommer finds no evidence of direct historical and literary influence of Cusanus on Schleiermacher. Sommer also claims that Schleiermacher's so-called Spinozism and sympathy for Spinoza is best understood as an affinity between his thought and that of Cusanus. I believe that Sommer is correct and that his interpretation explains and accounts for Schleiermacher's criticism of Spinoza's concept of God as *natura naturans* in his *Dialektik* from the standpoint of the negative theology. Sommer's article is all the more remarkable in that he too deals primarily with Schleiermacher's *Reden* and *Monologen,* and neglects what in my opinion is the prime evidence for Schleiermacher's resemblance of Cusanus, namely his doctrine of God in the *Glaubenslehre*.

24. Lewis White Beck, *A History of Early German Philosophy* (Cambridge, Mass.: Belknap Press, 1969); also F.C. Copleston, *A History of Philosophy,* 8 vols. (New York: Doubleday & Co., 1963), 3: pt. 2.

25. At least two contemporary philosophers of religion have argued that this is the position to occupy, even if it sounds like a contradiction (like "round-square") and even if it is like trying to walk on a razor's edge. See Paul Ricoeur's self-description as a "post-Hegelian-Kantian" in "The Specificity of Religious Language," *Semeia,* no. 4 (Fall 1975). See also John E. Smith's discussion of the "Kant-Hegel syndrome" in philosophical theology in his *Reason and God,* and his own version of this position in *Experience and God.*

PART ONE

THE RELIGIOUS A PRIORI

1

Experience and God

Although Schleiermacher never formulated a comprehensive account of feeling or immediate self-consciousness, his thought on consciousness and experience exhibits unity and coherence. Elsewhere I have made a study of his theory of consciousness, and I shall be drawing upon and summarizing that study here.[1] This chapter is a commentary and exposition of paragraphs three and four of *The Christian Faith*: "Piety, which is the basis of all religious communities, is, considered in and for itself, neither a knowing nor a doing, but a determination of feeling or immediate self-consciousness."[2] What Schleiermacher means by feeling has long been a matter of dispute. We shall argue that feeling is not to be understood in a merely psychological way as a subjective, emotive, or noncognitive state, but rather it should be understood as immediate self-consciousness as such, which is a global consciousness of self in correlation with the world. Feeling is a direct, prereflective apprehension of reality. In developing this contention, we shall compare Schleiermacher with Edmund Husserl's account of the natural attitude and the life-world (*Lebenswelt*). Such a comparison will facilitate a nonpsychologizing reading and interpretation of Schleiermacher, which in turn will open up his distinctive thesis about religious consciousness and experience: "The common element . . . which distinguishes piety from all other determinations of feeling . . . is this: that we are conscious of ourselves as utterly dependent, or, which amounts to the same thing, we are conscious of ourselves in relation with God."[3]

Not all feeling is religious, but only that distinctive modification and determination of feeling which qualifies it as feeling of utter dependence. The feeling of utter dependence has a structure which is determined by and dependent on its distinctive object. Intentional analysis of utter dependence will disclose the distinctive mode of being of its object or Whence. Moreover, such analysis will constitute a pretheoretical version of the ontological argument; it will bring to light the pretheoretical, existential grounds underlying the ontological argument as an objective proof. In developing this section, we shall compare and contrast Schleiermacher with Anselm, and with Kant's discussion of the feeling of the sublime. The latter will illumine the intentional structure and intentional object of prereflective religious consciousness, and the former will clarify the metaphysical implications of Schleiermacher's account of experience and God.

THE INTENTIONALITY OF FEELING

TWO ERRONEOUS VIEWS OF FEELING

There are two reductive interpretations of feeling and the emotions that have surfaced from time to time in the history of philosophy. The first view is that feeling is a direct, self-transcending apprehension of reality, that is, feeling is intentional. However, feeling is regarded merely as a primitive, confused form of knowledge. In other words, this view concedes the intentionality of feeling, that it is a direct apprehension of reality,[4] but denies that feeling is relatively autonomous and independent of cognition. It is simply a primitive form of clear and distinct knowledge. The second view is that feeling is autonomous and *sui generis* as a faculty; however, feeling is not considered to be a direct grasp of reality beyond the self. It is regarded as merely psychological, an emotive, noncognitive mode of consciousness. Its self-transcendence and intentionality are denied.

The first interpretation is found in continental rationalism, Leibniz in particular. He held that feeling is a self-transcending, preconceptual apprehension of reality. Hence the emotional and aesthetic life is not reducible to a mere stomachache.[5] However, while feeling is reality-apprehending, it is regarded as an inferior, confused form of theoretical knowledge. Although feeling directly apprehends reality, it differs from theoretical knowledge only in degree of clarity and distinctness. This view denies or overlooks the fact that the affective, emotional life is an autonomous stratum of life with an independence, sense, and validity of its own. The "darker" subjective elements of emotional apprehension are passed over or suppressed on the way to pure, theoretical cognition of being.

The second view of feeling emphasizes the autonomy and independence of feeling from cognition. Tetens, and Kant after him,[6] recognized that feeling is not simply reducible to cognition, and does not amount merely to the lowest form of knowledge. Feeling is more than theoretical knowledge because it is richer and more concrete; it does not abstract the values and other "subject-relative" elements from things. However, Kant denies that feeling is self-transcending or intentional. The emotional life is autonomous but blind; in feeling the self encounters only itself. Feeling does not express the object, but only the structures of subjectivity. In his noncognitive interpretation of feeling, Kant in effect denies that feeling is a meaningful mode of encountering something besides the self; the emotions are not different in principle from a mere stomachache.

SCHLEIERMACHER'S ALTERNATIVE: FEELING IS AUTONOMOUS AND INTENTIONAL

Schleiermacher seeks a middle ground between the foregoing interpretations. Each view presents an element of the truth, but distorts it in a one-sided fashion. With Locke and Leibniz, Schleiermacher believes that feeling is a direct, intuitive apprehension of reality. It cannot be reduced to a merely psychological state because it is the general organ of receptivity of the subject. As such, feeling is essentially in correlation with the world at the prereflective level: "What we here call feeling is the immediate presence of whole, undivided being, both spiritual and sensible, the unity of the person with his spiritual and sensible world."[7] Feeling is both the immediate consciousness of the world transcendent to the self, and the original response of the self to the world.

However, feeling cannot be reduced to a primitive form of cognition. Since feeling is neither a knowing nor a doing, it is an irreducible, autonomous aspect or dimension of the self. But this assertion is misleading because it suggests that feeling is a third faculty alongside the cognitive and practical faculties. Schleiermacher repudiates a faculty psychology such as Kant's because it tends to personify and treat as agents the abstract capacities of the self, thereby obscuring the totality and unity of the self as agent. Thus, feeling is not a faculty in contrast and opposition to others such as reason, understanding, judgment and sensation (or the senses). All of the latter are partial aspects and/or abstract capacities of the subject. In contrast, feeling is Schleiermacher's term for the totality and unity of the self; feeling is global self-consciousness. Feeling is neither cognitive-theoretical subjectivity, nor ethical subjectivity, but subjectivity as such, or consciousness as such. It is the common, generic element present in and rendered determinate in the more specific and circumscribed forms of self-consciousness. Feeling therefore is global human existence in its prereflective, lived interaction with the world. As such it underlies and mediates knowing and doing as partial aspects of human being. Thus feeling has a knowing and a doing which are implicit in it, but it is not knowing per se or doing per se. It is that in which knowing and doing contrast, the horizon or background against which now one and now the other element/function predominates.[8]

Schleiermacher unites both the autonomy and intentionality of feeling in his identification of feeling with immediate self-consciousness. Feeling qualifies consciousness as immediate, prereflective apprehension of the correlation between self and world. On the other hand, consciousness qualifies feeling. First, it excludes feelings which are not conscious. Schleiermacher does not deny the existence of such, but differentiates his understanding of feeling from Leibniz' theory of subliminal or unconscious feelings, which occur below the level of apperception.[9] Schleiermacher's identification of feeling with immediate consciousness is meant as a thesis about the fundamental form of wakeful human life: "From this description it follows that feeling should not be thought of as something confused or as something ineffective, for on the one hand, it is the clearest in our most vivid, vital moments, underlying immediately or mediately all expressions of the will, and on the other hand it can be grasped by reflection and its essence can be conceived by thought."[10] The above passage also makes it clear that feeling is not to be identified with bare sensation, or as mere experience minus the intellectual-conceptual component. Schleiermacher's understanding of feeling is not that of abstract sense-data empiricism or sensationalism. Feeling is not abstract sensation, nor a confused form of theoretical cognition, nor a merely psychological state. It is already meaningful, clear in vivid and vital moments; in short, it possesses intrinsic meaning even in prereflective form. Meaning does not have to be added to it or imposed upon it from abstract concepts, judgments, and inferences. Schleiermacher's thesis concerning feeling as immediate self-consciousness cannot be adequately understood against the background of continental rationalism or British empiricism. It is best understood as an anticipation of the thought of Edmund Husserl.

SIMILARITIES BETWEEN SCHLEIERMACHER AND HUSSERL

The purpose of this comparison is to illuminate Schleiermacher's account of feeling, namely, its intentionality and autonomy. What follows is not a full-scale treatment of Husserl's thought, or even a comprehensive historical comparison, but merely an attempt to highlight some important similarities. However, there is an historical and intellectual lineage between Schleiermacher and Husserl; the mediating figure is Wilhelm Dilthey, one of Schleiermacher's outstanding interpreters.[11] In his delineation of the human sciences (*Geisteswissenschaften*) Dilthey both continues Schleiermacher's fundamental distinction between the ethical and physical sciences, and is influential on Husserl's development of phenomenology. Husserl's work after his *Logical Investigations* can be viewed as a refinement and continuation of Dilthey's program of *Geisteswissenschaften,* and consequently as an indirect refinement and continuation of Schleiermacher's. Both Schleiermacher and Husserl reject merely naturalistic interpretations of human being as reductive and insufficient; both maintain the primacy of spirit (*Geist*) and freedom in human being, and present similar accounts of human being and freedom, even using similar if not exactly the same terminology.

I have selected the following topics for further explication and comparison: Schleiermacher's account of feeling as the immediate presence of whole undivided being bears resemblance to Husserl's account of the natural attitude. Both feeling and the natural attitude are "shot through" with a thesis, namely, the direct, straightforward acceptance of the world, or *belief* in the world. Second, the world which is directly believed in and lived in is an intersubjective, cultural life-world. In other words there is a resemblance between the spiritual and sensible world which is directly present in feeling (Schleiermacher) and the *Lebenswelt* (Husserl). Third, the relation between human being and the life-world is characterized by reciprocity, which includes both receptivity and spontaneity, dependence and freedom. Husserl and Schleiermacher both characterize human freedom in terms of receptivity and spontaneity. Against idealism both stress the finitude and contingent existence of human being in correlation with the world.

Feeling and the Natural Attitude

Schleiermacher finds immediate consciousness structured by a contrast and correlation between self and world. Immediate self-consciousness is constituted by a contrast between an identical and a variable element, a being and a having by some means come to be, or a being-for-self and a coexistence-with-other.[12] The contrast and correlation between self and other at the most general level is a contrast between self and world.[13] The world is the totality of relative contrasts, a totality of reciprocal interaction and interdependence. It is directly present to and accepted by the self in feeling. Schleiermacher's account of the self-world correlation anticipates Husserl's account of the natural attitude and its thesis, namely belief in the reality of the world. Husserl writes:

> I find continually present and standing over and against me the one spatiotemporal fact-world to which I myself belong, as do all other men found in it and related to it in the same way. This "fact-world" as the world already tells us, I find to be out there, and also take it just as it gives itself to me as something that exists out there. All doubting and rejecting of the data of the natural world leave standing the general thesis of the natural standpoint. The world is as a fact-world always there . . . it remains ever in the sense of the general thesis, a world that has its being out there.[14]

This general thesis of the reality of the world is designated as *Urglaube,* or primary, original belief in the world.[15] The world is the general intentional correlate of consciousness, not an object "in" the world, but the horizon of consciousness. Although the natural attitude is transcendentally constituted, it is the primary, the "natural" intentionality of consciousness which is expressed in the thesis of the reality of the world. This general thesis is presupposed by and underlies all further determinate modifications of consciousness, such as occur in scientific, theoretical cognition. The physical sciences are sciences of the natural attitude and standpoint, which take for granted and presuppose the thesis of the reality of the world. The thesis of the natural standpoint is the primary belief (*Urglaube, Urdoxa*) to which all further determinate modifications refer, and which they constantly take for granted.[16]

Urglaube is not merely chronologically prior, but logically prior to its determinate modes. It is primary in the sense that doubt about this or that aspect of the world leaves intact and indeed presupposes the general thesis. Thus the scientific-realist critique of ordinary experience presupposes and is logically derivative from the general thesis of the natural standpoint. Husserl observes that far from denying the general thesis of the natural standpoint or calling it into question, natural science seeks to know the "real world" better than ordinary consciousness and experience. Thus it presupposes and is carried out on the basis of the natural attitude. Even the skeptic does not doubt the general thesis; Hume's relief from his skeptical despair by playing billiards with his friends illustrates and confirms Husserl's point about the primacy of the natural attitude.

In designating the thesis of the natural attitude as a general one, Husserl means to deny that it is empirically derived. Belief in the reality of the world is not derived or induced from particular empirical observations or from explicit judgments about experience. Rather it is constitutive of and presupposed by such observations and judgments:

> It is this universal ground of belief in a world which all praxis presupposes, not only the praxis of life, but also the theoretical praxis of cognition. The being of the world in totality is . . . *not first the result of an activity of judgment, but that which forms the presupposition of all judgment.* Consciousness of the world is consciousness in the mode of certainty of belief; *it is not acquired by a specific act which breaks into the continuity of life as an act which posits being or grasps the existent,* or even as an act of judgment which predicates existence. All of these acts presuppose consciousness of the world in the certainty of belief.[17]

Belief in the reality of the world is a transcendental thesis, a transcendental thesis which is not an abstract, formal a priori, but a *concrete* a priori, which expresses the primary intentionality of consciousness. Husserl is challenging the Western philosophical tradition from Plato to Hegel by contending that knowledge in the strict sense (*episteme*) is founded upon *doxa,* or belief. Theoretical cognition is founded upon pretheoretical, prereflective immediate consciousness. In his last work, *The Crisis,* Husserl develops this thesis as the primacy of the life-world as the foundation of theoretical judgment and cognition.[18] However, what distinguishes Husserl from the Protagorean sophistry and relativism against which Plato struggled is precisely his insistence that the belief which founds theoretical cognition is a *transcendentally constituted one,* the general thesis of the natural attitude.

Is all of this to be found in Schleiermacher? As an explicit analysis or set of developed ideas, the answer must be no. Nevertheless, there are indications that Schleiermacher anticipates and is in substantial agreement with Husserl. For example, the structure of world-consciousness is the reciprocal correlation between self and world (other). This is not a merely accidental or contingent correlation, but an essential one; the world is the horizon of sensible consciousness. This is something like the general thesis of the natural attitude. Moreover, Schleiermacher's account of feeling as consciousness as such situates feeling on something like the transcendental level; feeling is both presupposed by and immanent in the more determinate modes of self-consciousness. However, although feeling is transcendental, it is not a formal structure or set of a priori categories as in Kant, or a pure absolute spontaneity as in Fichte. Schleiermacher shares with Husserl the peculiar concept of the transcendental as conscious life, as shot through with the thesis or belief in the reality of the world.

The relation between pretheoretical feeling and theoretical knowing is conceived by Schleiermacher in much the same way as Husserl, namely, as the prior foundation of theoretical cognition. Prereflective, immediate consciousness is not a confused, second-class form of theoretical cognition, nor does it refer to a merely abstract relation between ideas: "What I understand by . . . feeling does not at all proceed from a representation [*Vorstellung*], but rather it is the original expression of an immediate existential relation."[19] Theoretical knowledge is founded in feeling in the sense that it has its point of departure in the pregiven unity of self and world in feeling:

> If in general the immediate self-consciousness is the mediating link between moments in which knowing predominates and moments in which doing predominates . . . it will belong to piety [a modification of feeling] to stimulate and arouse knowing and doing, so that every moment in which piety predominates will include one or the other in germ. . . . Consequently, there are a knowing and a doing which belong to piety [feeling], but neither of these constitutes the essence of piety; rather they belong to it only as the aroused feeling comes to rest in a thought which fixes it, or in an action which expresses it.[20]

Schleiermacher does not explicitly say that feeling is the pretheoretical source of logical validities; however, he does think that knowing has a pretheoretical concrete genesis in feeling, for there is an affective moment presupposed by every genuine cognition: "Every impulse which tends towards perception and cognition, which has essence, attributes, and nature of things for its objects, begins with a stimulation of self-consciousness which accompanies the operation of cognition. . . . Wherever there is an objective consciousness, there is always an already-stimulated self-consciousness."[21]

Finally, Schleiermacher himself uses the term "belief" to designate the pretheoretical, affective correlation between self and world. He writes that in general, belief means to take something as true on the basis of feeling or immediate self-consciousness, that is, it is an intuitive certitude.[22] Belief is a pretheoretical certitude concerning the codeterminant of self-consciousness which is "different from, but not less certain than the certainty which accompanies the objective consciousness."[23] Not only is this subjective certitude different in kind from objective certainty, it has its own standard of measure.[24] It is an intuitive certitude prior to and independent of representations, inferences, and explicit judgment. It is a certitude generated by the direct, concrete interaction with and apprehension of the things themselves *as they give themselves*. It is irreducible to sense perception or inference, but forms the horizon and presupposition of all such particular cognitive acts. In this sense belief is the foundation, the transcendental source of theoretical knowledge.

The Life-world as the Object of Urglaube

In Husserl's late writings, the life-world (*Lebenswelt*) is the correlate of *Urglaube*. The life-world is an intersubjective, sociocultural world whose existence is straightforwardly accepted and taken for granted. As subject-relative, the life-world is directly intuitable in principle, in contrast to the mathematized idealizations of natural science. Yet the life-world is not simply subjective, since it exhibits nonsubject-relative structures and general features. Moreover, others fall within the sphere of the intuitable as delineated by Husserl. To be sure, others are not directly intuitable in their subjectivity; rather the other ego is appresented by (but not inferred from) his body.[25] The life-world presents two aspects or dimensions: on the one hand it is the correlate of transcendental consciousness in the sense that belief in the life-world is the transcendental condition of possible experience. On the other hand, the life-world is concretely experienced as a determinate social and cultural world. Thus it can be approached both from the perspective of transcendental phenomenology, and from the perspective(s) of history, psychology, and sociology.

There are hints of something like the life-world in Schleiermacher. For example, we have seen that he thinks consciousness is never simply consciousness or merely self-identical, but rather is essentially constituted through contrast. The question is, what is meant by the contrast between self and other constitutive of feeling? Is it merely a logical contrast between ego and non-ego as idealism contends? In the *Psychologie* he rejects the idealist interpretation because it construes the contrast as merely logical; it posits nothing real besides consciousness itself. Schleiermacher favors a realistic existential interpretation of the contrast: the primary contrast constitutive of consciousness is the contrast between I and thou, which he calls the "fundamental condition of all experience."[26] The non-ego, to which the concrete human ego is contrasted, is another human ego. Thus he contends that the ego is deficiently actual without its thou. Schleiermacher's designation of the contrast between I and thou as the fundamental condition of all experience implies that it is not a mere contingent or empirical apprehension, but rather a fundamental structure. Schleiermacher is not far from Husserl's thesis of transcendental intersubjectivity, that is, that the world is intersubjectively constituted at the transcendental level. It belongs to the very meaning of the world that it is a world for everyone, and not merely a world for me.

Schleiermacher also adopts an empirical, historical-cultural approach to human existence. Each individual learns of his origins not by inspecting an absolute, self-positing absolute ego, but from the stories of others who comprise the community which precedes and antedates him.[27] The historical-cultural approach is also employed in the *Glaubenslehre,* which juxtaposes the transcendental and historical approaches to the study of religion. It is a contributing factor in Schleiermacher's rejection of natural religion and theology in favor of historical religious communities. The world—including religion—is concretely a determinate historical-cultural world. Religion concretely exists in the form of historical religious communities.

The above similarities between Schleiermacher and Husserl can neither be pressed too far nor simply ignored. Schleiermacher is not far from Husserl's thesis concerning the priority and foundational character of the life-world, nor from his understanding of the social character of the life-world.

The Receptivity and Spontaneity of Human Freedom

In his discussion of human freedom and self-transcendence, Husserl uses the same terminology that Schleiermacher does, namely, receptivity (*Rezeptivität, Empfänglichkeit*) and spontaneity (*Spontaneität, Selbsttätigkeit*). It is also evident that Husserl follows a Schleiermacher-type interpretation of these terms, not a narrowly epistemological Kant-type interpretation. For Schleiermacher and Husserl, receptivity and spontaneity are more nearly modes of being in the world than merely psychological terms for the reception of impressions and the virtually automatic production of concepts. That is, they are concrete, existential modes of coexisting with others. For Schleiermacher these terms are an implicit criticism of Leibniz' windowless monads; receptivity and spontaneity imply that not only do monads have windows, they exist in concrete reciprocal interaction and interdependence.

We have noted that Schleiermacher observes that self-consciousness is essentially constituted by a contrast between a being-for-self and a coexistence-with-other, that is, a self-caused and non-self-caused element. The former self-caused element, or being-for-self, Schleiermacher calls the spontaneity of the self. The common element in all spontaneity-determinations of the self is the feeling of freedom.[28] However, freedom does not mean self-origination in an absolute creative sense, but rather a self-originated influence on other, whether this other be another human being, a mundane entity or the world. Without the free act of the self the other would not exist in the determinate state that it actually does. Conversely, the non-self-caused element in immediate consciousness Schleiermacher calls receptivity. The common element in all receptivity-determinations is the feeling of dependence.[29] The self is dependent on its other, such that the self would not exist as it actually does without its codetermining other. Note that freedom and dependence, spontaneity and receptivity are not mutually exclusive; they are different contrasting elements constitutive of immediate self-consciousness. The self is both free and dependent, dependent and yet free.

Husserl's discussion in *Ideen II* resembles that of Schleiermacher. Receptivity and spontaneity are determinate modes of the correlation between consciousness and world. Husserl indicates that receptivity is not a mere passivity opposed to freedom; rather receptivity is the lowest level (*Stufe*) of free activity.[30] He thereby agrees with Schleiermacher that receptivity is a condition of freedom, and that freedom is not absolute. Moreover, Husserl continues Schleiermacher's critique of determinism: the relation between self and other is not simply a causal relation. Receptivity is not a simple passivity like a block of stone which is to receive form from an external source. Rather, receptivity is itself a free condition, through which others and the common, intersubjective world are pregiven, that is, prior to the self-originated action of the self. Such pregivenness does not contradict or violate freedom, rather it is a condition of such. The correlation between self and other is not a relation of efficient causality, but rather an intentional relation. The causality effective in such an intentional relation is a causality of motivation, a causality inclusive of freedom and not antithetical to it. The life-world is pregiven to the self as a source of motivation and a field of potential action, and the self bypasses itself towards the world and other.

Schleiermacher and Husserl agree that freedom is finite; this means that freedom essentially includes receptivity. Receptivity in turn means that the self is not self-creating or producing, nor does it create its world. Rather the world is pregiven to the self as the field of its free activity and response. Schleiermacher writes: "If the objects are not created by our activity, it follows that they are as they are independent of us."[31] Even if this does not strictly "follow," Schleiermacher agrees with Husserl that the correlation between self and world is structured by contingency and the transcendence of the world and mundane entities to consciousness.

Conclusions

The point of the above comparisons of Schleiermacher with Husserl is that feeling as Schleiermacher understands and uses the term is not merely psychological, but essentially involves self-transcendence and intentionality. Schleiermacher stretches the psychological language of his day to say something more than psychology; feeling is primal consciousness of the world. If, as Husserl indicates, the clue to the intentionality of consciousness is its free self-bypassing and self-transcendence towards the world, then Schleiermacher clearly understands feeling or immediate consciousness to be intentional in this sense.

This conclusion is supported by a casual observation of the various types of feeling which Schleiermacher mentions. The diversity of feeling indicates that it undergoes differentiation through diverse objects, in short, that it is consciousness of ——, and exhibits an act-object correlation. The whole class of sensible or mundane feelings, including sympathy, compassion, honor, and patriotism, all are determinate modes of coexistence with other, exhibiting the general structure of reciprocal interaction.[32] Significantly, the distinctive religious feeling of utter dependence also exhibits the general structure of coexistence with other. However, it is distinguished from other modes of feeling by its codeterminant, which is nonmundane; hence it is a mode of coexistence with other which is not structured by reciprocity but by nonreciprocity or *utter* dependence. We shall turn our attention to this topic in the next section. For the present it is sufficient to observe Schleiermacher's contention that religion or piety is not simply synonymous with feeling as such, but rather is a special modification of feeling. This contention by itself gives the lie to Feuerbach's psychologizing interpretation of Schleiermacher, to the effect that feeling per se is declared to be the divine. That is simply not true. Feeling in its various intentional act-structures is the medium of access to many different objects, both mundane and divine.

THE FEELING OF UTTER DEPENDENCE

The feeling of utter dependence has freedom as its limiting condition in the sense that without a feeling of freedom, no feeling of utter dependence and no God-consciousness would be possible.[33] We have already found that Schleiermacher and Husserl regard receptivity as intrinsic to freedom; Husserl calls it the lowest grade (*Stufe*) of freedom. Schleiermacher's thesis concerning religious consciousness is that receptivity for God or the codeterminant of utter dependence is not the lowest, but rather the highest grade (*Stufe*) of freedom.[34] He is contending that without a feeling of freedom no God-consciousness would be possible, and without God or the transcendent Whence of utter dependence, there would be no freedom. Freedom is the *ratio cognoscendi* of God, and God is the *ratio essendi* of freedom. Schleiermacher acknowledges that this contention includes the God-consciousness in the self-consciousness in such a way that the two can neither be separated nor identified.[35] In order to understand Schleiermacher better, it will be helpful to sort out and discuss separately the following topics: freedom, utter dependence, and the codeterminant of utter dependence. In addition, we shall seek to clarify the sense of the feeling of utter dependence and its codeterminant through a comparison with the feeling of the sublime. The justification for such a comparison between Schleiermacher and Kant is that Schleiermacher himself mentions an analogy between the religious feeling and the feeling of the sublime, while offering a different interpretation of the latter from Kant. He even goes so far as to identify the sublime as such with God.

SCHLEIERMACHER'S ACCOUNT OF FREEDOM

Schleiermacher is distinguished from German idealism in his rejection of freedom interpreted as absolute autonomy. In a temporal being such as man, a feeling of absolute freedom (claimed by Schiller and Fichte) can have no place.[36] Schleiermacher does not agree with idealism in identifying human being or its freedom with the formal, noumenal freedom of transcendental subjectivity or an absolute ego. That sort of freedom is really an abstraction from human existence. To be sure, this is not to deny that human being is self-determining or autonomous; however, such self-determination is qualified and limited. In contrast to idealism, Schleiermacher sees human freedom as situated partly on the transcendental level, and partly on the historical and social level. He agrees with Kant that freedom is transcendental to the phenomenal realm. It is a causality without antecedents, or a spontaneously self-originated act. Freedom is either a transcendental act or it is not free. This excludes determinism; Schleiermacher thinks that freedom is man's capacity for self and world transcendence.

However, while man is free and self-originating, his freedom is not absolute; it is not a capacity for absolute self-origination or self-creation. The consciousness (feeling) of freedom is accompanied by a consciousness of limit: "the whole of our being does not present itself to our consciousness as having proceeded from our own spontaneous self-activity."[37] Human being cannot be identified with an absolute self-positing ego because it is not self-originating. Man is born into an antecedently existing community which sets real limits and conditions upon his freedom.[38] Moreover, human freedom is not simply or entirely noumenal, but it is also embodied in and exercised through an involuntary, biological organism. Consequently, while freedom is a transcendental act, it is not concretely exercised *ex nihilo* or *de novo,* but always in a context of and in reciprocity with the social and natural orders of being. Freedom exhibits both autonomy and receptivity, or limitation. Although freedom is a transcendental capacity for self-originated action, it is concretely actualized in degrees of more and less. Schleiermacher sees that while human freedom is transcendental, it can actually fail to be or coincide with itself. This possibility of noncoincidence with self is the condition of evil; it presupposes the temporality of freedom, and exhibits its finitude.

UTTER DEPENDENCE

We have found that man does not create either himself or his world; the receptivity of human freedom forbids such Promethean suggestions. Yet, both self and world are contingent, and point beyond themselves to a transcendent Whence: "The self-consciousness accompanying our entire self-activity (and because this is never zero, it accompanies our entire existence) and which negates absolute freedom, is already in and for itself the consciousness that the whole of our free, self-active being derives from elsewhere."[39] The feeling of utter dependence is a peculiar, distinctive receptivity-determination of the self in that although it exhibits the structure of coexistence with other, it qualifies that structure as nonreciprocal. This qualification has given rise to several questions and criticisms. First, it does not follow from the fact that the self is contingent and dependent that there is something on which the self depends. One cannot infer the satisfaction of indigence from the mere fact of indigence.[40] Second, Schleiermacher makes this illicit inference because he tacitly reads into religious experience the traditional metaphysical conception of the relation between God and world. Thus, not only does he violate his own methodological stricture that the feeling of utter dependence is not dependent on a prior conceptual knowledge of God, he makes use of the questionable Aristotelian scheme in which the world is dependent on and related to God, but God is not related to the world. Hegel has pointed out the disastrous consequences of this conceptual scheme: "A one-sided relation . . . is not a relation at all. If in fact, we are to understand by religion nothing more than a relation between ourselves and God, then God is left without any independent existence. God would, on this theory, exist in religion only, He would be something posited, something produced by us."[41] In the traditional conception, the relation between the world and God is one-sided. The God whose existence is thus inferred from the ontological indigence of the self or world is nothing more than a projection, a mere postulate, and has no existence transcendent to and independent of religious consciousness.

The above criticism of Schleiermacher is completely mistaken. God is not *inferred* from man's utter dependence. Consider what the feeling of utter dependence is: it is a receptivity-determination of the subject. As such, it is that through which the existence and causality of the codeterminant is *pregiven,* that is, given prior to and thus independent of the productive spontaneity of the self. Thus the codeterminant of receptivity cannot be a product or projection or an inference of the self. It is either pregiven, prior to such acts, or not at all. The feeling of utter dependence, therefore, is not an inference of the existence of something absent, but rather a discovery of a presence, a codeterminant, *das Woher.* In short, whatever else it is, the feeling of utter dependence signifies a mode of coexistence with other, and as such discovers and presupposes the other. It can only be understood as a correlation between self and this distinctive other.

This interpretation is borne out and supported by Schleiermacher's discussion in the *Psychologie.* There he mentions an analogy between the religious feeling and the feeling of the sublime. He describes the latter in the following passage: "Here the impression [of the sublime] is bound up with—I will not say a life-hindrance—but with the consciousness that we concede to the object beyond us a power over us, and we surrender ourselves to its power."[42] The feeling of the sublime is constituted by the power of the object over the subject; it is a mode of coexistence with other in which the being and power of the object are pregiven, that is, given antecedently to finite, free spontaneity. The object of the feeling of the sublime is overwhelming and surpassing; the experience it constitutes is both humbling and exhilarating. The self in its freedom is related to the sublime as that which the self cannot equal, much less surpass, master, and control. Kant writes concerning the sublime that "as the mind is not merely attracted by the object but is ever being alternately repelled, the satisfaction in the sublime does not so much involve a positive pleasure, as admiration and respect."[43] It is clear that the sublime is not the nemesis or annihilation of freedom; man is not wholly passive at the sublime. Rather the sublime is the occasion for man to measure himself against it, and to find in it a limit which he cannot equal or surpass.

Schleiermacher thinks that religion is similar to the feeling of the sublime. In his early *Speeches on Religion* he wrote that religion is "glorious reverence, both exalting and humbling."[44] This suggestion is developed further in the description of religion offered in the *Psychologie:* "What we mean by devotion [*Andacht*] in its simplest and most general sense is a finding of self under the control of another, a sinking as it were, under the infinity of the other, and yet a being attracted to it again and again. It is a losing of self in the infinite, accompanied by the recognition that every resistance is completely impossible."[45] The religious feeling exhibits a hum-

bling and exaltation similar to that of the sublime. The religious is both attracted to the infinite and terrified by it. The being laid hold of by the infinite is terrifying because it appears to imply loss of self and autonomy. If
this were the only feature of the nonreciprocal coexistence between self and
other constitutive of utter dependence, the charge that Schleiermacher reads
into experience the traditional metaphysical relation between world and
God would be plausible. However, although the self is terrified by the
infinite and the loss of control, it is also fascinated and attracted to the
infinite willingly. The self would not be willingly attracted to the infinite if
such attraction meant total annihilation and extinction. Rather Schleiermacher's meaning is that the self is attracted to the infinite because it is akin
to the infinite and finds its true being and destiny—including its full
freedom—in union with the infinite. This is Schleiermacher's version of the
Augustinian theme that the self is restless until it surrenders to and abides
in the infinite. This surrender is not annihilation; rather Schleiermacher is
appealing to the attractiveness and irresistibility of God, which alone can
satisfy man's longing for the infinite and eternal (*Seligkeit*).

These considerations make it evident that Schleiermacher is not treating
God as a mere projection of religious consciousness. The feeling of utter
dependence is a distinctive mode of coexistence with other, a distinctive
correlation between self and other. And this implies that that on which the
self utterly depends is pregiven, discovered as something already present,
and not merely inferred or postulated. As Schleiermacher's account of the
sublime indicates, he is not portraying the relation between God and world
in traditional terms. Not only is the self attracted to the infinite; the infinite
is related to the self. It has the self under its control, and the self is its
vehicle of expression. To be sure, this description is not a metaphysical
formulation or analysis; on the other hand, it is clear that it does not quite
fit the traditional metaphysical conception.

THE CODETERMINANT OF UTTER DEPENDENCE

Granted that the codeterminant of utter dependence is not the result of an
inference or postulation of the subject, but rather directly apprehended and
pregiven, what is the other so apprehended? It is clear that the other is the
whence of human being understood in its entirety as receptive and spontaneous. Both finite dependence and finite freedom have their basis in the
Whence. Further, the simultaneous humbling and exaltation of the self have
their basis in the Whence. Thus, there must be something in the Whence
which supports and is correlative to the dialectic of abasement and

exaltation on the one hand, and the polarity of freedom and dependence on the other. Schleiermacher's conviction is that the Whence is apprehended as living and dynamic, and that it exhibits a bipolar structure which he describes as absolute inwardness and absolute vitality.

In order to understand Schleiermacher's conviction and account of the transcendent Whence, some further discussion of the sublime is required. Specifically, Kant's account of the sublime object will illumine Schleiermacher's account. According to Kant, the sublime is infinite, that is, it is formless or boundless.[46] Such boundlessness inspires awe, fascination, and even terror at the sublime. Kant writes that "the transcendent [towards which the imagination is impelled in its apprehension] is for the imagination like an abyss in which it fears to lose itself."[47] Schleiermacher's early description of religious experience may reflect this very passage in Kant: "We . . . have strange, dread, mysterious emotions when the imagination reminds us that there is more in nature than we know."[48] The transcendent Whence of utter dependence exceeds the limits of imagination and is the limit principle of the imagination. It is formless, beyond form.

However, although the sublime is formless, even an abyss, it is not simply negative or nothing. How could merely abstract, conceptual nothingness inspire awe and dread? The formlessness of the sublime is something alive and dynamic. Kant proceeds to distinguish two contrasting elements in the formless: the mathematical sublime and the dynamical sublime. The mathematical sublime is the infinite or transcendent qua magnitude. An infinite magnitude humbles human cognitive powers because it is greater than can be conceived. The dynamical sublime is the infinite qua power; as such, it humbles human vital powers and cannot be equaled or surpassed by human spontaneity. Thus the sublime is infinite both in respect to magnitude and power. Kant writes: "We call that sublime which is absolutely great."[49] The absolutely great is not merely great in comparison with something else, but rather is "great beyond all comparison."[50] Thus the sublime is great in and of itself; it cannot be measured by any criterion external to itself or by anything besides itself. It is its own standard. The sublime is its own standard because it is the absolute maximum, that beyond which there is nothing greater. The sublime is its own measure and the measure of everything else, which, compared with the sublime, appears small and insignificant.

Kant's account of the sublime bears a resemblance to Anselm's idea of God as that beyond which nothing greater can be conceived. This apparent resemblance raises several questions. Is Kant tacitly reading a theological concept into aesthetic experience? Kant would deny this on two grounds:

First, he maintains that the sublime pleases without concept, "without reasoning about it, in the mere apprehension of it."[51] In short, the sublime is directly and pretheoretically apprehended as the codeterminant of aesthetic feeling. The experience of the sublime itself therefore exhibits the above-noted features of the sublime at the prereflective level. Although one might contend that Kant stands within and resembles a philosophical tradition concerning the sublime including Nikolaus Cusanus, Anselm, and Plotinus,[52] his appeal concerning the sublime is not to the tradition, but to experience itself as the source and foundation of his account, and of the account offered by the tradition. Thus Kant could reply that the experience of the sublime as that which is absolutely great in and of itself is the foundation and source of Anselm's concept. This is Schleiermacher's thesis, as we shall see shortly.

However, Kant would deny that the sublime is theological in the above Anselmian sense. Although he softened his attitude, he never dropped his opposition to the ontological proof. He offers therefore a different philosophical interpretation of the sublime. His account of the sublime appears in his *Critique of Judgment*. This has the effect of obscuring the interpretation of the ontological status of the sublime. It is never clear whether Kant means that the sublime is transcendent to consciousness, that is, "out there" in the world, or whether he means that the sublime resides merely in a feeling which accompanies the reflective judgment. Kant's psychological interpretation of feeling and his philosophical interpretation of the sublime take the latter, noncognitive course: The sublime is located "not so much in the object as in our own state of mind in the estimation of it."[53] The sublime is identified with the self-determination and self-legislation of autonomy. Consequently, the sublime present in the world is but a projection of the sublime in man.[54]

Schleiermacher accepts Kant's phenomenological description of the sublime, but not his philosophical-moral interpretation. What is sublime, inspiring awe and respect because it is great in and of itself, transcends the self and cannot be simply identified with the self as Kant does. The seriousness of the sublime (Kant's term) forbids a merely immanent interpretation of it; the sublime is more than reason or a postulate of reason. Schleiermacher identifies the sublime with God: "The absolute sublime object is God . . . because his self-determination is the ground and basis of the whole of being."[55] Schleiermacher agrees with Kant that the original sense of the sublime is that which is absolutely great in and of itself. It is the self-sufficiency of the sublime which inspires awe and respect. In this sublime self-sufficiency lies the objective, experiential foundation of theology: God, or the Sublime as such, is that which is great in and of itself, and not merely great in comparison with other things. The Sublime as such is the maximal being, the Most High, which is qualitatively different from all other beings. There is substantial agreement between Schleiermacher and the other great theologian of religious experience, Jonathan Edwards, concerning the objective correlate and foundation of religious experience. Edwards writes that "The first objective ground . . . of [religious] affections is the transcendently excellent and amiable nature of divine things as they are in themselves, and not any conceived relation they bear to self or self-interest."[56] As the Sublime as such, God is great in and of himself, transcendent to and greater than human being. Schleiermacher and Edwards are in striking agreement in their independent descriptions of God as the codeterminant of religious experience.

Schleiermacher goes beyond Edwards in distinguishing two contrasting elements of the Whence of utter dependence. We shall see that he contends that the best, least speculative terminology for the Whence is that God is absolute inwardness and absolute vitality. The latter (vitality) roughly corresponds to the dynamical sublime as described by Kant. However, the former goes beyond the mathematical sublime; it suggests that God is not merely substance, but also subject. Despite his criticism of anthropomorphisms, Schleiermacher contends that God must be conceived as living and dynamic. Life essentially involves contrast and opposition, dynamism and movement; God's life is exhibited in the contrast between absolute inwardness and absolute vitality. There will be more to say about this later.

To conclude this section, we do not claim to have presented Schleiermacher's idea of God, much less his full doctrine of God. We have unearthed some background elements in the prereflective, pretheoretical apprehension of the original sense of God. These include the analysis of feeling as intentional, the distinctive modification of feeling qua feeling of utter dependence, and the distinctive mode of coexistence with other which constitutes the latter. We now turn to the *Glaubenslehre* to see how Schleiermacher derives the idea of God and constructs a doctrine of God as the source and correlate of utter dependence.

THE CONSTITUTION OF THE IDEA OF GOD

There are two essential features of the idea of God in the *Glaubenslehre*. First, the idea is concrete; it expresses the object pole of an immediate existential relation, and involves a real apprehension of its object. Second, the idea of God has two distinct strata or dimensions, the transcendental and the historical. The full idea of God is a concrete, determinate synthesis of the transcendental and historical strata. For purposes of analysis, Schleiermacher considers the transcendental stratum in abstraction from its concrete determinacy. That element of the idea of God comprising its transcendental stratum I propose to call the *Transcendent as limit,* in recognition of the fact that the Whence of utter dependence functions as the limit principle of human freedom and self-transcendence. The full, concrete determinate idea of God, inclusive of the transcendental and historical strata, I propose to call the *Transcendent as God,* in recognition of the fact that for Schleiermacher the concrete historical elements are decisive in determining the meaning of the idea.

THE CONTRAST BETWEEN REAL AND NOTIONAL APPREHENSIONS

Before discussing the genesis of the idea of God, it will be helpful to prepare the way by sketching briefly the contrast between real and notional apprehensions which is central to Schleiermacher's argument concerning God in the *Glaubenslehre.* Following Locke, Schleiermacher distinguishes two modes of apprehension, one directed towards concrete particular things, and the other directed primarily to ideas or notions, which are the abstract creations of the mind. John Henry Newman formulated this contrast explicitly as a contrast between real and notional apprehension.[57] In real apprehensions, the mind is directed to concrete things in and through their images, while in notional apprehensions it is directed primarily towards abstract, general ideas, rather than the things themselves.

Closely related to these two modes of apprehension are two different modes of thought and knowledge, the one concrete, the other abstract. The former Newman calls belief or assent; the latter he calls inference. What Newman terms belief Schleiermacher calls subjective consciousness, and also subjective certitude or belief; and what Newman terms inference Schleiermacher calls objective consciousness or knowing. The two are contrasted as follows: "We may call it the normal state of inference to apprehend propositions as notions; and we may call it the normal state of assent to apprehend propositions as things . . . An act of *inference includes in its object the dependence of its thesis upon its premises,* that is, upon a relation which is abstract; but an act of *assent rests wholly on the thesis of its object,* and the reality of the thesis is almost a condition of its unconditionality."[58] Inference is a mode of apprehension mediated by abstract general concepts and which is intellectually derived from premises by discursive reasoning. It includes the dependence of its thesis upon relevant antecedent conditions; the conclusion follows provided that the concepts are clear and distinct, the premises in which they appear are true, and the reasoning is valid. Since this entire complex of notions, premises, and conclusion is the object of inference or objective knowledge and consciousness, inference is conditional. In contradistinction, belief or assent is a mode of apprehension directed to particular concrete things and is immediate, direct, and unconditional. It is not derived from ideas or premises, but from its object as directly given and apprehended. The thesis of assent directly reflects and depends upon the pregivenness of the thing itself (compare Locke's simple idea) prior to intellectual formation, conceptualization, and judgment. Its unconditionality depends on the independent reality and pregivenness of its object.

It should be noted that although real apprehension and notional apprehension are in contrast with each other, they are not in opposition or conflict with each other. They are different ways of holding the same thesis. In principle there is no conflict between belief and inference. Schleiermacher observes that since these are the subjective and objective forms of self-consciousness, a conflict in principle between the two would mean that self-consciousness, and therefore human being, were self-contradictory.[59] Newman notes that a single proposition may admit of both interpretations. For example, it may have a real sense as used by one man, and a notional sense as used by another; moreover, the same proposition may express both a notion and a concrete matter of fact, for example, as Dido embodies the essence of femininity.[60] Real and notional apprehensions are not related as the true and the false, but as the abstract and the concrete. Each is a different and independent mode of apprehending and holding the same content, the same thesis. It is erroneous either to identify them—as in rationalism—or to play them off against each other—as in sentimentalism and existentialism.

THE CONCRETE GENESIS OF THE IDEA OF GOD

Scheleiermacher's discussion of the feeling of utter dependence is meant to show that the idea of God essentially involves a real apprehension. Schleiermacher writes that "the pious feeling does not at all proceed from a representation or concept; rather it is the original expression of an immediate existential relation."[61] The term *god* originally signifies the Whence of utter dependence: "In the first instance God signifies for us simply that which is the codeterminant in this feeling and that to which we refer our being in such a state."[62] The sense of God is passively pregiven in and through the feeling of utter dependence, prior to all spontaneous conceptualization and judgment. Like the sublime, God inspires awe, reverence, and respect—as Kant expresses it—"without concept . . . without reasoning about it, in the mere apprehension of it."[63] The passive genesis of the idea in receptivity (feeling) presupposes and points to the being and act of the codeterminant; as Newman says, the reality of the thesis of assent depends directly on the reality of its object. And Schleiermacher writes that belief in God is a "certitude concerning the feeling of utter dependence as such, that is, as conditioned by a being outside of us, and expressing our relation to that being."[64] Hence Schleiermacher declares belief in God independent of objective knowledge of God. To refer belief to mere abstract ideas, which are after all merely the creations of the human intellect, is to misplace the concreteness of belief and to run the risk of idolatry.

However, although the concrete sense of the idea of God is passively pregiven, God is not given as an external mundane object. God is not externally or contingently given.[65] Although the idea involves a real apprehension and is thus experiential, it is nevertheless not derived from experience or from any particular positing of the object. The idea of God is transcendental, at least in part. Schleiermacher calls this aspect of it the transcendent ground, the *terminus a quo* of thought and being, and defends its innateness against Locke.[66]

THE TRANSCENDENTAL DIMENSION OF THE IDEA OF GOD

Schleiermacher's discussion of the transcendental dimension is an account of the conditions of possibility of an idea of God, and not an account of any particular God-concept. It runs something like this: The feeling of utter dependence is the highest grade of human self-consciousness, and thus is a universal life-element of human existence. This means that man is essentially constituted such that he has an inner or innate tendency and disposition towards God-consciousness.[67] Man is not only utterly dependent like the rest of finite, temporal being, he is also immediately conscious of utter dependence. When the ontological situation of utter dependence is concretely apprehended, the idea of God comes into being as the expression of the Whence of utter dependence.[68]

It is apparent that this transcendental dimension of the idea of God is closely related to the ontological argument. It is particularly close to those interpretations which develop the argument as a reflexive one, and which interpret the idea of God as a limit-concept. McGill describes this version as follows: "The idea of God is simply the mind's recognition of what lies at the root of its own intellectual activity. Human thinking has the idea of God and is constantly seeking for God . . . because it is sustained and activated *from within* by God. This is an idea in the *active* sense. It is that by which and toward which the mind is moved and provoked in its thinking."[69] Schleiermacher presents such a reflexive version of the ontological argument in his *Dialektik;* God is identified with the transcendent ground, the *Urgrund,* and the *terminus a quo* of thinking.[70] In this interpretation the argument for God is transcendental rather than a traditional demonstration from premises to conclusion: "It does not discover what is given to consciousness, but what is at the foundation of consciousness. It moves in a regressive manner from an activity to its inner ground. It produces . . . what the mind does not embrace in any of its objective representations, but . . . what embraces it and stands at the origin of its dynamism."[71]

However, despite similarities, there are important differences between the transcendental argument given above and the feeling of utter dependence. The above argument is a regressive quest for what lies at the foundation of the intellectual activity and dynamism of the mind. But the feeling of utter dependence intends what lies at the foundation of human spontaneity as such; Schleiermacher does not restrict the mode of recognition of the Transcendent to an intellectual one. Rather the Transcendent is grasped as the Whence of entire human being, including its freedom. Neither theoretical nor practical reason is given primacy. Moreover, the feeling of utter dependence reflects the passive pregivenness of the Transcendent; the movement is from the pregivenness of the thing itself to its idea, and not a regressive movement from the idea to its condition of possibility. The feeling of utter dependence is distinguished from all forms of argument in that it is a real apprehension, and not a merely notional apprehension. Stated othewise, the feeling of utter dependence refers to the movement of the Transcendent towards man, rather than the attempt of man to grasp the Transcendent. This does not mean that the two are in conflict or opposition, but merely to observe with Schleiermacher that such striving after the Transcendent "is a separate act with which we are not here concerned."[72]

The most radical divergence of Schleiermacher from Anselm is his refusal to allow that the ontological principle by itself constitutes the entire idea of God. The ontological principle comprises merely the abstract, formal-transcendental structure of the idea of God, but not its full concrete reality. Considered by itself it does not express an actual God-consciousness, but only the inner disposition towards God-consciousness. To be sure, this inner disposition is not blank, or wholly empty and formal; however, its object, the Whence, is indeterminate. Let us call the disposition towards God-consciousness, considered in abstraction from the actual God-consciousness, an unfulfilled intention, which aims at the Transcendent as limit. Let us call the actualized disposition towards God-consciousness a fulfilled intention towards the Transcendent, which apprehends the Transcendent as God. What fulfills the intention and actualizes the disposition towards God-consciousness is the being and causality of the Transcendent. Schleiermacher describes the objective element of such codetermination of feeling as a "transcendent determination of consciousness . . . in which the transcendent Ground or the Highest Being itself is represented."[73] In the fulfilled intention towards the Transcendent, "the *Urgrund* is posited in us just as in perception things are posited in us."[74] The concrete, actualized God-consciousness is more than the merely abstract formal structure, and cannot be deduced or derived from the merely abstract structure, since it depends on the act of the Transcendent which is not deducible from its abstract structure and concept.

THE HISTORICAL DIMENSION OF THE IDEA OF GOD

The preceding account of utter dependence considered it in abstraction from its full, concrete determinacy. Although the feeling of utter dependence is a universal life-element, there is no absolutely universal consciousness of utter dependence in general: "It is impossible for anyone to be in some moments exclusively conscious of his relations within the [finite] sphere of contrasts, and in other moments exclusively conscious of his utter dependence in and of itself in a general way, because it is as a particular person within the sphere of contrasts, determined in a particular way in a particular moment, that he is conscious of his utter dependence."[75] The feeling of utter dependence is always historically and culturally shaped. Abstractly considered it is the same in all, but concretely it is differently determined in each.[76] The concrete determinacy of the feeling of utter dependence is reflected in its correlative idea of God: "There is no purely monotheistic piety, in which the God-consciousness alone and by itself constitutes the sole content of religious experience. Rather, just as in Christian piety a relation to Christ always occurs with the general God-consciousness, so also in Judaism there is always a relation to the lawgiver."[77] The abstract, generic God-consciousness is modified in its concrete acutalizations. Thus, in the faith-community of Judaism, the Whence of utter dependence is concretely represented as commanding will.[78] In Christianity the general thesis is: "no general God-consciousness without a relation to Christ, and no relation to Christ without a copositing of the general God-consciousness."[79] Thus the Whence or the Transcendent is concretely represented as sovereign redemptive love and as the Father of the Redeemer.

Such historical determinacy of the God-consciousness is not simply a particular instantiation of the abstract, formal scheme. Schleiermacher seeks to correct precisely such a formalist view of the idea of God. The way in which the general abstract features come to concrete realization is meaning-determining. The Transcendent as limit is indeterminate; its concrete significance and meaning is to be grasped from the standpoint of its concrete actualization as part of a larger, more inclusive whole, namely, the Transcendent as God. The transcendental dimension of the idea of God makes possible its concrete determinacy, and in turn the transcendental generic features undergo modification in their actualization. For this reason the Transcendent as God is not deducible or derivable a priori from the Transcendent as limit; the concrete is more than the merely abstract and cannot be derived from the merely abstract. Hence the determinate features of the Transcendent as God are equally constitutive of the meaning of the term "god." In fact, Schleiermacher goes so far in his correction of formalism that he allows one concrete feature to be identical with and decisive for the meaning of the abstract term "god," namely, love. We shall subsequently show in the chapter on trinity that, contrary to widely held opinion, Schleiermacher finds the basis of the historical determinacy of the Christian God-consciousness in God himself.

THE FEELING OF UTTER DEPENDENCE
AS A REPLACEMENT FOR THEOLOGICAL PROOFS

Schleiermacher's contention that the feeling of utter dependence takes the place for the *Glaubenslehre* of the so-called objective proofs for the existence of God has been widely interpreted as sentimentalism, that is, as subjectivism and noncognitivism in theology. The theological assertions of the *Glaubenslehre,* it is said, reflect nothing more than a condition of pious sentiment; they express merely the feeling of utter dependence, or man's relation to God, but not God himself. Hence they are nothing more than theological belief and opinion, not objective theological knowledge.[80] By severing the *Glaubenslehre* from the theological proofs and objective consciousness, Schleiermacher appears to rest his case for God on mere subjective belief and opinion. The *Glaubenslehre* appears as an antimetaphysical, anti-intellectual, noncognitive theology.

Such appearances are deceptive. Schleiermacher seeks to locate theology in prereflective, lived experience. His phenomenological description of the feeling of utter dependence is neither for nor against, but prior to the objectifying metaphysical enterprise. The close kinship between Schleiermacher's descriptions of utter dependence and the reflexive transcendental versions of the ontological argument make it clear that Schleiermacher is far from a noncognitive or antimetaphysical interpretation of religious consciousness and its object. Rather he is tracing the argument to its experiential foundations; in this respect he is quite Augustinian.

Schleiermacher refuses to conceive belief and knowledge as the noncognitive and the cognitive respectively. *Both* belief and knowledge are in contrast with the noncognitive. Both belief and knowledge are modes of holding the same proposition, the same truth, although each has its own grounds for doing so. Belief, as a mode of feeling, is a direct intuitive apprehension of the thing itself, while knowing holds the same content mediately in abstract notional form, on the basis of intellectual spontaneity, including conceptualization and inference. Feeling and belief, and knowledge or inference, are thus different modes of apprehension. The contrast and independence of these two modes of apprehension gives rise to Newman's paradox: "When inference is clearest, assent may be least forcible, and when assent is most intense, inference may be least distinct . . . while apprehension strengthens assent, inference often weakens apprehension."[81] In principle there is no conflict between belief and objective knowledge, rather, the two are related as the concrete and the abstract. Thus, while they may agree, there are irreducible differences in the mode of apprehension. Objective knowledge is more explicit but less certain than belief, while belief is more certain but less explicit conceptually than knowledge. Moreover, objective knowledge is not always superior to belief, for "what is gained in depth and exactness is lost in freshness and vigor."[82] For these reasons Schleiermacher declines to join Hegel in the bacchanalian revelries of objective logic or in the faustian quest for absolute knowledge. Hegel's enterprise leads to an illusory reversal of the concrete relation between thought and experience which makes it appear as if religious experience is merely a derivative moment of speculative conceptual knowledge. Schleiermacher's view of the relationship between belief and knowledge finds expression in his discussion of Anselm.

SCHELEIERMACHER AND ANSELM:
BELIEF AND OBJECTIVE KNOWLEDGE

We have already said that the feeling of utter dependence is related to the ontological proof. However, we distinguished the former as a real apprehension dependent on the givenness of its object, from the latter as a notional apprehension mediated by concept and inference. In Schleiermacher's view the argument does not move merely at the level of abstract ideas, and thus is not an ontological argument which infers existence from concept. Rather the proof, including its concepts, is grounded in religious experience; in Tillich's language, God (as the Whence of utter dependence) is the presupposition of the idea of God. Schleiermacher describes Anselm's procedure as follows: "He proceeds from the indubitable, invariant God-consciousness given in self-consciousness, and he postulates that this is to be made explicit in concept [that is, in objective consciousness]."[83] Thus, the ontological argument *qua* argument presupposes religious experience in the sense that the latter furnishes the idea with which the proof begins. Belief in God, which is immediately certain of the object of utter dependence, is prior to and independent of objective theoretical knowledge and proof. Belief includes an underlying real apprehension of its object. However, such subjective certitude falls short of apodicticity: the existence of God is naïvely presupposed and taken for granted in historical religious experience. It usually is not even explicitly asserted; the original belief in God is not an explicit assertion that God exists, in opposition or a negation to another assertion, namely, that there is no God. Such opposition reveals that belief has already become reflective, perhaps even challenged. Furthermore, the proposition "God exists" is not held originally as an explicit reflective judgment, the denial of which is self-contradictory. The original, life-world objective self-evidence of God's existence is not in the form of self-evident propositions; the latter self-evidence is grounded in the former. But the former pretheoretical self-evidence of the thing itself is subject-relative in form, that is, it is felt, it is a belief.

Anselm's explication of what faith believes concerning God changes the form but not the content or the intentionality of belief. This explication involves a translation of the content from its subject-relative determinacy into general notional form, into concept and proposition. It involves the transformation of a real apprehension into a notional apprehension. The transcendent Whence, experienced as the Sublime as such, great in itself, is now expressed notionally as that than which nothing greater can be conceived. Since the latter is a general concept, a notion, no feeling of utter dependence is needed in order to apprehend and understand it. The conclusion of the argument is that the necessary existence of God is so certain that, even if one did not believe it, one could not fail to understand it. Such an objectifying translation of the content of belief into notions goes beyond experience and apparently gives belief foundation in objective knowledge. Assuming that the proof is successful, its objective certainty is so great that only a fool would deny the existence of God. Such certainty appears to achieve for belief a virtually unshakable objective foundation by converting it into knowledge.

Schleiermacher is not a fool, nor does he wish to challenge the success and adequacy of the proofs as products of conceptualization and inference. His point is rather that the Western intellectual tradition has tended to overestimate the accomplishments of such proofs. He points out that the proofs have limits, since "No science can by means of mere ideas reach and elicit what is individual, but must stop short with what is general."[84] Even if the argument succeeds in establishing that God necessarily exists, necessary existence is not found within experience, but is something which is abstract and notional. Anselm himself concedes this point when he says, "If you have found God, why don't you feel that you have found Him? Why, O Lord, does not my soul feel Thee if it has found Thee?"[85] In this perhaps the most rationalistic of all proofs for God, we find illustrated Newman's paradox: what is gained in conceptual depth, precision, and exactness, is lost in concreteness and subjective certitude Hence the objective proof of Anselm is not superior in all respects to the naïve belief which it seeks to understand and explicate, for reasons which Newman explains: "The margin between the abstract conclusions of science and the concrete facts we wish to ascertain, will be found to reduce the force of inferential method from demonstration to mere determination of the probable."[86] Theological proofs are not demonstrations in the strict sense, but merely determinations of probability because they cannot reach what is concrete and particular, that is, they fall short of real apprehensions. Consequently they do not create belief, but rather presuppose it, and what they extend is not belief or subjective certainty, but objective consciousness. For this reason therefore, they have no place in a *Glaubenslehre,* and cannot be given a theological form. They should be replaced by reflection on the feeling of utter dependence, and the latter will thus take the place of the theological proofs for phenomenological theology.

However, Schleiermacher is not thereby denying that belief is meaningful, or cognitive, or that it has metaphysical implications and assumptions. The *Glaubenslehre* is not an antimetaphysical theology, but a pretheoretical, phenomenological theology. Schleiermacher's point is that phenomenological description and clarification must precede objectifying metaphysical formulation. In order to properly understand theological assertions, one must understand their pretheoretical foundations in religious experience, that is, both the object as it originally gives itself to consciousness, and the modes of consciousness correlative to its self-givenness. Thus, Schleiermacher does not seek to eliminate the language of metaphysics from the *Glaubenslehre,* rather he seeks to bring it under control of the given.

Consequently it is a serious mistake to regard the *Glaubenslehre* as a theology of mere belief, or of mere private, subjective opinion. The *Glaubenslehre* sets forth the social, intersubjective belief of the Christian faith-community. To call this mere opinion is to assume that there is a higher objective standpoint above mere faith from which it can be judged as merely subjective, and its images determined as mere images. Such a standpoint is abstract and formal: "Science working by itself, reaches truth in the abstract, and probability in the concrete, but what we aim at is truth in the concrete."[87] Schleiermacher anticipated the objection that the *Glaubenslehre* is merely a theology of subjective opinion:

> Many theologians are in complete agreement with the definition of dogmatic theology which we have here established, but assign this dogmatic to a pretty low level, as being concerned only with the presentation of ecclesiastical opinions. They contend that there must stand above it another and higher theology which would *set aside those ecclesiastical opinions in order to bring out and make clear the essential truths of religion.* However, the Christian doctrine of God and Salvation cannot possibly recognize such a distinction between church doctrines and the essential truths of religion (which, after all, are supposed to be Christian as well, since otherwise there could be no talk of them in connection with dogmatic theology). . . . Therefore, if anybody is disposed to say that the ecclesiastical doctrine . . . is mere opinion . . . it must be replied that nevertheless there is nothing superior to it in the realm of Christian knowledge, except the purer and more perfect ecclesiastical doctrine which may be found in some other period and in other presentations.[88]

Schleiermacher challenges the dualism between theoretical knowledge and the noncognitive, merely emotive. First he denies that the abstract formal standpoint from which one grasps the so-called essential truths of religion is epistemologically superior and primary. That view is speculative folly and needs to be restrained by a sober recognition of the life-world as the foundation of all human praxis, including the theoretical.

Second, to propose to study the essential truths of religion by setting aside the actual beliefs of the church is not only a self-contradictory, mindless objectivism and formalism, it is also to lose sight of the given, the actual living data which theology studies. In Christianity the so-called essential truths of religion find concrete embodiment and modifications. A theology which abstracted from and simply set aside such concrete embodiment of the essential structures would cease to be a genuine Christian theology. It would subvert the essence of Christianity and result in generic formalism.

Third, since the essential and universal features of religion find concrete embodiment and modification in the essence of Christianity, it follows that a *Glaubenslehre* cannot be an antimetaphysical, noncognitive theology. For Christian faith in God and in redemption has metaphysical implications and presuppositions. For example, certain world-views are excluded, namely, those which deny there is a god, and which consequently have no way of relating and distinguishing God and world, and the higher and the lower grades of feeling or self-consciousness in man. Without those metaphysical assumptions it is impossible to speak about sin as alienation from God, about the need of redemption and the reality of redemption.[89] Although the *Glaubenslehre* has metaphysical implications, not any metaphysics will do as a vehicle of communication; some are better than others. We shall see in the following chapters that Schleiermacher finds it necessary, largely for reasons intrinsic to Christianity itself, to revise the metaphysical language of theology in order to produce better, more adequate statements of the meaning and significance of Christian faith. In particular, it will be necessary to revise traditional theism in order to set forth the distinctive meaning of Christian faith and its central affirmations about God. In the next chapter we shall examine the historical precedent and background of Schleiermacher's concept of God in the thought of Nikolaus Cusanus.

NOTES

1. Robert Williams, "Consciousness and Redemption in the Thought of Friedrich Schleiermacher" (Ph.D. diss., Union Theological Seminary, 1971).

2. *Gl,* § 3.

3. *Gl,* § 4.

4. I am following Max Scheler, *Formalism in Ethics and Non-Formal Ethics of Values,* trans. by Manfred S. Frings and Roger L. Funk (Evanston: Northwestern University Press, 1973). This statement concerning intentionality needs qualification. The intentionality of consciousness does not settle or establish the reality-status of the intentional object. Intentionality means that it belongs to consciousness to be directed to an object, that is, to be consciousness of ———. The object intended, however, could be real, imaginary, fictional, dreamt, wished for, and so forth. However, intentionality does clarify somewhat the psychological status of consciousness, namely, that it is not merely subjective or merely consciousness of an inner psychological state. It belongs to consciousness to transcend itself and be directed to meanings, including real meanings. For a discussion of intentionality and reality, see *EM,* pp. 65 ff.

5. Scheler, *Formalism,* pp. 262 ff.

6. J.N. Tetens, *Philosophische Versuche ueber die menschliche Natur und Entwicklung* (Leipzig, 1777); Immanuel Kant, *Critique of Judgment,* trans. J.H. Bernard (New York: Haffner Publishing Co., 1951). For helpful discussions see Lewis White Beck, *A History of Early German Philosophy* (Cambridge, Mass.: Belknap Press, 1969); Harold Hoffding, *A History of Modern Philosophy,* 2 vols., trans. B.E. Meyer (New York: Dover Publications, 1955), vol. 2.

7. *Gl,* § 3.2; Schleiermacher is citing his friend Henrich Steffens, *Von der falsche Theologie und dem Wahren Glauben* (Breslau, 1823), cited in *Der Christliche Glaube,* ed. Martin Redeker (Berlin: Walter de Gruyter & Co., 1960), p. 17 n.

8. Ibid.

9. Ibid.

10. *Gl,* § 3.5.

11. Dilthey was a foremost interpreter of Schleiermacher, whose *Leben Schleiermachers* and *Schleiermachers System als Philosophie und Theologie* are standard works. Dilthey was influenced by and sought to develop further Schleiermacher's theory of hermeneutics in the direction of an historical interpretation of culture, which he distinguished from natural sciences and to which he gave the name, *Geisteswissenschaft.* Husserl regarded Dilthey as one of the first to see the inadequacies of a "natural science of the soul" (*Ideen II: Phaenomenologische Untersuchungen zur Konstitution,* ed. Marly Biemel [*Husserliana,* vol. 4], The Hague: Martinus Nijhoff, 1952, p. 172). Husserl seeks to provide a philosophical foundation for the distinctive *Geisteswissenschaften* through an intentional and constitutional analysis of their sense. In such analysis, Husserl continues and furthers the concerns and program of Schleiermacher and Dilthey. See Hans-Georg Gadamer, *Truth and Method* (New York: Seabury Press, 1975) pp. 58 ff.

12. *Gl,* § 4.1.

13. *Gl,* § 4.2.

14. Edmund Husserl, *Ideas: A General Introduction to Pure Phenomenology,* trans. W.R. Boyce Gibson (New York: Collier Macmillan, 1962), p. 96.

15. Ibid., p. 274.

16. Ibid., pp. 274–78.

17. Edmund Husserl, *Experience and Judgment,* ed. Ludwig Landgrebe, trans. James Churchill and Karl Ameriks (Evanston: Northwestern University Press 1973), p. 30 (italics by R.R.W.).

18. Edmund Husserl, *Crisis of European Science and Transcendental Phenomenology,* trans. David Carr (Evanston: Northwestern University Press, 1970) p. 124.

19. Schleiermacher, *Sendschreiben an Luecke,* ed. Hermann Mulert (Giessen: Toepelmann, 1908), p. 13; cited in Redeker ed., p. 21 n.

20. *Gl,* § 3.4.

21. *Gl,* § 46.1.

22. *Gl,* § 14.1.

23. Ibid.

24. *Gl,* § 3.4.

25. Husserl, *Ideen II,* pp. 162–72. See also Edmund Husserl, *Cartesian Meditations,* trans. D. Cairns (The Hague: Martinus Nijhoff, 1960), pp. 108 ff.

26. Friedrich Schleiermacher, *Psychologie,* ed. Ludwig George (Berlin: G. Reimer, 1862), pp. 17–20. Hereafter cited as *Psychologie.*

27. Ibid., pp. 40 ff.

28. *Gl,* § 4.2.

29. Ibid.

30. Husserl, *Ideen II*, p. 213.

31. *Gl*, § 4.3.; Redeker ed., p. 27, n. "c."

32. *Gl*, § 4.2. See also § 5.1, Redeker ed., p. 32, n. "a."

33. *Gl*, § 4.3.

34. *Gl*, § 4; 5; 32.2.

35. *Gl*, § 4.4.

36. *Gl*, § 4.3 This analysis of how the self is temporalized and temporalizes itself distinguishes Schleiermacher from idealism. See Friedrich Schiller, "On the Sublime," *Essays Aesthetical and Philosophical* (London: Bell & Sons, 1884).

37. Ibid.

38. Friedrich Schleiermacher, *Soliloquies,* trans. and with an introduction by Horace Friess (Chicago: Open Court, 1957), p. 18: "Freedom finds its limit in another freedom, and whatever happens freely bears the marks of limitation and community."

39. *Gl*, § 4.3.

40. See Van A. Harvey, "A Word in Defense of Schleiermacher's Theological Method," *Journal of Religion* 42 (July 1962).

41. G.W.F. Hegel, "Lectures on the Proofs for the Existence of God," in *Lectures on the Philosophy of Religion,* 3 vols., trans. E.B. Speirs and J.B. Sanderson (New York: The Humanities Press, 1962), 3:192.

42. *Psychologie,* p. 200.

43. Kant, *Critique of Judgment,* p. 83 (§ 23).

44. Schleiermacher, *On Religion: Speeches to Its Cultured Despisers,* trans. John Oman (New York: Harper & Row, 1958), p. 67.

45. *Psychologie,* p. 211.

46. Kant, *Critique of Judgment,* p. 82 (§ 23).

47. Ibid. p. 97 (§ 27).

48. Schleiermacher, *On Religion,* p. 69.

49. Kant, *Critique of Judgment,* p. 86 (§ 25).

50. Ibid.

51. Ibid., p. 83.

52. See Plotinus, *The Enneads,* trans. Stephen McKenna (London: Faber & Faber, 1956), pp. 587, 619; Nikolaus Cusanus, *De Docta Ignorantia,* in *PTS,* vol. 1; and Anselm, *Proslogion,* trans. M.J. Charlesworth (Oxford: Clarendon Press, 1965).

53. Kant, *Critique of Judgment,* p. 94; see also p. 104: "Sublimity therefore, does not reside in anything of nature, but only in our mind, insofar as we can become conscious that we are superior to nature."

54. See Beck, *Early German Philosophy,* p. 501.

55. Schleiermacher, *Aesthetik* (Rudolf Odebrecht, *Friedrich Schleiermachers Aesthetik* [Berlin: Walter de Gruyter, 1931]), p. 104.

56. Jonathan Edwards, *A Treatise Concerning Religious Affections,* ed. John E. Smith (New Haven: Yale University Press, 1957), pt. 3.

57. John Henry Newman, *A Grammar of Assent* (New York: Doubleday Image Book, 1955). There is common philosophical background between Edwards, Schleiermacher, Newman, and Husserl, namely, John Locke. It is well known that both Edwards and Newman read and were influenced by Locke (although with important revisions). Schleiermacher refers to Locke as the originator of *Gefuehlsphilosophie.* See Schleiermacher, *Geschichte der Philosophie* ([*Saemmtliche Werke,* III/4], Berlin: G. Reimer, 1839), p. 263. Husserl read and

commented on Locke and Hume, regarding the latter as a superior phenomenologist to Kant. See Husserl, *Erste Philosophie I: Kritische Ideengeschichte* (1923–24), ed. Rudolf Boehm (The Hague: Martinus Nijhoff, 1956).

58. Newman, *Grammar of Assent*, p. 51 (italics by R.R.W.).

59. *G1*, § 28.3.

60. Newman, *Grammar of Assent*, pp. 30–31.

61. See n. 19 above.

62. *G1*, § 4.4.

63. Kant, *Critique of Judgment*, p. 83.

64. *G1*, § 14.1.

65. *G1*, § 4.4; 4.1.

66. *Dial. (J)*, p. 434. Cf. *Dial. (O)*, p. 307.

67. *G1*, § 4.4, 5; 33.1; 50.4.

68. *G1*, § 4.4.

69. Arthur C. McGill, "Recent Discussions of Anselm's Argument," *The Many-Faced Argument* (New York: Macmillan, 1967), p.90; see also pp. 83 ff.

70. *Dial. (J)*, p. 430.

71. McGill, "Anselm's Argument," p. 91.

72. *G1*, § 4.1.

73. *Dial. (J)*, p. 430. In the *Dialektik*, Schleiermacher deliberately uses abstract speculative language for the Transcendent. In this respect he resembles Paul Tillich, who called the Transcendent the *Ground of Being*. However, there is an important difference between Schleiermacher and Tillich. The latter holds that there is one nonsymbolic, literal statement about the Transcendent, namely, that it is Being itself. Tillich uses this concept to measure and determine the meaning of the concrete Christian symbols, that is, they are interpreted as symbols of Being itself. Schleiermacher, on the contrary, thinks that the one nonsymbolic statement that can be made about the Transcendent is that God is love. This is an assertion not about the speculative Transcendent as limit, but about the Transcendent as God. It is a determinate image derived from redemption, and expresses the full reality of the God-consciousness and its object. Schleiermacher's actual procedure, that is, his carrying out of the method of correlation, is less reductive than Tillich's.

74. Ibid.

75. *G1*, § 5.3.

76. *G1*, §10.2.

77. *G1*, § 32.3.

78. *G1*, § 9.2.

79. *G1*, § 62.3.

80. Isaac August Dorner, *A System of Christian Doctrine*, vol. 1, trans. Alfred Cave and J.S. Banks (Edinburgh: T & T Clark, 1888), p. 37.

81. Newman, *Grammar of Assent*, p. 52. Schleiermacher differs from Newman in his contention that belief or intuitive certainty is different in kind and to be judged by its own measure rather than simply by the criteria of objective knowledge (*G1*, § 3.4; 14). Newman's argument may not be entirely consistent, since he attempts to combine a basically intuitive view of assent with an Aristotelian-inferential view of the intellect and knowledge. The distinction between reflex assent and inference is not very clear. Schleiermacher might have the following comments about Newman's treatment of reflex assent or assent to assent: "It may . . . be objected that the assertion that piety is a matter of knowing refers not . . . to the content of that knowledge but to the certainty which characterizes its representations; so that the knowledge of doctrines is piety only in virtue of the certainty attached to them, and thus only

in virtue of the strength of conviction, while a possession of doctrines without conviction is not piety at all. Then the strength of conviction would be the measure of piety; and this is undoubtedly what those people have in mind who . . . paraphrase the word faith as "fidelity to one's convictions." But in all other more typical fields of knowledge the only measure of conviction is the clearness and completeness of thought itself. Now if it is to be the same with this conviction, then we would be back to our old point, that he who thinks religious propositions most clearly and completely . . . must likewise be the most pious man. If then, this conclusion is to be rejected, but the hypothesis to be retained (namely, that conviction is the measure of piety) the *conviction in this case must be of a different kind and must have a different measure*" (*G1,* § 3.4). The underscored words represent Schleiermacher's own position. Newman's treatment of certitude and reflex assent tends to blur the distinction which Schleiermacher makes and insists upon.

82. Newman, *Grammar of Assent,* p. 177.

83. Schleiermacher, *Geschichte der Philosophie,* p. 184.

84. *G1,* § 2.1.

85. Anselm, *Proslogion,* chap. 4, p. 135. The translation is my own.

86. Newman, *Grammar of Assent,* p. 215.

87. Ibid., p. 223.

88. *G1,* § 19, Postscript (italics by R.R.W.).

89. *G1,* § 28.1.

2

The Platonic Background of Schleiermacher's Thought

Schleiermacher's description of the generic a priori structures of religious experience provides a general ontology of human existence in coexistence with world, and of the utter dependence of this mundane totality on God. This general ontological scheme exhibits features which resemble Plato's account of empirical being and its relation to the intelligible realm of the forms. As the translator of Plato, Schleiermacher was thoroughly acquainted with Plato's thought and literature. However, the extent of Plato's influence is a question which has yet to be determined for Schleiermacher's thought as a whole.[1] Moreover, if there are Platonic features present in Schleiermacher's writings, it is a further question whether this presence indicates wholesale acceptance and borrowing, or whether Schleiermacher independently reached such conclusions on his own. The truth probably lies somewhere between these extremes; in any event I shall not attempt to decide the influence of Plato on Schleiermacher, but rather to clarify the text of Schleiermacher's *Glaubenslehre* in light of certain Platonic conceptions of empirical being.

However, while there are important similarities between Schleiermacher and Plato, there are also important differences. Schleiermacher does not simply repeat Plato; there are other factors which shape his thought. It has already been noted that Schleiermacher's existential proof for God is closely related to Anselm's proof and his theological program of faith in search of understanding. This "locates" Schleiermacher within the broad tradition of Augustinian Christian Neoplatonism. However, Schleiermacher stands closer yet to the other major Neoplatonic tradition stemming from Nikolaus Cusanus and from Pseudo-Dionysius and Eriugena. In particular, he is close to this tradition in respect to its stress on the negative theology, and is very close to Cusanus' conception of theology as learned ignorance. As Cassirer has noted, Cusanus attempts to combine a negative theology based on the limitations of the finite discursive understanding with a positive theology based in religious experience.[2] This is something very similar to Schleiermacher's early thesis that religion is the sense of the infinite in the finite.

Schleiermacher is critical of certain aspects of the Augustinian tradition of theology. He is critical of its interpretation of creation as essentially perfect, in which a "fall of man" nevertheless occurs. In short, he is critical of the Augustinian view of creation and original sin. In place of this view Schleiermacher seeks to work out an Irenaean theology of history, in which there is a two-stage creation. Man is initially created imperfect so that he might develop ethically and religiously to perfection in a temporal process. Such a temporal development is essential to the development of genuine ethicoreligious perfection; it is absurd to assert that God has "ready-made" a human being complete with such moral and religious perfection at the very outset. For if man truly had such perfection, no fall would have taken place! In Schleiermacher's view, redemption is not a restoration of man to perfection mysteriously lost in a "fall," but rather an elevation of man from a lower to a higher, perfect state of being in coexistence with God. Thus redemption is not a re-creation, but a completion and perfection of creation.[3]

Schleiermacher conceives the perfectibility of human being in Platonic terms, specifically as an imposition of limit on an indefinite element. This conception will be explained further shortly; however, its importance consists in the following thesis: While man is capable of being perfected, such perfection is not an autonomous human possibility or capacity. Man is capable of being perfected, of receiving and developing such perfection. And this implies that such a capacity for perfection, or for redemption, is not an active capacity, but a passive one. Man requires help from an outside source in order to be perfected, and that is why redemption is necessary in order to bring creation to its fulfillment and final telos.

Schleiermacher's doctrine of God combines elements drawn from both Anselm and Cusanus, and it is the presence of the latter elements that make Schleiermacher's conception of God bipolar. At first sight, the contention that both Anselm and Cusanus are important for Schleiermacher's conception of God may appear strange and implausible. However, there are some important motifs common to both Anselm and Cusanus, which are also found in Schleiermacher's doctrine of God. First, both Anselm and Cusanus seek to develop a single fundamental concept of the Most High which will not only exhibit its distinctive mode of being, that is, necessary being, but which also will serve as the basis for the divine attributes which are subsequently developed and expounded.[4] Second, both Anselm and Cusanus think that the concept of the Most High as that beyond which there is nothing greater requires dialectical interpretation. Anselm indicates that not only is God that than which nothing greater can be conceived, but that as such, God is greater than can be exhaustively conceived, and thus surpasses finite thought and experience. Thus, although Anselm undoubtedly stands close to the Augustinian tradition and affirmative theology, he also indicates an important sense in which his basic conception requires dialectical interpretation which balances the positive or affirmative theology against the negative theology. Anselm does not pursue this idea very far, and never abandons the Neoplatonic idea of the hierarchy of being.

Cusanus makes the dialectical interpretation of the Most High central to his interpretation of divine existence and attributes. If God is unsurpassable he must be conceived not only as the greatest, but also as the least; thus God is coincidence of opposites, that is, in him both absolute maximum and absolute minimum coincide. Cusanus seeks to show that such a dialectical interpretation is both inherent in and required by the Anselmian notion of the greatest being, and is crucial to the proper understanding of divine immanence and transcendence. In addition, Cusanus criticizes and rejects the idea of a hierarchy of being; he seeks to replace it with a concept of finite being as a homogeneous and continuous whole which is limited and bounded by the infinite.

Third, both Anselm and Cusanus posit distinctions in the divine being itself which are essential to conceiving God as living. To be sure, Anselm presents the more traditional Augustinian concept of trinity; yet even that concept is an attempt to state and relate the immanence and the transcendence of God implicit in Anselm's formula. In part the doctrine of trinity is an analysis of God as absolute and God as related. Similarly, Cusanus' concept of God as absolute coincidence of opposites is an attempt to conceive the divine being as bipolar and thus as living. Later we shall consider whether the doctrine of trinity can be stated in these terms, but for the present it is sufficient to observe that such a concept is a radical departure from *actus purus*.

These three elements noted above are present in Schleiermacher's doctrine of God. Schleiermacher's conception of God is bipolar, and such a structure underlies his account of the relation between God and world in creation and preservation, and his account of the divine attributes. In this respect Schleiermacher continues the Anselmian motif that the conception of the Most High predelineated in religious experience and made explicit in the ontological argument is fundamental for determining the doctrine of the divine attributes. The doctrine of God Schleiermacher presents in his *Glaubenslehre* is the most systematic and full-scale treatment of this Anselmian motif in all of Christian thought.

However, it should be noted at the outset that the focus of concern in this chapter is on only the generic elements of Schleiermacher's doctrine of God, and the relation between God and world. The concern is deliberately abstract: neither the concrete modifications of the generic elements, nor the telos of Christian religious consciousness will be considered here. Such historical determinacy is bracketed. That is why we must postpone the analysis of Schleiermacher's two-stage creation theory until later, for that involves Schleiermacher's account of the specifically Christian teleology derived from redemption. Consequently, owing to such abstraction, any apparent resemblance between Schleiermacher's thought and any particular version of Platonism can only be provisional and tentative, pending further concrete elaboration of the argument of the *Glaubenslehre*.

A BRIEF SKETCH OF PLATONIC ONTOLOGY

The following account of Platonic ontology is drawn primarily from the dialogue *Parmenides* and the helpful introduction and commentary by F.M. Cornford.[5] It is in no sense a comprehensive, systematic account of Plato, although those elements applicable to Schleiermacher happen to be found here. The following ideas are important for Schleiermacher. Finite being is described as a mixture of opposites, whose general structure is presented as an indefinite dyad, something which fluctuates between "more" and "less" without being anything definite. Considered in and for itself, this indefinite dyad is indeterminate, but it is capable of receiving determination, in which case it is determined as either more or less of any given pair of opposite qualities. Prior to such determination, finite being qua dyad is indeterminate, but at the same time it is determinable.

The process of determination of the dyad is both the process of its coming to be, and its coming to be something definite. To be finite is to be something definite, not indeterminate. Such determination is the completion or the perfecting of an entity; that is, the indefinite dyad is rendered determinate, and thereby becomes something definite and particular. Such process of becoming is teleological, and has as its telos approximation to form, without ever becoming the form itself. Thus, such an approximation to form reduces the indefiniteness of the indefinite dyad, but not the duality inherent in the dyad itself. Thus every approximation to form is always limited and conditioned by another opposing element; this is the reason nothing finite ever becomes the form or archetype itself. Nevertheless, one can speak of the perfecting of a thing, which consists not in the elimination of duality, but in the effecting of harmony or a ratio, between the opposing elements.[6]

In contrast to the Aristotelian concept of becoming as a transition of form from potency to act, Platonic becoming is the effecting of a harmony or ratio between two qualities which are and remain irreducible. While the harmony may be characterized as an overcoming of indefiniteness, it does not overcome contrast and opposition as such, nor does it mediate contrasts in effecting a higher synthesis. Form does not become immanent in things through a transition from potency to act; rather form effects a harmony between opposing qualities which remain irreducible.[7] There is a transition from indeterminacy to determinacy, but this is not the same as a transition of form from potency to act. Rather it is a determination of ratio between opposing qualities by a transcendent cause or limit principle. In contrast to the Hegelian logic, such a determination involves a setting and fixing of limits and not a transcendence of limits. Thus the coming to be of a finite entity is neither an evolutionary process from lower elements (as in Hegel) nor an emanation from a higher level of reality (as in Plotinus). Rather it is a determination of an already-existing but indefinite contrast, which sets limits to indefiniteness and indeterminacy.[8] Plato calls this the imposition of form or limit, on an unlimited (indefinite) element or matter. The indefinite dyad and its process of determination are the common elements of finite being.

This account of finite being as a mixture of opposites has dialectical significance. On the one hand, being is constituted by an irreducible, qualitative opposition. Yet on the other hand, as an irreducible dyad, finite being forms a continuum embracing all such relative oppositions, which prevents them from being absolute oppositions. Hence all finite contrasts, while irreducible, are also relative. Any given finite "thing" is "something" with opposite qualities, fixed in some ratio which determines the range of fluctuation and opposition. Thus any definite thing is a relative coincidence or ratio of opposites, which requires apparently contradictory statements concerning it, for example, it is both one and many, both great and small. But such contradictions are merely apparent and reflect merely relative contrasts. Such contrasts are "relativised" and mediated by a limit principle which in itself admits of no more or less, and as such is opposite in kind from such mutable and transient being.

Although they agree with Plato's account of finite being, Schleiermacher and Cusanus differ in their conception of the limit-principle. According to Plato, the limit-principle is form, ultimately the Good. Moreover, the contrasts between relative opposites are real and irreducible, because Sameness and Difference are both forms, essential elements of the intelligible world.[9] But the forms are not identified with God; they appear to be located "outside" of God in the mythical account presented in the *Timaeus,* that is, they are extradeical.[10] In contrast, Schleiermacher and Cusanus conceive the divine being itself to be a coincidence of opposites, and thus the divine being itself is the basis and the cause of the relative contrasts of finite being.[11] Thus, on the one hand, all finite contrasts are real and irreducible because they express aspects of the divine polarity qua absolute coincidence of opposites. On the other hand, all finite contrasts are relative, none is absolute, because all are relative to and mediated by God's being. This concept of God will be developed further in the subsequent sections. In what immediately follows, I shall attempt to show that Schleiermacher makes use of the indefinite dyad and its determination.

PLATONIC ELEMENTS IN SCHLEIERMACHER

The identification of certain Platonic elements is not meant to suggest that Schleiermacher simply foists on or reads into experience such concepts in an external fashion; rather Schleiermacher's descriptions and analyses elicit and engender such concepts. For example, his account of self-consciousness as essentially including an identical element (being for self) and a mutable element (coexistence with other) leads to his conclusion that the self is inherently constituted as a mixture of opposites. Such relative opposition makes possible the changes of the self and its experience. It should come as no surprise that Schleiermacher thinks human existence is a mixture of being and nonbeing.[12] Moreover, such a thesis is adumbrated in the sense of utter dependence, which discloses the gratuitous, contingent participation of the self in existence.[13]

Schleiermacher also reflects the Platonic conception of finite being as determinable and perfectible. To be sure, the latter element is not derived entirely from Plato, for Plato has a conception of matter as preexisting and recalcitrant to form, which is included in his judgment that genuine perfection is never attained in the lower sensible realm, but only approximated. Although Schleiermacher agrees with Plato that human existence is originally imperfect and unstable, this imperfection is not the result of a recalcitrant matter existing "prior" to creation. Rather, such imperfection is an essential requirement of the kind of being that God creates, that is, a being which is free and which is to become ethically and religiously perfected as a result of its free temporal development. On the other hand, Schleiermacher's thesis that human being is perfectible and does not strive endlessly after an impossible ideal goal is dependent on two basic Christian beliefs. The first is christological, namely, the belief in the sinless perfection of the Redeemer.[14] A sinless humanity is therefore possible. The second is theological, namely, God has no opposite, and is the sole originator and lord over being, including both matter and form. This thesis is implicit in Schleiermacher's criticism of Schelling's theory that creation is the result of a primal fall from essence to existence.[15]

However, one of the most important texts in evidence of a Platonic type of thought in Schleiermacher is found in the important postscript to the discussion of creation and preservation. Consider the following passage:

> Our propositions retain their purely dogmatic character and content, and do not depend on speculation, in spite of their connection with it, because they are all implied in the principal proposition [that is, creation and preservation as equivalent expressions for utter dependence]. Their common relation to it is not everywhere apparent. It consists in this, that each in its own sphere puts forth a greatest and a least, and then it is shown that the feeling of utter dependence holds good in an equivalent way for both limiting cases such that this equivalence becomes the rule for all religious expression. Thus, the contrast between the ordinary and the miraculous refers to the greatest and the least in the sphere of nature from which both are to be explained. The contrast between good and evil refers to the greatest and the least in the harmony of universal reciprocal activity with the being-for-self of the individual. The contrast between freedom and mechanism refers to the greatest and the least of the individual life.[16]

It is scarcely possible to overestimate the significance of this passage for Schleiermacher interpretation and for the argument of the *Glaubenslehre*. Schleiermacher clearly indicates his Platonic conception of the structures and limits of sensible being and experience. Such structures are essential to his reconstruction of creation and preservation as equivalent expressions for the feeling of utter dependence. The greatest and the least are the limit-principles of sensible experience and the limits within which reciprocal interaction is possible. Schleiermacher's treatment of creation and preservation is an application of such limit-principles; creation and preservation are expressions of the utter dependence of both the minimum and the maximum of finite being on God. A critical investigation and analysis of Schleiermacher's contentions concerning the mediation of such opposites lie beyond our present task. Interesting as these issues are—and they are related to Plato's *Parmenides* and Kant's third antinomy—they are secondary to our concern with Schleiermacher's doctrine of God. The question is, what must God be such that the feeling of utter dependence holds true for both limiting cases of maximum and minimum of finite being? The answer is that God must be an absolute coincidence of opposites.

CUSANUS' PANENTHEISM

THE INFINITE AS COINCIDENCE OF OPPOSITES

It has already been observed that Cusanus and Schleiermacher have a different concept of the limit-principle than Plato. Although it is true for all of these thinkers that the limit is qualitatively different from the finite because it is not subject to degrees of more and less, the distinctive feature of God as limit is that as Creator, God does not have a merely negative relation to the contrasts of finite being. As absolute coincidence of opposites, God both supports and reconciles such contrasts. Although Cusanus is representative of the Platonic tradition, he differs significantly from that tradition in his concept of God's infinity as coincidence of opposites, which is a development of Anselm's idea:

> I call this greatest something beyond which there can be nothing greater. This surpassing abundance belongs to One alone. The greatest coincides with unity, which is also entity. If this unity is absolute, without qualification and limitation, then it is clear that nothing can be opposed to it. The absolute, therefore is the absolute unity of all things, and everything exists in it . . . But, since nothing is opposed to it, it coincides immediately with the least, and therefore exists in all. Since it is absolute, it is also in actuality every possible being, since all derive from it, and it derives nothing from things.[17]

It is apparent that such terminology recalls Anselm and the ontological argument. God is that beyond which there is nothing greater, and necessarily exists. However, Cusanus goes beyond Anselm in contending that divine infinity requires dialectical interpretation: the greatest being has no opposite. It is great in and of itself, and not merely great by comparison. But if nothing opposes it, the maximum coincides with the minimum. Such dialectical interpretation leads to Cusanus' fundamental idea that God is coincidence of opposites. This means that God is bipolar. The interpretive problem is to pin down the precise sense of Cusanus' fundamental idea.

There is little consensus concerning how Cusanus is to be interpreted and classified. Some view him as a medieval thinker (Beck); others see him as a modern thinker who anticipates German idealism, particularly Schelling (Cassirer); still others see him as a Plotinian (Flasch). Copleston despairs of adequate classification and treats Cusanus in a separate chapter as a transitional figure.[18] Cusanus does appear to be all things to all people! Some recent studies shed new light on the traditional interpretations and favor Cassirer's interpretation. They even suggest that Cusanus represents a third alternative to classical theology and process theology. We shall try to indicate the originality of Cusanus' thought by allowing it to emerge as an alternative to others.

Kurt Flasch sees Cusanus basically as a Neoplatonist, who, like Plotinus, offers a metaphysics of the One.[19] Flasch interprets the coincidence of opposites in God as a return to a simple, hyperessential unity. Thus coincidence of opposites means simple identity, or better, unity. God is the One who is above being and form, excluding any characteristic besides unity. In this interpretation, Cusanus appears to be a continuation of monopolar theological thought, a rationalism which culminates in a mysticism. Unfortunately, this interpretation simply misses the subtlety and novelty of Cusanus; Flasch fails to see that the infinite requires dialectical interpretation and is bipolar.

Cusanus' fundamental idea is found in the following passage: "The greatest in its absoluteness is all actuality, since it is everything that can be. And since it is everything that can be, there can be none greater, and conversely, there can be none 'lesser.' For the absolute is that beyond which there can be nothing greater, or nothing 'lesser.' Since the absolute maximum is that beyond which there is nothing greater, it is clear that the maximum coincides with the minimum, and vice versa."[20] God is that beyond which there can be nothing greater, and thus is everything that can be. God is not beyond being, but rather maximal being. Hence God's uniqueness is not his unity, but his maximal, unsurpassable being. God is unique in that he has no opposite, nothing besides himself to which he can be contrasted as "other than." Rather, God is his own opposite. But if God is his own opposite, he is both greatest and least, or the absolute maximum and minimum. And if he is both maximum and minimum, then in God opposites coincide. Uebinger explains: "God . . . is the absolute maximum in comparison with which there is nothing greater. He is the absolute minimum, in comparison with which there is nothing lesser. Why? . . . because God is everything that can be."[21]

As maximal infinite being, God is qualitatively different from finite being. The infinite does not exist in degrees of more or less; it does not exist or possess perfections contingently. It is maximal actualization, beyond which there is nothing greater. Such maximal actualization cannot be increased or diminished, and since it has no opposite but is its opposite, there is nothing which can be added to it or diminish it. Cusanus would agree with Hartshorne that God is bipolar and that divine perfection is best conceived as modal coincidence.[22] However, Cusanus interprets modal coincidence differently than Hartshorne. In God coincidence is absolute, and different from all finite relative coincidence of opposites which are actualized in degrees of more and less. Opposites completely coincide in God because God is everything that can be. God's actuality is absolute and does not exist in degrees of more or less: "Everything in the infinite is infinite."[23]

Cusanus would find Hartshorne's version of divine modal coincidence strange, since God is both infinite and finite. God's concrete actuality is finite, but includes and surpasses God's infinite or absolute aspect. However, this means that God is actualized in degrees, although only "more" and not "less." Despite such qualification, such a conception is too anthropomorphic for Cusanus, and falls short of the genuine or proper infinite. Moreover, divine self-surpassing contradicts the very idea of modal coincidence; self-surpassing presupposes *modal noncoincidence,* and implies relative imperfection. To evade the objection that a finite-infinite God is a contradiction by distinguishing levels of being within God and conceiving God as a society of occasions[24] renders both modal coincidence and divine unity even more problematic. If modal coincidence is the clue to divine bipolar perfection—the perfection of that than which nothing greater can be conceived—it must mean that opposites completely coincide in God. Modal noncoincidence is an imperfection, and imperfection is incompatible with the fundamental idea of God.

Such assertions appear to indicate that Cusanus' theology, although bipolar, is simply another version of classical theology's *actus purus.* However, this is not the case. What distinguishes Cusanus from traditional theology is his use of negative theology, and his interpretation of coincidence of opposites through negative theology. As coincidence of opposites, God transcends, but does not violate, the law of contradiction.[25] Coincidence of opposites has its epistemological correlate in learned ignorance, not nonsense. However, traditional theology is based on and makes use of discursive reason or understanding. Affirmative theology and analogy of being are based on the traditional Aristotelian theory of analogy and categories of being. It presupposes the law of contradiction. Cusanus regards Aristotelian logic and the system of categories as a logic of the finite. It is inadequate to the infinite, for between finite and infinite there is no proportion. Negative theology therefore is truer than affirmative theology. However, Cusanus goes further; he introduces negativity into the concept of God itself, and accomplishes a tour de force of negative theology.[26]

In his early writing on *Learned Ignorance* Cusanus indicates that coincidence of opposites in God can be formulated as equality of unity. This concept of equality of unity introduces duality into God. God is not simply hyperessential unity, but unity which is also entity. Hence God is both unity and something else, namely, being. This duality requires mediation. Mediation occurs in the formulation that God is absolute equality of unity. Throughout his writings, Cusanus experiments with different names of God. His experimentation shows that he was aware of the standard objection that negative theology presupposes some positive knowledge of God. Still he favors negative theology because it preserves the infinite qualitative difference between God and world and prevents idolatry. The best name for God, which may be truly affirmed of him without violating the negative theology, is that God is Not-Other (*Non-Aliud*). The complete formulation of this name is that the Not-Other is not-other than the not-other.[27] Formally the statement is a simple identity. It is equivalent to the formula absolute equality of unity. However, unlike the latter it introduces negativity as an essential element in God, or better, makes explicit the negativity implicit in the original formula of coincidence of opposites. As Not-Other, God is the negation of otherness. And since otherness is itself a negation, Cusanus' idea now means that God is a negation of negation. Coincidence of opposites does not mean simple indifference, or simple, undifferentiated identity, but rather negation of negation, an identity of identity and nonidentity.

Thus there are two negative moments or elements in Cusanus' doctrine of God. The first is the thesis that God is maximal being, everything that can be, and therefore a coincidence of opposites. Such coincidence of opposites is qualitatively other than finite being and knowledge. God is thus wholly other, and greater than can be thought. However, it is true that God is greater than can be thought—namely, by discursive understanding. This observation initiates the second moment of negation which unifies and integrates the negative theology: God is not only wholly other, but Not-Other. There is in God a power of self-negation which is at the same time the power of self-manifestation, namely, as Not-Other. Thus God's being is most correctly thought of as a negation of negation, a negation of otherness. This does not abolish negative theology, but elicits its positive significance; it is closely related to Cusanus' discussion of God hidden and God revealed.[28] God has the power of self-movement and self-determination through which he manifests and hides himself. God can both posit and oppose his own positings. Consequently it must be affirmed that God is both living and dynamic.

Cusanus is not representative of classical theology with its concept of God as *actus purus*. Cusanus' God does not simply exclude potentiality and/or possibility as does *actus purus*. God is not simple negation or exclusion, but double negation, a negation of negation. This means that possibility is posited in the first moment of negation, that is, God is everything that can be, or everything possible. There is possibility in God to this extent, namely, God's freedom and power of self-movement and negation is the ground of possibility. Hence God is possibility itself or *posse ipsum*. [29] Dangelmayr characterizes this view as the "new ontology of *posse ipsum*" which consists in affirming the primacy of God's free, dynamic power over his abstract, static structure. [30] Classical theology spoke only of the latter element in its concept of *actus purus;* its absolute was conceived as substance and not free self-negating subject. Classical theology is therefore monopolar. While Cusanus agrees with classical theology that God is maximal actualization of being, this does not mean a simple negation or exclusion of possibility from God. For God does not cease to be free, that is negating, in his maximal state of actualization. Since freedom is the source of possibility, possibility is retained even in God's maximal actualization.

Consequently, this bipolar concept of God represents an alternative to classical theology. Instead of static substance, God is free, self-moving, dynamic, and living. Such a deity is able to be immanent in and related to the world without loss of being or perfection. To be related is not to be dependent, because God remains free even in relation. This is the decisive difference between Cusanus and classical theology: God is both absolute and related. However, since God is maximal being, he needs nothing and derives no self-increment from the world, and thus is not dependent on the world (while nevertheless related to it). Since coincidence of opposites is understood as negation of negation, God is not threatened with dissolution either from within or from without. In these respects Cusanus differs from process theology (Hartshorne).

HOW SCHLEIERMACHER RESEMBLES CUSANUS

Schleiermacher resembles Cusanus' fundamental idea to a remarkable degree. This resemblance is all the more remarkable because in all probability, Schleiermacher did not read Cusanus! He did read Schelling, who read Cusanus, but Schelling was more influenced by others, including Jakob Boehme. Thus he resembles Cusanus less than Schleiermacher! However, although there is resemblance between Schleiermacher and Cusanus, this is not an historical influence; Schleiermacher in all probability reached his position independently of Cusanus. Still, owing to the common *type* of thought, comparison between Schleiermacher and Cusanus is philosophically and theologically fruitful.

We have found that Cusanus speaks of God as absolute equality of unity. This equality is the absolute coincidence of opposites, qualitatively different from finite equalities and similarities which approximate it in varying degrees. Schleiermacher's introductory remarks on theological predication recall Cusanus' formulation: God is equal in scope, but opposite in kind to mundane being and causality:

> The divine causality is equal in scope to the finite only insofar as it is opposite in kind. For if it were like the finite in kind—as is often the case in anthropomorphic ideas of God—it too would belong to the sphere of interaction and therefore would belong to the natural order as a part of it. In the same way, if the divine causality were not equal in scope to the finite, it could not be set over and against it without disrupting the unity of the natural order, for there would be some finite causality for which there would be some divine causality, but not for some other finite causality.[31]

Schleiermacher reflects Cusanus' reasoning that God has no opposite, but is his own opposite. God is thus bipolar: he is like the world and related to it, but qualitatively other than the world. Conversely he is qualitatively other than the world, but related to it and immanent in it. God is different from the world because his being is not actualized in degrees of more and less. On the other hand, God is expressed in the world in the natural order, and does not disrupt the unity of the natural order. While this assertion may sound like Spinoza, it also reflects Cusanus' ideas about divine providence, namely that God works in and through relative contrasts. Everything, good and evil alike, is sent by God. This idea, which influenced Luther, is also found in Schleiermacher.[32]

However, Schleiermacher's resemblance to Cusanus' type of thought is even clearer in the following passage, which contains the key to the organization of Schleiermacher's account of the divine attributes:

> But, to express the identity of all these attributes in the briefest manner, still another expression may be chosen. If time and space everywhere represent externality [*Aeusserlichkeit*], and we . . . always presuppose something which, by extending itself in space and time, becomes an external object; the contrast between God and space-time may be represented by the term "absolute in-

wardness." Likewise, if the term omniscience emphasizes that omnipotence should not be thought of as a dead, lifeless power, the same result would be attained by the term "absolute vitality." And this pair, absolute inwardness and absolute vitality, would be just as exhaustive a mode of representation, perhaps even more secure against dilution with alien elements.[33]

God is both absolute inwardness and absolute vitality; Schleiermacher is conceiving God as coincidence of opposites. As coincidence of opposites, God is not subject to more or less, but is beyond the greatest and the least of finite being. Furthermore, Schleiermacher's choice of terms reflects something like Cusanus' later development, namely, that God is not simply substance, but also and primarily subject. Absolute inwardness suggests that God has the power of negation, and that this is the clue to his transcendence of the world. In view of Schleiermacher's subsequent assertion that God is love, it would seem that God is a subject and/or spirit in some sense. This appears to be what Schleiermacher has in mind when he says that God is living and dynamic.[34] As absolute inwardness and absolute vitality, God is living and dynamic, both absolute and related.

Schleiermacher's entire discussion of the doctrine of God and divine attributes is organized around the principle of coincidence of opposites in God, and around the contrast between God and world. God is both opposite in kind (namely absolute coincidence of opposites) and equal in scope to the world. This amounts to a novel synthesis of affirmative and negative theology. The tendency of traditional affirmative theology is to identify God with the world *(via eminentiae)*; the tendency of negative theology is to separate God from the world, and thus to become wholly negative, positing nothing real. The former thinks of God simply as absolute vitality, but tends to identify God with the world or as a simple extension of the world. The latter thinks of God as absolute inwardness and overemphasizes his qualitative difference from the world. Schleiermacher's proposal is to combine the negative and affirmative theologies by combining negative and positive divine attributes in pairs. Thus, instead of saying that God is eternal or that God is omnipotent, we should rather say that God is almighty-eternity and/or eternal-omnipotence. The justification for such paired theological predication is that God is coincidence of opposites, both opposite in kind and equal in scope to the world. Thus, Schleiermacher's unique theory of theological predication is an additional piece of evidence that he resembles Cusanus in conceiving God as coincidence of opposites. Schleiermacher's pairing of negative and positive attributes reflects his attempt to construct the doctrine of God on the fundamental phenomenological contrast between God hidden and God revealed. There will be more to say about this contrast later.

NOTES

1. Werner Schulz, "Das griechische Ethos in Schleiermachers *Reden* und *Monologen*," *Neue Zeitschrift für systematische Theologie und Religionsphilosophie* 10(1968): 261–88. Schulz's article is a valuable start in assessing Schleiermacher's Platonic background. However, as the title indicates, he deals only with the *Reden* and the *Monologen*.

2. Ernst Cassirer, *The Individual and the Cosmos in Renaissance Philosophy*, trans. Mario Domandi (New York: Harper & Row, 1964).

3. *Gl*, § 89.

4. Cf. the interesting paper by Siegfried Dangelmayr, "Anselm und Cusanus: Prolegomena zu einem Strukturvergleich ihres Denkens," in *Analecta Anselmiana* 3, ed. F.S. Schmitt (Frankfurt: Minerva GMBH, 1972), pp. 112–40. Dangelmayr contends that one of the major points of agreement between Anselm and Cusanus is that each derives divine attributes from his basic conception of divine being. Anselm indicates that his argument will show that God possesses anything it is "better" or "greater" to have than not to have. On the other hand, Cusanus makes use of his dialectical treatment of Anselm's formula to show that all divine names are qualified approximations, balancing the negative theology against the affirmative theology. Schleiermacher too continues this procedure. If the apprehension of the Most High is pretheoretical, then the original, least speculative "theory" concerning God will be the explication of the divine attributes implicit in the original apprehension. The result is a genuine phenomenological theology based upon religious experience itself; like Anselm's argument, such theology is prior to and independent of any particular "theory" or speculative conception.

5. F.M. Cornford, *Plato and Parmenides* (New York: Liberal Arts Press, 1957).

6. John Wild, *Plato's Modern Enemies and the Theory of Natural Law* (Chicago: University of Chicago Press, 1953), pp. 137–57.

7. Cornford, *Plato and Parmenides*, p. 157.

8. Ibid., p. 144–57.

9. F.M. Cornford, *Plato's Theory of Knowledge*, a translation and commentary on *Theaetetus* and *Sophist* (New York: Liberal Arts Press, 1957) pp. 228–52.

10. H.A. Wolfson, "Extradeical and Intradeical Interpretations of the Platonic Ideas," *Religious Philosophy* (New York: Atheneum, 1965), pp. 27–68.

11. What distinguishes both Cusanus and Schleiermacher from classical Platonism is the Christian conception of creation. However, what is central in the idea of creation is the contingency of finite being. The question then arises whether the contingency of created being requires an assertion of creation in time, such that it is necessary to posit a time when the world did not exist. According to Schleiermacher, theology does not have any basis on which to assert such an event. On the other hand, the power required to bring the creation into being is displayed and exhibited in redemption as the completion of creation. I shall subsequently attempt to show that this scheme requires a change in the exercise of divine power corresponding to the two stages of creation. Cf. below chap. 7.

12. *Gl*, § 81.

13. *Gl*, § 46, Postscript.

14. *Gl*, § 68.3; 91–94.

15. *Dial. (J)*, p. 166: "Schelling's assertion that finite being is a primordial apostasy from God is completely inadmissible. For if God cannot be conceived without his primordial

apostasy [*seinen Abfall*], then good is conditioned by evil, and evil has a reality equal to the necessary being of God."

16. *Gl*, § 49, Postscript.

17. Nikolaus Cusanus, *De Docta Ignorantia* 1.2, in *PTS,* vol. 1. Hereafter the first citation will be to the Latin original in the above German edition and translation; the second citation will be to the English translation. Thus: *De Docta Ignorantia,* 1.2. (*PTS,* vol. 1, p. 199; Cusanus, *ET,* p. 9).

18. Lewis White Beck, *A History of Early German Philosophy* (Cambridge, Mass.: Belknap Press, 1969); Cassirer, *The Individual and the Cosmos;* Kurt Flasch, *Die Metaphysik des Einen bei Nikolaus von Kues* (Leiden: E. J. Brill, 1973); F. C. Copleston, *A History of Philosophy,* 8 vols. (New York: Doubleday & Co., 1963), 3: pt. 2, pp. 40 ff.; see also Etienne Gilson, *History of Christian Philosophy in the Middle Ages* (London: Sheed and Ward, 1955); Luis Martinez Gomez, "From the Names of God to the Name of God: Nicolaus of Cusa," *International Philosophical Quarterly* 5 (1965): 80 ff.

19. Flasch, *Die Metaphysik des Einen.*

20. *De Docta Ignorantia,* 1.4. (*PTS,* vol. 1, p. 205; *Cusanus, ET,* p. 12). While Cusanus' interpretation and elaboration of Anselm's idea is highly original, it is as though he were interpreting it through Plato's dialectical reasoning concerning the one entity in the *Parmenides* 154. Conversely, the entity in which opposites coincide absolutely is infinite and perfect, unsurpassable.

21. J. Uebinger, *Die Gotteslehre des Nikolaus Cusanus* (Münster: Paderborn, 1888), p. 18, cited in Gerhard Schneider, *Gott—das Nichtandere: Untersuchungen zum metaphysischen Grunde bei Nikolaus von Kues* (Münster Westfall: Verlag Aschendorff 1970 [*Buchreihe der Cusanus Gesellschaft,* vol. 4, ed. Rudolf Haubst, Erich Meuthen, and Josef Stallmach]).

22. Charles Hartshorne, *The Logic of Perfection* (La Salle, Ill.: Open Court, 1962); see also his essay, "What Did Anselm Discover?" *The Many Faced Argument,* John H. Hick and Arthur C. McGill (New York: Macmillan, 1967).

23. *De Docta Ignorantia,* 2.1. (*PTS,* vol. 1, pp. 269; 321; Cusanus, *ET,* p. 70).

24. See Charles Hartshorne, "Perfection," in *An Encyclopedia of Religion,* ed. Vergilius Ferm (New York: Philosophical Library, 1945), p. 573; Eugene Peters, *Hartshorne and Neoclassical Metaphysics* (Lincoln, Nebraska: University of Nebraska Press, 1970), p. 68; Hartshorne, "The Dipolar Conception of Deity," *The Review of Metaphysics* 21(1967): 273–89. Hartshorne's idea of levels of being within God and that God is a society of occasions has provoked considerable discussion and disagreement in the process theology movement. The most serious problem facing Hartshorne appears to be whether his version of God is compatible with relativity theory [see John T. Wilcox, "A Question from Physics for Certain Theists, *The Journal of Religion* 41(1961): 293–300]. For an alternative interpretation of God as a single entity, see Lewis S. Ford, "Is Process Theism Compatible with Relativity Theory?" *The Journal of Religion* 18(1968):124–35. Cusanus and Schleiermacher are much closer to Ford's interpretation than to Hartshorne's.

25. See Schneider, *Gott—das Nichtandere,* pp. 155 ff.

26 Ibid.; see also Siegfried Dangelmayr, *Gotteserkenntnis und Gottesbegriff in den philosophischen Schriften des Nikolaus Cusanus* (Meisenhem am Glan: Verlag Anton Hain, 1969 [*Monographien zur philosophischen Forschung,* no. 54]), pp. 226 ff. Herafter abbreviated as *Gotteserkenntnis.*

27. Cusanus, *De non aliud,* 1.4 (*PTS* 2, pp. 447 ff.); see also Schneider, *Gott—das Nichtandere,* and Dangelmayr, *Gotteserkenntnis.*

28. Cusanus, *De deo abscondito* (*PTS,* vol. 1., pp. 299 ff.); see Reinhold Weier, *Das Thema vom verborgenen Gott von Nikolaus von Kues zu Martin Luther* [*Buchreihe der Cusanus Gesellschaft,* 2nd. ed.] (Münster Westfall: Verlag Aschendorff, 1967).

29. Cusanus, *Trialogus de possesst* (*PTS,* vol. 2, pp. 267 ff.); see Dangelmayr, *Gotteserkenntnis,* pp. 293 ff.

30. Dangelmayr, *Gotteserkenntnis,* p. 289.

31. *G1,* § 51.1.

32. See Weier, *Thema vom verborgenen Gott;* also Wilhelm Pauck's comments on Schleiermacher in "Schleiermacher as Contemporary," *Journal for Theology and Church,* no. 7, pp. 172 ff. Schleiermacher belongs very much to this theological tradition of Cusanus and Luther: "Even what appears to be evil . . . exists as a result of utter dependence and therefore is to be regarded as ordained by God. Otherwise we should not be . . . able to think of . . . any world at all as dependent on God, and this would contradict our fundamental proposition" (*G1,* § 48.2).

33. *G1,* § 51.1.

34. *G1,* § 55.1; see the first edition formulation in Martin Redeker, *Schleiermacher: Life and Thought,* trans. John Wallhausser (Philadelphia: Fortress Press, 1973), p. 122.

PART TWO

————————

THE DOCTRINE OF GOD

3

Divine Attributes Expressed in Generic Religious Consciousness

THE STRUCTURE OF THE DOCTRINE OF GOD

Schleiermacher's use of the phenomenological method is nowhere more in evidence than in his discussion of the doctrine of God and divine attributes. Specifically, the original idea of God as the codeterminant of utter dependence, and the first four divine attributes are set forth by means of an abstraction or epoché from the full, historically determinate Christian religious consciousness. He repeatedly calls attention to this methodological abstraction throughout his discussion of the divine attributes, warning the reader not to mistake the abstract, formal schematism presented therein for the full doctrine of God. The following passage is typical, and appears at the beginning of his exposition:

> Here we have not yet to do with the actual appearance of religious consciousness in the concrete forms of pleasure and pain, but only with that which uniformly underlies these appearances, i.e., the inner productive tendency towards God-consciousness, in abstraction from its hindrance or furtherance. Thus, we call those attributes which are set forth in the first half [of the *Glaubenslehre*] original or innate, and those attributes set forth in the second half, derived.[1]

Such an abstract, formal schematism of God and divine attributes is both presupposed by and immanent in the Christian consciousness of sin and grace. The universal, formal and generic features of the Christian God-consciousness—which it shares to a greater or lesser extent with other types of monotheistic God-consciousness—are accessible as a common generic structure only through an epoché or abstraction. The result of such abstraction, that is, that which is set forth concerning the codeterminant of utter dependence, is itself abstract and indeterminate, an indirect schematism of the Transcendent, and not a living representation of the Transcendent as God.

Consequently, Schleiermacher repeatedly indicates that the first set of divine attributes, considered by themselves, cannot and do not represent a doctrine of God. They set forth merely the abstract generic features of the Transcendent, implicit in the original apprehension of the Sublime as such. While it is no doubt correct to assert that God is eternal and omnipotent, these assertions are fragmentary, incomplete, and indeterminate. Even the four generic attributes taken as a whole cannot be regarded as a complete account of God, but only as an indeterminate structure coinherent in an actual God-consciousness and to be taken account of in a doctrine of God:

> Hence, even these attributes, however completely viewed together and related to each other, can in no way suffice for a description of the divine being. But it must be clearly understood in advance, that whatever additional attributes may emerge later on, those described here will always have to be thought of as inhering in the others; thus an activity which cannot be conceived under the general form of eternal-omnipotence, ought not be regarded as divine.[2]

Thus the ontological proof and the first four divine attributes yield an abstract, generic, formal schematism and structure. They do not in and of themselves express the full doctrine of God because they are set forth by means of an epoché or abstraction from a determinate concrete God-consciousness.

However, it would be a serious mistake to think that such an abstract schematism of the Transcendent is purely formal and merely abstract, like Kant's Ideas of reason. The ontological principle, namely, that God is the presupposition of the idea of God, forbids a purely formal, merely abstract, and merely notional reading of the Transcendent. Conversely, the innate productive tendency towards God-consciousness is not a mere projection, but is a response to and aims at a reality and not merely an abstract idea. Schleiermacher would find useful Charles Hartshorne's distinctions between divine essence, existence, and actuality: "Existence is that the defined abstract nature is *somehow* concretely actualized; but how it is actualized, in what particular state, with what particular content not deducible from the abstract definition, constitutes the actuality. . . . actuality is always more than bare existence."[3]

The ontological proof yields an abstract, indeterminate schematism of the Transcendent as existing *somehow* in *some* concrete state and with *some* concrete, determinate content. But the proof says nothing about that concrete state or with what particular concrete content the Transcendent exists. This is precisely the abstract sense of the Transcendent and its generic attributes that Schleiermacher is after in the first half of the *Glaubenslehre*.

THE TRANSCENDENT AS LIMIT AND THE TRANSCENDENT AS GOD

Schleiermacher hints at an important distinction between the Transcendent as limit and the Transcendent as God. The former is discovered or reached as the limit of the productive innate tendency towards God-consciousness. This is the philosophical impulse and aspect of human being; it represents man's efforts at questioning back to the transcendental conditions of possible experience, and the attainment of the Transcendent as limit, that is, the *terminus a quo* of free, self-active human existence. Such a quest yields general indirect schematisms of the Transcendent. In contrast, the theological impulse reflects the movement of the Transcendent itself towards man, the transcendent, unconditional determination of human existence constitutive of religious consciousness. From this movement and action of the Transcendent towards man there arise living, even anthropomorphic representations of the Transcendent as God, for example, as commanding will in Judaism, and as sovereign, redemptive love in Christianity.[4]

Such living representations of God cannot be deduced from or otherwise derived from the Transcendent as limit because the concrete is more than the merely abstract and because the actual cannot be derived from the merely abstract. Consequently, objective theological proofs at best are demonstrations of the Transcendent as limit, but not of the Transcendent as God. The latter concrete actuality, as expressed in constitutive images such as love, cannot be proven, but merely set forth and accepted or rejected. Nevertheless, precisely because the concrete and the actual is more than the merely abstract, the abstract generic nature of the Transcendent is rendered determinate and concretely modified in its state of actualization. Schleiermacher—and only Schleiermacher—has made this a central concern and guiding principle of theological construction. Consider the following passage from his *Sendschreiben an Luecke:*

> The first part [of the *Glaubenslehre* and the four "original" divine attributes] belongs, to be sure, to the structure, but only as the entrance and anteroom, and the propositions there are really . . . only an empty framework. They receive their actual content only from the subsequent sections. Would I not be justified in postponing this entire section and cycle of attributes until later, when they could appear in their full meaning? For it is certain that an omnipotence whose purpose and motive I do not know, an omniscience whose arrangement and valuation of its objects I do not know, and an omnipresence whose illumination and attraction I do not know—these are all indeterminate

and scarcely living representations. But it is quite otherwise if this omnipotence manifests itself in the consciousness of the new spiritual creation, the omnipresence in the efficacy of the Holy Spirit, and omniscience in the consciousness of the divine grace and good pleasure.[5]

Underlying this analysis is what one writer has called the "very cornerstone"[6] of phenomenological theology, namely, the principle of positivity. This principle derives from the consideration that the concrete is more than the merely abstract. It means that the generic or essential features of religion and theology are not simply in correlation within the concrete historically determinate elements, but undergo modification and transformation in their concrete realization. Conversely, the concrete realizations are more than simple instantiations of the abstract generic features. Consequently, the way in which the abstract generic features of the God-consciousness come to concrete, determinate expression is not dispensable, but is meaning-determining.

The implications of these considerations for the structure of the doctrine of God can be stated as follows: the doctrine of God is a multifaceted, multistrata synthesis consisting of generic features common to monotheism, together with particular, historically determinate, distinguishing features. To use the rubric above, the doctrine of God is a synthesis of the Transcendent as limit with the Transcendent as God. Since the concrete cannot be deduced or derived from the merely abstract, but includes the abstract, the principle of synthesis—and the clue to the meaning of the whole—lies in the concrete distinguishing features. This makes it mandatory to take the doctrine of God as a whole, and to reject any piecemeal approach or interpretation. Since understanding divine attributes presupposes a prior understanding of the concrete correlation between the Transcendent and religious consciousness, the doctrine of God can be understood only together with the entire argument of the *Glaubenslehre*.

SCHLEIERMACHER AND THE PROBLEM OF DIVINE ATTRIBUTES

THE OVERTHROW OF THE TRADITION OF NATURAL THEOLOGY

Given Schleiermacher's project of a *Glaubenslehre,* that is, a theology in which God is set forth as the correlate of the various elements and strata of religious consciousness, the traditional problem of divine attributes is bypassed. For the traditional problem of divine attributes is that of naming God from the standpoint of creation, as opposed to a knowledge of God through his essence. Stated otherwise, God's essence is not known; only his attributes, that is, modes of activity and operation in the world, are known. Divine attributes are terms for these mundane or cosmological features which are not God himself, but expressions of God. Thus a knowledge of God through his attributes falls short of a knowledge of God in himself, that is, through his essence. There is a gap to be bridged between knowing God in his attributes and the unknowable divine essence, by means of analogical predication and removal of limits (*via eminentiae*).

Schleiermacher bypasses and discards this entire speculative problematic. This claim, which breaks new ground in Schleiermacher interpretation, may appear to be contradicted by Schleiermacher's initial assertion concerning the divine attributes: "All attributes which we predicate of God do not designate anything special in God, but only something special in the way in which the feeling of utter dependence is related to him."[7] Without exception this proposition has been read as evidence that Schleiermacher embraces and in fact falls back upon classical theism and traditional natural theology, particularly its distinction between the abstract, simple divine essence, and the concrete multiplicity of divine attributes. Thus Schleiermacher has been accused of theological agnosticism, of saying that theological predication has no basis in God himself, but derives instead from religious consciousness. Consequently, theological language is anthropomorphic, and with the possible exception of the bare abstract assertion that God exists, theology is reducible to anthropology.[8] Schleiermacher did himself considerable injustice in the above proposition, for it has invited the Hegelian and Barthian caricature just presented. However, a more careful reading reveals that Schleiermacher is moving in an entirely different direction.

It should be noted that in his subsequent discussion Schleiermacher rejects and dissociates himself from the speculative distinction between divine essence and attributes.[9] He tells us that he intends to make no use of this distinction and its speculative apparatus. He notes that the distinction itself has inherent dialectical problems: it presupposes some speculative knowledge of the supposedly unknowable divine essence.[10] More important, however, the distinction violates the cardinal principle of phenomenological theology, namely, it separates God's being (essence) from God's act (attributes).[11] This is Schleiermacher's fundamental objection to traditional or classical theology, and the reason why he seeks an alternative both at the level of theological method and at the level of substance.

As phenomenological theology, the *Glaubenslehre* develops the doctrine of God on the basis of the actual correlation between God and world as directly given in religious consciousness. It focuses explicitly on God as the objective correlate, but prior to and independent of speculative metaphysical concepts and theories of the relation between God and world. Prior to metaphysical conceptualization and formulation of the doctrine of God, Schleiermacher follows two rules or axioms in setting forth the concrete correlation between God and world: 1) Anything which would annul God's presence in religious consciousness must be explicitly denied of him, and 2) That which unconditionally manifests his presence in religious consciousness must be specially affirmed in God.[12] These two axioms are related to and possibly even derived from the ontological principle, that God is the presupposition of the idea of God, and that it consequently belongs to God to manifest and express himself.[13] Schleiermacher correctly points out that these two axioms amount to a distinctive version of the *via negativa* and *via eminentiae,* which is "far removed from customary usage."[14]

Schleiermacher is by no means asserting theological agnosticism; he is not saying that theological language has no basis in God, or that God exists only in relation to the world (and so has no independent being of his own). Such contentions derive from and depend on speculative metaphysics. To be sure, if we take paragraph fifty of the *Glaubenslehre* out of context, it may appear as if Schleiermacher contradicts himself by embracing speculative classical theism. But this is not Schleiermacher's actual meaning. His point is that the only way to guarantee that theological language is really grounded in God and not derived from speculative natural theology is to develop such language by reflection on religious consciousness and its correlative object. Consequently, when Schleiermacher develops his doctrine of God and affirms that element in God which supports unconditionally his presence in Christian religious consciousness, he offers the following comments about theological language: "Already it has been repeatedly stated that in God there can be no distinction between essence and attributes, and just for this reason the concept of attribute is not very well suited to express the divine being. This implies that, insofar as something true is asserted concerning God . . . what is thus truly predicated is true of the divine being itself."[15] Thus the indeterminate, abstract schematism of the Transcendent is rendered determinate and filled with concrete content through its inclusion within the concrete Christian God-consciousness. What is truly said about God as manifest in religious experience is truly said about the divine being itself. God's being is grasped through his act of self-manifestation. The sense and significance of God's essence and attributes, transcendence and immanence, are to be derived from God's actual self-manifestation in religious experience.

SCHLEIERMACHER'S ALTERNATIVE: GOD HIDDEN AND REVEALED

If Schleiermacher rejects the distinction between essence and attributes, his doctrine of divine "attributes" must appear very strange. He is not doing a doctrine of attributes in any traditional sense. Rather, for Schleiermacher an attribute is an element of the divine self-manifestation, that is, an element of the objective correlate of religious consciousness. How does this differ from the tradition? The intention is the same: theological predication is grounded in God himself. The way of fulfilling this intention is radically different.

Schleiermacher's proposal is to replace the traditional distinction between God's essence and attributes with the phenomenological contrast between God hidden and God revealed. God's hiddenness is not the same thing as the divine essence as conceived by the speculative tradition (despite itself). For the divine essence tends to be assimilated to the Neoplatonic One, which is beyond being and essence. And this concept in turn tends to be assimilated to Aristotle's abstract unmoved mover. In contrast, God hidden does not mean God in his abstract eternity and aseity, utterly transcendent to and absent from the world. Rather, "God hidden" is meant as the phenomenological limiting feature of God's self-disclosure or self-manifestation. God hidden is the *terminus a quo* of divine self-disclosure. In other words, God hidden is an essential feature of "what appears," namely, God revealed. And this differs radically from the tradition, because it means that God's hiddenness is or can be experienced, and is coconstitutive of the divine attributes. An attribute is apprehended as a divine attribute only if it is seen as proceeding from God hidden as the *terminus a quo* of divine self-disclosure.

Conversely, a divine attribute is something more than a mere accidental or contingent expression of God in relation to the world; it is an expression of God himself. Given the ontological principle, Schleiermacher could not make sense of a divine attribute which expressed merely or only God's contingent relation to the world, not God himself.

At the same time, however, God does not completely unveil himself. Although he manifests himself and expresses himself in and through the world, he also conceals himself. That is, even in his revealedness God does not cease to be hidden. Despite such disclaimers, however, Schleiermacher really stands with the assertion that God communicates and manifests himself. This is at once quite Platonic and quite Christian; we shall not be able to say with confidence which is the decisive element until we have examined his entire doctrine of God, and learn how such divine communication comes to actual expression.

SCHLEIERMACHER'S CORRECTIVE TO THE
NEGATIVE AND AFFIRMATIVE THEOLOGIES

Given the fundamental concept of God as coincidence of opposites and Schleiermacher's replacement of the distinction between essence and attributes with the contrast between God hidden and revealed, we can make explicit and appreciate the principles presiding over his theological predication. Given the contrast between God hidden and God revealed, one would naturally expect that theological language would seek to express this contrast. No one has worked this contrast out more systematically or more dialectically than Schleiermacher. He seeks to correct the one-sidedness of the affirmative and negative theologies by incorporating them as elements within a larger dialectical whole. This extra-philosophical "whole" is the divine self-disclosure constitutive of religious experience, and it is the object of reflection in the *Glaubenslehre*. Schleiermacher writes that

> as long as philosophy does not set forth any generally accepted formula to express the relation between God and the world, and while even in dogmatics there is no longer talk about the origin of the world, but only about its coexistence with God and its relatedness to God, we cannot avoid an oscillation between formulas which, on the one hand approximate an identification of God with the world [namely, affirmative theology] and which, on the other hand, approximate a separation and opposition between the two [negative theology].[16]

Religious experience forbids two mutually exclusive theses concerning the relation between God and world; God cannot be identified with or separated from the world.

A separation and total opposition between God and world would involve a transcendence of the limits of possible experience, and contradict the experiential foundations of the *Glaubenslehre*. A claim to knowledge of God apart from the world would be wholly speculative and notional, transcendent to possible experience. Whether advanced as a claim of ecstatic, mystical union, or as a theoretical speculative knowledge of God in himself prior to creation, such a thesis is acosmic, or world-negating. Moreover, a separation between God and world, to the extent that it involves anything real, would in effect conceive God and world as externally related and as independent. Such a deist interpretation likewise contradicts the experiential foundations of the *Glaubenslehre*.

On the other hand, if God and world cannot be separated, neither can they be identified. Such identification contradicts the intentionality of religious consciousness and explains away the feeling of utter dependence; it removes the ontological difference between God and world and replaces it with an identity. If the former principle qualifies the negative theology, this principle qualifies the affirmative theology or *via eminentiae,* for its latent tendency is to identify God with the world. In such a scheme God tends to be regarded as the highest being in the more or less continuous hierarchy of being, and thus is a member of the chain of being, not qualitatively and ontologically different from other members of the chain. Schleiermacher shares Cusanus' thesis that there is no proportion between finite and infinite. Hence God and world cannot be identified.

Schleiermacher's third alternative to complete separation and to complete identification of God and world can be stated in a succinct formula: God is both opposite in kind and equal in scope to the world.[17] To assert that God is opposite in kind to the world means that he cannot be identified with the world. On the other hand, to affirm that God is equal in scope to the world means that he is adequately, even fully expressed in and through the world. The world is not an alien, distorting medium through which God is apprehended, but is in some sense the self-manifestation of God. However, this is far from a simple identification of God with the world because God does not pass over and become the world; he remains qualitatively and ontologically different from everything mundane.

If then, God is opposite in kind and equal in scope to the world, this principle must also be reflected in theological predication. Schleiermacher's original contribution to the doctrine of God is his theory of dialectical combination of divine attributes; those attributes which tend to separate God from the world must be combined with and qualified by those which tend to identify God with the world, and vice versa. We have seen that Schleiermacher's term for God's qualitative difference from the world is *absolute inwardness,* which includes the negative attributes of eternity and omnipresence. Conversely, his term for God's equality in scope to the world is *absolute vitality,* which includes the positive attributes of omnipotence and omniscience. Schleiermacher's proposal is that negative and positive attributes must be paired and qualified through such pairing. Thus, instead of saying that God is eternal or that God is omnipotent, we ought to say that God is almighty-eternity or eternal-omnipotence. In this way the very being of God as coincidence of opposites—the coincidence of God hidden and God revealed—will be reflected in theological language, and limits will be placed on the objectifying language of metaphysics used to set forth the doctrine of God.

Objectification and objectifying language will be controlled in the following way. The *Glaubenslehre* sets forth neither God apart from the world nor the world of human existence apart from God, but rather the correlation between human freedom and God. This correlation implies two limiting principles. The first is that no statement can be made concerning God or God's causality which negates or undermines human freedom. Freedom is the limiting condition of utter dependence; conversely utter dependence, while involving elements of control of the self by the Transcendent, does not mean an heteronomous objectification and determination of human being which strips it of its freedom. Rather, utter dependence and the theological language used to set forth the divine causality constitutive of utter dependence are in part an expression of human freedom *coram deo*. Therefore any objectifying language subsequently used to interpret and expound religious consciousness and its object must be qualified and interpreted in such a way that it does not destroy but expresses human freedom in relation to God. This excludes, or at least qualifies, theological determinism. Divine sovereignty is not the destruction of human being, but rather its liberation and salvation.

The second principle is that no statement can be legitimately made concerning human freedom which negates or nullifies its utter dependence on God. Human being is essentially and ontologically indigent; therefore finite freedom requires both God and theological language to express and to interpret its actual condition. While man is capable of redemption, redemption is not something he can give to himself; he can only receive it, and such redemption refers to and presupposes divine causality or, what is the same thing, prevenient grace. Consequently any objectifying language used to interpret and expound religious consciousness must be qualified in such a way that the theological requirements and presuppositions of human freedom are preserved and expressed. This principle excludes from the *Glaubenslehre* the following contentious theses: that God is superfluous to human autonomy, that God is merely a projection of man, and that God is simply another word for the human species.

DIVINE ATTRIBUTES EXPRESSED IN THE
RELIGIOUS A PRIORI

INTRODUCTION TO THE FORMAL-GENERIC DISCUSSION

The best, least speculative formula for God's being, which structures Schleiermacher's discussion of divine attributes, is that God is absolute inwardness and absolute vitality. The concept of God is bipolar: absolute inwardness is the inner or freedom pole; absolute vitality is outer or necessity pole. God is the perfect coincidence of both. Thus God is both immanent in the world as world-ordering omnipotence, and at the same time transcendent to the world in his freedom. God is both absolute and related, both hidden and revealed. The negative attributes (eternity, omnipresence) express God's absolute inwardness, and the positive attributes (omnipotence, omniscience) express God's absolute vitality.

However, Schleiermacher's actual discussion of the divine attributes in the first half of the *Glaubenslehre* is not fully coincident with the above scheme. For three of the attributes (eternity, omnipresence, and omniscience) are qualifiers of the fourth (omnipotence); conversely, God appears to be primarily omnipotence. Thus it is by no means apparent that Schleiermacher actually conceives God as a free subject. God is basically eternal-omnipotence and this appears to mean that God is more nearly like substance than subject. The necessity pole or aspect of God appears dominant, and thus Schleiermacher appears rather close to Spinoza.

Such appearances are misleading. It should be noted that according to Schleiermacher none of the first four attributes can be identified with God or taken as a full doctrine of God; they are simply empty schematisms and structures which appear in the larger whole. Although omnipotence predominates in the initial abstract discussion, it cannot be identified with the entire reality of God. Moreover, if the fundamental contrast in the doctrine of God is between God hidden and God revealed, and if God's self-disclosure presupposes and exhibits God's freedom, then the apparent "absence" of the freedom pole in the first half of the doctrine of God can be explained: qua abstract, the first part of the discussion abstracts from God's actual free self-disclosure. The full account of the doctrine of God, as an account of the free divine self-disclosure, will make explicit the inwardness and subjective aspect of God. In the second half of the *Glaubenslehre* we shall discover that it is God's inwardness or subjectivity as love which is predominant over God's vitality or omnipotence. The necessity of conceiving God as subject as well as substance is derived from the second half of the argument of the *Glaubenslehre,* namely, the contrast between sin and grace and the consciousness of redemption. Conversely, redemption is the decisive modification and exhibition of divine eternal-omnipotence.

With these qualifications in mind, we can follow Schleiermacher's order of exposition. For historical and polemical reasons, Schleiermacher treats each attribute separately. This is a further abstraction and is not without dangers, but it does allow greater focus and clarity of discussion. It permits Schleiermacher to review and criticize received opinions.

GOD AS ABSOLUTE INWARDNESS: ETERNITY AND OMNIPRESENCE

Divine inwardness is not a speculation about God's inner life apart from or prior to the creation of the world. Rather it presupposes and expresses God's self-disclosure; it is the limiting principle or *terminus a quo* of such self-disclosure. Similarly, divine vitality is the *terminus ad quem* towards which God's self-disclosure proceeds. Taken in abstraction, absolute inwardness means that God is both unconditioned and wholly other with respect to time and space. But what does this mean?

According to Schleiermacher, there is no consciousness of divine eternity as such, rather eternity comes to expression in the consciousness of God's eternal power. Eternity ought not be abstracted or separated from omnipotence; otherwise it is a merely negative and abstract attribute. Eternity means neither timelessness, that is, no relation to time, nor boundless time, that is, time with the limits of beginning and end removed. Schleiermacher seeks a third alternative to mere timelessness and boundless time:

> If eternity be taken as pure timelessness, nothing real or actual is affirmed. But this can happen only if eternity is placed among the inactive attributes and it is further supposed that every attribute by itself expresses some part of the divine essence. On the other hand, this objection disappears if, as we demand, the concept of eternity is combined with the concept of omnipotence. For then a living divine reality is affirmed, and while this reality may not be fully known or exhibited intuitively, it is by no means merely nothing.[18]

The eternity of God should be understood positively as the "absolutely timeless causality of God conditioning all times and time itself."[19] This absolutely timeless causality is not apprehended by itself apart from the world, but only along with the world as it conditions and constitutes time and temporal succession.[20] The order of time is based in divine eternity. Eternity does not mean divine remoteness from the world or an infinite "before" prior to the creation of the world. Eternity is a constituent element in the divine presence in the world. When combined with omnipotence, eternity means the constancy and immutability of the divine causality. It exists and is active in such a way that *more* and *less* do not apply to it.

Omnipresence denies that place, or the category of space, applies to God: "By omnipresence we understand the absolutely spaceless causality of God conditioning all spaces and space itself."[21] Nevertheless, God's absoluteness here is likewise an absoluteness inclusive of relation, for his spaceless causality is apprehended only as it conditions space. And so the point is that the divine causality is uniformly present throughout the world. This uniformity sets it in contrast to finite mundane causality:

> For we have to admit that finite causality is greater and less at different points in space. It is least where space is occupied with so-called dead forces, and greater where there is a greater development of life, and greatest where clear human consciousness is active . . . as completely spaceless, and consequently not as greater or smaller at different places.[22]

God is equally "near" and equally "far" from all finite being and places. He is present to all, but not "in" any particular place. Moreover, like Cusanus, Schleiermacher rejects the notion of hierarchy of being in which the greater the perfection the greater or the "closer" one is to God. The notion of a hierarchy of being is undercut by the recognition that God is equally near and far from any particular place, and that more and less do not apply to his causality as it conditions space.

Consequently, Schleiermacher thinks that the question of the "location" of God in the universe or cosmos is confused: "The distinction (always a rather curious one, and if I may say so, crudely drawn) between a God who is outside of and above the world, and a God who is in the world, does not exactly meet the point. For nothing can be said about God in terms of the contrast between 'inner-worldly' and 'other-worldly' without imperilling in some way the divine omnipotence and omnipresence."[23] Divine omnipresence is the negation of remoteness, as well as local presence. This concept of omnipresence undercuts the Neoplatonic view of the cosmos as a graded hierarchy of being, with God at the top. Both Schleiermacher and Cusanus are critical of such a view and think that it imperils the divine omnipresence. All finite being forms a continuous whole, and God as coincidence of opposites is equally and uniformly related to all parts of the whole. He is equally near and equally far from each.

The common element in both attributes of eternity and omnipresence is the rejection of an abstract, unrelated absolute. Eternity and omnipresence are not merely abstract or purely negative, but have positive significance as qualifications of omnipotence. God is apprehended as immanent in the world only as the wholly other who is not subject to degrees of more or less. Thus God and world, while closely related and inseparable transcendentally, cannot be identified: "The world does not allow of being completely conceived [as totality and unity] except in and with God, and there is no other revelation of God than the world."[24] In some sense the world is a theophany.

GOD AS ABSOLUTE VITALITY: OMNIPOTENCE AND OMNISCIENCE

We turn now to the so-called positive attributes, which express God's immanence and relation to the world, that is, his equality in scope. Such equality in scope or divine immanence is controversial; it is advanced by Schleiermacher as a critique of supernaturalism and miracle. The question is whether he goes too far and identifies God with the world, that is, pantheism. Our contention is that no such identification occurs because God's equality in scope or immanence in the world is qualified by God's infinite qualitative difference from the world. God in relation to the world is but one polar aspect of God's bipolar being. The bipolar concept of God prevents such a pantheistic identification of God with the world and makes possible both radical divine immanence and radical transcendence. This contention must now be tested in greater detail in our examination of Schleiermacher's treatment of absolute vitality.

Omnipotence

Schleiermacher's discussion of omnipotence has been a source of controversy, as he himself predicted.[25] Yet few critics have really gone to the heart of the issue by interpreting his discussion of omnipotence in light of his theological method, that is, the epoché of temporal determinacy, the pairing of negative and positive attributes, and in light of his bipolar conception of God. Failure to deal with these issues means failure to come to terms with Schleiermacher. His formulation of omnipotence runs thus:

> The concept of omnipotence contains two elements: first, that the natural order comprehending all space and time is grounded in the divine causality, which as eternal and omnipresent is opposite in kind to all finite causality; and second, that the divine causality expressed by our feeling of utter dependence is fully exhibited in the totality of finite being, and therefore everything for which there is a causality in God happens and becomes real.[26]

The first element of omnipotence excludes dualism; God has no opposite and there is nothing which can resist or oppose him. All being other than

God is produced by God and is dependent on God; it does not limit, but exhibits God's power and perfection. This brings us to the second thesis or element of omnipotence, namely, all being other than God is the complete exhibition of his power: there is nothing held back. God is fully manifest in the finite. If God could not create everything of which he is capable that would imply either that God is limited by something he did not create, or that God is a bungler. In either case God is imperfect and limited, and this is incompatible with the fundamental idea of God as unsurpassable.

Schleiermacher advances his contention against supernaturalism and miracles, specifically the concept of *potentia dei absoluta,* or God's unordered power by which he intervenes and contravenes the natural order. Not only are miracles in this sense *antithetical* to religion, they imply that God is imperfect, a bungler who must keep correcting his previous mistakes:

> Now some have represented miracle in this sense as essential to the perfect manifestation of omnipotence. But it is difficult to conceive how omnipotence is shown to be greater in the suspension of the interdependence of nature than in its original course which was no less divinely ordained. Indeed, the capacity to make a change in what has been ordained is a merit in the ordainer only if a change is necessary. But if a change is necessary, this can only mean that there was some imperfection, either in the artificer or in his work. If such an interference be postulated as one of the privileges of the Supreme Being, it would first have to be assumed that there is something not made by Him which could offer Him resistance and thus invade his work. But such an idea would utterly destroy our fundamental religious feeling.[27]

Religious consciousness is not hindered but enhanced by the divine ordering of the world; religion is precisely belief in the power of the Transcendent to disperse the chaos, and order and found a world. Supernaturalism and its miracles amounts to the view that the cosmos is ruled by chance or arbitrariness, and this is the opposite of genuine omnipotence and piety:

> It is true that one frequently encounters the view that the more prominent the system of nature is in self-consciousness, the more the feeling of utter dependence recedes, and that, conversely, the feeling of utter dependence is most prominent when something . . . abrogates the interconnection of nature, i.e., something miraculous. This we can only regard as an error. The real fact is that we most abrogate the interconnection of nature when we posit either a dead mechanism or chance and arbitrariness; and in both cases the God-consciousness recedes—a clear proof that it does not exist in inverse proportion to our consciousness of the interrelatedness of nature.[28]

The traditional distinction between *potentia dei absoluta* and *potentia dei ordinata* tends to undermine rather than support belief in one supreme power ordering and ruling the universe. Divine interventions contrary to nature connote not order, but chance and arbitrariness; they imply a return to chaos. Divine omnipotence is better conceived as power which is unified and coherent. Thus Schleiermacher proposes the following conservative revision: God is not simply absolute or simply related as the abstractions *potentia absoluta* and *potentia ordinata* suggest. Rather God is both absolute and related; in him absolute power and ordered power coincide. There is but one unified divine causality: "The entire omnipotence is, undivided and unabbreviated, the omnipotence that does and effects all."[29] The divine causality forms a unity, such that "there is no point at which we can relate only to the absolute (which by way of stricter contrasts we ought to call not "unordered" but "ordering") exercise of omnipotence and not the ordered exercise, and vice versa."[30] God's power is ordered power, equal in scope to finite causality, but opposite in kind.

The coincidence of absolute and ordered powers in God means that there is no higher "absolute" or "unordered" power in God by which he might interfere with or contradict the natural order. Given the feeling of utter dependence there is no basis for attributing to God such unordered power beyond or in addition to the one divine causality manifest in the world. Assuming such an unordered power in God nullifies the unity of the feeling of utter dependence and makes God out to be a bungler. But if there is no higher power in God than world-ordering omnipotence, then God must be fully manifest in the whole of finite being: nothing hinders and nothing is held back.

It is important to note that although Schleiermacher's assertions are very bold, they actually say very little because the analysis is abstract and indeterminate. Everything, the actual and the possible, good as well as evil, is in some as yet unspecified way conditioned by God's causality. Let us recall Schleiermacher's caveat that an omnipotence whose motive and telos are unknown is scarcely a living representation: "Although we explain omnipotence as the attribute by which all finite things are through God as they are, while we certainly . . . posit the divine act in its entirety, it is without motive, and therefore as an act wholly indeterminate in character."[31]

As is well known, Barth is sharply critical of Schleiermacher's treatment of omnipotence because it appears to imply that God is exhausted in his work. If God is exhausted in his work, then God is no longer a free subject over his works, and with this God's freedom—and therefore God himself—is denied. Barth writes:

> The question of a divine power beyond the totality of the actual did not exist for Schleiermacher. . . . Because will and power . . . are not separated in God, "the entire omnipotence, undivided and unabbreviated, is the omnipotence

that does and effects all," and beyond this, i.e., the divine omnicausality, there is no more to be said about divine omnipotence. . . . Here . . . the divine power is simply dissolved and disappears into his actual willing and action. We can now appreciate the full consequences of the nominalists' doctrine of the divine attributes, what it means when the identity of divine attributes is understood as a real *simplicitas,* but not as a real *multiplicitas.* God is his own prisoner because the identity of his attributes is understood only as something single.[32]

Barth's interpretation and criticism raise three issues: first, his entire criticism presupposes that Schleiermacher's assertions about omnipotence are exhaustive and fully determinate; second, that Schleiermacher has a monopolar concept of God (last sentence), and third, that God is exhausted in his works and therefore is a prisoner of his own attributes and actions. Barth is wrong in each case.

Concerning the first issue, Barth's whole interpretation and criticism commits the fallacy of misplaced concreteness and mistakes the part for the whole. Omnipotence is not the whole doctrine of God, but only one aspect of it, and is set forth in abstraction from the full concrete reality. The omnipotence Schleiermacher describes is an omnipotence whose motive and telos are "unknown" because they have been bracketed. Hence, whatever is said about omnipotence remains indeterminate, tentative, and provisional. Schleiermacher says nothing concerning how God is fully expressed and manifest in the totality of finite being. There is one possibility that seems not to have occurred to Barth, namely, that omnipotence is fully exhibited in the finite in redemption and incarnation. The full self-disclosure of God in the finite is to be found in the person of the Redeemer. We shall see later that this is precisely what Schleiermacher intends to say.

As for the second issue, Barth's discussion is a telling critique of classical monopolar theology. In such a theology God is not living and dynamic, he is merely *actus purus.* There is no inwardness or freedom in God himself. This God is an eternal paralytic, the prisoner of his own being and act, whether this be directed essentially towards himself as in Aristotle, or towards the world as in Spinoza. The Scholastics, recognizing this, qualified such a conception by distinguishing *potentia absoluta* from *potentia ordinata* in order to preserve God's freedom over his works. But they did so by making his freedom an exception to order, thereby inviting Schleiermacher's critique. But Schleiermacher has no part of this; his theology is bipolar. Such a bipolar concept of God challenges the traditional assumption that to be related is to be dependent. Precisely because God is bipolar, he has inwardness as well as vitality. God is living and thus can remain free and independent of the world even though he is radically immanent and manifest in it. Because God has inwardness as well as vitality, his relation to the world does not render him dependent on it, or a prisoner of his attributes constitutive of that relation. He can be both fully manifest in the world and yet not exhausted in such manifestation. These remarks also serve as a reply to Barth's third criticism that God is supposedly exhausted in his works.

Perhaps Barth is objecting to what he thinks is an identification of God with the finitely actual, that is, the status quo. However, Schleiermacher knows as well as Barth that any simple identification of God with the finitely actual is idolatrous. The conclusion follows from Schleiermacher's own premises. Moreover, God and world are transcendental a priori correlates of consciousness, or its limit-principles. The world is the transcendental *terminus ad quem,* or the spatial-temporal horizon of finitude. It is conceived as a quantitative infinite magnitude, or a potential infinite.[33] It is difficult to see how God's power could be exhausted in a potential infinite. At the formal ontological level, Schleiermacher is saying that God produces both finite actuality and the potential infinity of the world. This means that God's power is both always manifest in every time and yet never exhausted in any.[34] Formally at least, Schleiermacher adheres to the principle of plenitude. But we shall see that he is led to modify it significantly when he pursues new thematic inquiries into sin and grace.

If God is the source of the finitely actual and the potential infinity of the world, then God cannot be identified with either the finitely actual or with merely abstract possibility. As the being whose nonexistence is impossible, God is not simply abstract possibility, but the ultimate limit to possibility. On the other hand, God does not simply exclude possibility as does *actus purus;* rather God's relation to possibility is a negation of negation. God is the source of possibility, or possibility itself (*posse ipsum*). Since God is living, his freedom and inwardness are the source of possibility, and his being is the actualization (negation of negation) of all that can be. Thus the contrast between the actual and the possible is not applicable to God. The idea of a potentiality outside of God, the actual infinite, is contradictory, because "that, the existence of which conflicts with the existence of everything else, is also contradictory to itself."[35]

Like Spinoza, Schleiermacher rejects the Platonic and Leibnizian image of God as an artificer who creates by surveying an infinitude of merely abstract possibles, selects the best set of compossibles, and actualizes them. Not only is the image of God anthropomorphic, it suggests that possibility is antecedent to or independent of God's power. Not only is the concept of pure unactualized possibility self-contradictory, it also contradicts the notion of God as Creator since it posits something not dependent on God. Schleiermacher objects that "the whole productive activity is assumed to be critical and selective, and therefore secondary."[36] Further, for God to create by selection and choice is not to enhance but to limit the perfection of creation, because to choose is to negate, and negation means limitation, and this implies that God does not do all that he can.[37] As *posse ipsum,* God is the ground of possibility and of actuality; he produces everything that can be, without limitation. Thus the creation is good, because God is sovereign over his work: "The world, as the whole content of the divine formation and production, is so perfectly enclosed within the divine causality that there is nothing outside of the whole which could gain an influence on the whole"[38] and undo God's work. Thus both elements in Schleiermacher's doctrine of omnipotence form a coherent whole, and express the Reformation view of divine sovereignty.

Omniscience

Schleiermacher's discussion of omniscience is perhaps the most elusive of all the divine attributes. On the one hand, omniscience is a qualification of omnipotence, preventing it from being misunderstood as dead power or necessity. On the other hand it is identical with omnipotence as an expression of absolute vitality. In addition, it does not actually appear in Christian consciousness, save in modified determinate form as *wisdom.* Yet, for all its obscurity, it provides an important interpretive clue to Schleiermacher's doctrine of God. Let us attempt to sort out the confusion.

The basic idea of omniscience is that omnipotence is not mechanistic or deterministic necessity, but a spiritual power to which man can be related in freedom. Without the qualification "spiritual," omnipotence might appear as fate or necessity, "and such necessity, conceived as equal to the whole of finite causality, yet contrasted with it, would really mean positing the latter alone."[39] In other words, unqualified omnipotence, or omnipotence conceived as sheer efficient causality, is equivalent to atheism, because it denies that God is living and free, and this is to deny God. However, as a qualification of omnipotence, omniscience should be identified with absolute inwardness and not absolute vitality: "Spirituality here means nothing more than what we previously called inner vitality."[40] If unqualified omnipotence tends to make God out to be substance, omniscience qualifies such substance as subject. In the first edition of the *Glaubenslehre* Schleiermacher explains himself more fully:

It is much more important to establish the difference between the feeling of dependence on the Supreme Being, and that feeling which might derive from a blind and dead necessity, than it is to determine precisely what the similarity is between God and that which we term Spirit [*Geist*]. . . . However, we know of no better way to designate that difference than to contrast the dead and the blind [necessity] with the living and the conscious, because for us consciousness is the highest thing. Even while we say this, however, we are aware that *we cannot think of God's consciousness as anything like our own* . . . and we must guard against thinking of God as some sort of perceiving and sensitive [that is, receptive] world soul.[41]

Thus Schleiermacher is attributing subjectivity and even consciousness to God; the unresolved question is, how and in what sense are such to be conceived in infinite being? Schleiermacher seeks the mean between two extremes: God cannot be conceived as blind, mechanical necessity or fate, because that amounts to atheism. On the other hand, God cannot be conceived anthropomorphically or as a finite world soul in simple, receptive interaction with the world. Nevertheless it cannot be denied that God is living and even a subjectivity; therefore the problem is to qualify the second alternative: "Our first rule must be to exclude from the spirituality of the divine being everything which necessarily contains in itself receptivity or passivity."[42] This means that God's knowledge is not dependent on or receptive to anything given to him independently of his own creative act: "The divine knowledge is exclusively a knowledge of the willed and produced, not a knowledge for which an object could be given from any other source."[43] Thus God's knowledge must be appropriate to his being as Creator, and therefore God cannot be conceived as a receptive world soul or Platonic artificer.

However, Schleiermacher's further elaboration of omniscience appears to be in tension, if not contradiction with his above assertion that God is not dead, blind necessity. Although omniscience is introduced as a qualification of omnipotence, Schleiermacher treats it as coordinate with omnipotence, as absolute vitality. The tension becomes apparent in the following passage:

Finite existence must merge as completely in the divine knowledge as in the divine omnipotence . . . in finite being the divine knowledge is as completely exhibited as the divine omnipotence, so that when the two are compared, there is nothing left in the divine knowledge to which there is no correlate in existence . . . Or, to put it briefly, God knows all that is, and all that God knows is, and these two are not different, but one and the same, because God's knowledge and his almighty will are one and the same.[44]

Schleiermacher's account lands in apparent contradiction: on the one hand, omniscience is a qualification of omnipotence as spiritual, on the other hand, it is identical with omnipotence. It almost appears subordinate to omnipotence, and so is virtually indistinguishable from the very necessity it is supposed to exclude. This language does appear to take Schleiermacher in the direction of Spinoza.[45]

However, despite similarities, Schleiermacher does not follow Spinoza here, and in fact is critical of Spinoza. He rejects Spinoza's concept of substance as *natura naturans-natura naturata* (God or nature) because it fails to do justice to the infinite qualitative difference between God and world, infinite and finite.[46] Spinoza is too close to the classical tradition of *actus purus* at this point, and fails to conceive of God as living and spiritual. Given this qualification and given the assertion of inwardness and freedom in God, Schleiermacher can follow both Spinoza and Schelling in maintaining that in God freedom and necessity coincide. Freedom means here the power to be what one essentially is, without external constraint; that is, freedom is self-realization. In finite beings, freedom is actualized in varying degrees of more and less. However, since God has no opposite, God is perfectly free, unlimited self-actualization: "It is self-evident that he on whom everything else depends is absolutely free."[47] But such freedom involves no arbitrariness or irrationality: unlimited self-actualization is ethically necessary. Thus Schleiermacher contends that nothing in God is free unless it is also morally necessary.[48] This puts some distance between Schleiermacher and Spinoza.

The above-noted antinomy in the account of omniscience is resolved by means of Schleiermacher's important distinction between omniscience and wisdom. Omniscience is a formal generic divine attribute; wisdom is its determinate modified form relative to redemption. At the abstract level, God is somehow omniscient, and his knowledge is somehow spiritual. However, what is abstracted from is the particular ordering and valuation of God relative to redemption. Considered abstractly, omniscience is coordinate with omnipotence, because the qualities appropriate to the subjectivity and spirituality of omniscience and omnipotence, namely their valuation and ordering, are bracketed. But it would be completely false to infer that omniscience-omnipotence have no such subjective aspects or dimensions because such aspects and dimensions of divine causality are not accessible apart from God's actual self-disclosure. This implies that God's subjectivity is accessible primarily from an historically determinate point of view,[49] and that God's being cannot be separated from his act.

Wisdom is the determinate form assumed by omniscience relative to redemption. It cannot be deduced or inferred from omniscience abstractly considered that wisdom is the principle ordering the world for redemption, that is, the art of realizing the divine love perfectly.[50] The reason why wisdom cannot be deduced from omniscience is that the concrete cannot be deduced from the merely abstract. God's historically determinate form is the result of God's free self-disclosure in incarnation and redemption. However, since the concrete includes, instantiates, and modifies the abstract, wisdom is identical with and inclusive of divine omniscience. This implies that absolute vitality or omnipotence is concretely subordinate to God's subjective or ethical essence. Although there is no higher *potentia absoluta* in God by which he might intervene in the natural order and contradict his own works of omnipotence, nevertheless omnipotence is subordinate to and guided by ethical principles. Omnipotence is power motivated by love and wisdom. It comes to actual expression as ethical power relative to sin and grace, that is, redemption. Since wisdom is the divine attribute ordering the world for redemption, it indicates how God deals with human beings who happen to be in bondage to sin, in alienation from God. Redemption is in part God's ethical response to the human situation; it assumes that God is spiritual and able to take account of the world and human being, and able to liberate man without annihilating him. The redemption effected is the redemption needed. If God's power is motivated by love and effects the liberation of man from the bondage of sin, it cannot be conceived as mere substance or fate. God's absolute vitality cannot be identified with physical necessity, for that is the antithesis of freedom and of redemption.

NOTES

1. *Gl*, § 50.4.

2. *Gl*, § 56, Postscript.

3. Charles Hartshorne, "What Did Anselm Discover?" *The Many-Faced Argument,* ed. John H. Hick and Arthur C. McGill (New York: Macmillan, 1967), p. 329.

4. *Gl*, § 9.2; 81; 166–67.

5. Friedrich Schleiermacher, *Sendschreiben an Luecke,* ed. Hermann Mulert (Giessen: Toepelmann, 1908), p. 32.

6. *EM.*

7. *Gl*, § 50.

8. See Karl Barth, *Theology and Church,* trans. Brian Cozzens (London: SCM Press, 1959), p. 164; also his *Church Dogmatics,* II/1, trans. T.H.L. Parker et al. (Edinburgh: T. & T. Clark, 1957), pp. 338 ff.; 529 ff.; see also Gerhard Spiegler, *The Eternal Covenant* (New York: Harper & Row, 1962), pp. 68; 153; 166 ff.

9. *Gl*, § 50.4: "We may hope to solve our problem equally well without this speculative apparatus and apart from any such collection of speculative attributes, if only we treat of each part of our scheme as adequately and completely as possible. However, we shall be able to make use of many of these speculative terms *in our own way*" (italics by R.R.W.). The interpretive problem is therefore considerably more complex than interpreters like Barth and Spiegler make it appear. If Schleiermacher makes use of some speculative metaphysical terminology, does it follow that he thereby embraces classical theology? I think not; rather

Schleiermacher is concerned to liberate theology from dependence on metaphysics: "A proposition which had originally proceeded from the speculative activity, however akin it might be to our propositions in content, would not be a dogmatic proposition" (*Gl*, § 16, Postscript). The point is not that Schleiermacher is primarily interested in finding another metaphysical alternative to classical natural theology. The point is rather that he is trying to get underneath or penetrate behind the metaphysical task of formulating theology, and seeking instead to ground the entire theological enterprise in actual religious experience. It is religious experience, and not an a priori speculative metaphysics which determines the actual sense of the doctrine of God and divine attributes.

10. *Gl*, § 50.3: "Such a derivation of the divine attributes from the divine essence would presuppose the latter as known, and would be a purely speculative procedure."

11. *Gl*, 1st ed., § 68.6.

12. *Gl*, 1st ed., § 64.4; cf. 2nd ed., § 50.4.

13. *Gl*, § 54.4; 57.1.

14. *Gl*, 1st ed., § 64.4.

15. *Gl*, § 167.1.

16. *Gl*, § 46.2.

17. *Gl*, § 51.1.

18. *Gl*, § 52.2. Nelson Pike in his book *God and Timelessness* (New York: Schocken, 1970) misinterprets Schleiermacher and much of classical theism on this issue. Pike takes Schleiermacher to assert a purely negative concept of divine eternity as timelessness, and from this infers that since creation and production are essentially temporal activities, a timeless God cannot create, and if he cannot create, then he is not omnipotent. This would come as news to Thomas Aquinas or to Spinoza! Moreover, Pike's contention that creation is essentially a temporal activity on the part of the creator is part of the crude supernaturalism and literalism which Schleiermacher rejects. Pike's reading and interpretation of Schleiermacher are questionable: (1) Pike is aware that Schleiermacher demands that eternity be combined with omnipotence so that the former not be conceived merely negatively and abstractly. Yet Pike proceeds to discuss both attributes separately, and without taking seriously Schleiermacher's point that each delimits and qualifies the other. As the quotation in the text makes clear, Schleiermacher does *not* assert that divine eternity is pure or unqualified timelessness. (2) Pike ignores Schleiermacher's declaration that, owing to the methodological abstraction from historical determinacy and concreteness practiced in the first part of the *Glaubenslehre*, the first four divine attributes are indeterminate and cannot serve as an adequate description of God. In short, Schleiermacher is here considering God in abstraction from his self-manifestation in Christian experience. The question is whether this abstraction is meant in a metaphysical sense (as in the case of the classical conception of *actus purus*) or in a non-metaphysical, methodological sense. I shall argue that the latter is the case, and that the full metaphysical sense of Schleiermacher's language can be determined only from the standpoint of the completion of the doctrine of God in part 2 of the *Glaubenslehre*.

19. *Gl*, § 52.

20. Gerhard Ebeling, "Schleiermacher's Doctrine of the Divine Attributes," *Schleiermacher as Contemporary* (New York: Herder & Herder, 1970), p. 144.

21. *Gl*, § 53.

22. *Gl*, § 53.1.

23. *Gl*, § 8, second Postscript.

24. Schleiermacher, *Die christliche Sitte nach den Grundsätzen der evangelischen Kirche*, ed. Ludwig Jonas (Berlin: G. Reimer, 1884), *Beilage* A, § 19.

25. *Gl*, § 54; see *Der Christliche Glaube*, ed. Martin Redeker (Berlin: Walter de Gruyter & Co., 1960), p. 279, n. "a."

26. *Gl*, § 54.

27. *Gl*, § 47.1.

28. *Gl*, § 34.2.

29. *Gl*, § 54.3.

30. *Gl*, § 54.4.

31. *Gl*, § 167.1.

32. Barth, *Church Dogmatics, II/1*, p. 530.

33. *Dial. (O)*, pp. 302 ff.

34. *Gl*, § 54.4.

35. *Gl*, § 55.2.

36. *Gl*, § 59, Postscript.

37. *Gl*, § 55.2; see H.F. Hallet, "Substance and Its Modes," *Spinoza: A Collection of Critical Essays,* ed. Marjorie Grene (New York: Doubleday, 1973), pp. 148 ff.

38. *Gl*, § 55.1.

39. Ibid.

40. Martin Redeker, *Schleiermacher: Life and Thought,* trans. John Wallhausser (Philadelphia: Fortress Press, 1973), p. 122.

41. Ibid.

42. *Gl*, § 55.1.

43. Ibid.

44. Ibid.

45. See Van A. Harvey, "A Word in Defense of Schleiermacher's Theological Method," *Journal of Religion* 42(July 1962): 160 ff.

46. *Dial (O)*, pp. 238 ff.

47. *Gl*, § 41, Postscript.

48. *Gl*, § 54.4.

49. *Gl*, § 55.1; 168.1.

50. *Gl*, § 165.1.

4

The Determinate
Christian God-Consciousness

INTRODUCTION

In the second half of the *Glaubenslehre,* Schleiermacher removes the brackets of the epoché in which he set forth the general ontology of the first half. The removal of brackets opens up new thematic inquiries; the task is now the description and analysis of the generic structures as they are combined with and modified by the historical and determinate elements of Christian faith, that is, sin and redemption. The following methodological comment makes clear the importance of the analyses in the second half of the *Glaubenslehre:* "The representations underlying the assertions of the first part attain to complete determinateness and living embodiment for the first time only in connection with this [that is, redemption]."[1] As we shall see, redemption affects not only the concrete "how" of the general structures, but also their actual meaning in the *Glaubenslehre.* In this chapter we shall offer a sketch of the God-consciousness in its general temporal determinacy, then consider the modification in the general structures of existence by the essence of Christianity, and finally relate the above modifications to views of the divine causality which are excluded by the essence of Christianity. These are necessary preparations for the analysis of the divine attributes derived from sin and grace in the second part of the *Glaubenslehre,* which will be presented in the following chapter.

TWO GENERAL MODES OF APPEARANCE
OF THE GENERIC GOD-CONSCIOUSNESS

Schleiermacher offers a brief glimpse of the God-consciousness in general temporal determinacy, but apart from the specifically Christian elements of sin and grace. The removal of the brackets from temporal determinacy means that the generic structures, for example, the feeling of utter dependence, now appear concretely in degrees of actualization, that is, as either more or less: "Clearly . . . our religious consciousness is not such that more and less do not apply to it; on the contrary, it oscillates between . . . extremes, sharing the variations of our temporal life."[2] The God-consciousness oscillates between an upper or maximum limit of actualization, called blessedness or perfect communion with God, and a lower limit of actualization, called God-forgetfulness.[3] However, more and less by themselves are not sufficient criteria to determine or express the fundamental contrast between the sacred and the profane. It is necessary therefore to distinguish stages in the development of the God-consciousness and correlate these with the relation of man to God.

The God-consciousness is the highest grade of human self-consciousness. However, its development is not linear from less to more because it develops in relation to human freedom: "A movement from less to more indicates that the disposition to God-consciousness is developing with increasing freedom, while a movement from more to less is a restriction of it, and implies the power of another impulse is greater."[4] Since man is free, he can hinder or restrict the dominion of the God-consciousness. We have learned that freedom is also subject to degrees of actualization, and that man can fail to coincide with himself. Freedom is the power to negate and strive against self, as well as coincide with self (qua free). It is also the power to turn away from God, as well as to turn towards him. In seeking sheer autonomy man not only strives against himself, but also against God. The result is a restriction of the God-consciousness.

Schleiermacher isolates two contrasting, fundamental existential stances of man towards God. The disharmony in man produced by the seeking of autonomy in opposition to God Schleiermacher calls turning-away-from-God (*Abwendung von Gott*).[5] Man rejects God and absolutizes himself. However, such self absolutization contradicts man's essentially finite nature, and does not result in an increase of freedom. Rather it leads to a decrease in freedom and a betrayal of self by itself into bondage; the self is bound to itself qua absolutized. Thus man is alienated and estranged from God. In contrast, Schleiermacher calls the attainment of dominion in man by the God-consciousness a turning-towards-God (*Hinwendung zu Gott*) which opens up fellowship or communion with God (*Gemeinschaft mit Gott*),[6] and makes possible the attainment of maximal freedom.

Both turning away from God and turning towards God are temporal determinations of the generic structure of the God-consciousness. Each presupposes the generic God-consciousness, but actualizes it in a fundamentally different way. It is of crucial importance to note that not all God-consciousness is fellowship with God, but only that God-consciousness which is actual as a turning towards God. Moreover, turning away from God and turning towards God are not identical with the dialectic of humbling and exaltation constitutive of generic utter dependence. Both turning towards God and its opposite exhibit in diverse ways the constitutive dialectic of humbling and exaltation. For example, in the rejection of God there is a distortion and inversion of the constitutive dialectic. Owing to the absolutizing of the self, humbling and exaltation in the infinite are transformed into pride and despair. In the case of fellowship with God humbling and exaltation appear as humility and joy in the Lord.

THE ESSENCE OF CHRISTIANITY

In his account of the essence of Christianity, Schleiermacher determines more carefully and explicitly the significance of the fluctuation of the God-consciousness in relation to other elements of life. The essence of Christianity means that the dominance of the God-consciousness, that is, its turning-towards-God, is specifically related to the redemption accomplished by Christ. In his initial, provisional description of redemption which precedes full and explicit dogmatic elaboration, Schleiermacher defines redemption in relation to the indeterminate fluctuation of the God-consciousness. The general sense of redemption is liberation, that is, a liberation of something from some constraint by the agency and aid of another.[7] That which needs liberation is the human God-consciousness, which is obstructed and arrested in its development to full dominion over the other aspects of human life. It appears to be "less" in relation to other "more" powerful elements. This means that man is frustrated in his development towards his essential perfection. This initial description is vague; it is not the full, dogmatic elaboration of redemption, and taken by itself, it is theologically untenable, since it is implied that the sensible self-consciousness of man is itself a bondage, or the cause of human bondage. Against this implication it should be noted that the sensible self-consciousness is the locus of relative freedom; according to Schleiermacher, the more developed and dominant the sense of utter dependence, the greater is the freedom of man. If the higher grade of consciousness is arrested in its development, so is the lower or sensible grade. Thus human being as a totality is essentially ordered, but existentially it appears to be disordered. Initially at least, man is ontologically unstable and imperfect; he fails to fulfill and actualize his essential features in their proper ratio and order.

Conversely, the initial description of redemption makes it appear as if the emergence and dominion of the God-consciousness per se were itself redemption. Thus both need of redemption and redemption itself tend to be defined exclusively in terms of the higher consciousness, and the Redeemer's help is merely the occasion for the development of man to maturity and perfection. This initial formulation requires greater precision and qualification; what it lacks are the analyses of sin and grace.

If it is true that in Christianity redemption is the central element in religion, then redemption must have implications for the way in which the God-consciousness emerges in self-consciousness and the specific manner in which the dominion of the God-consciousness is achieved. Schleiermacher indicates the principle of transformation as follows: "In the actual life of the Christian the two are always in combination: there is no general God-consciousness without a relation to Christ, and no relation to Christ without a relation to the general God-consciousness."[8] The point is not that there is no God-consciousness at all apart from redemption, but rather that there is no fellowship with God apart from the Redeemer. The centrality of redemption means that the Redeemer is the exclusive mediator of all true fellowship with God, but not necessarily all God-consciousness. While there is a general God-consciousness apart from redemption, fellowship with God is not achieved by simple autonomous human agency, rather it is mediated exclusively by redemption through Christ. Thus the fuller, more precise formulation of the essence of Christianity is as follows:

> Although in general we trace the manner in which the God-consciousness is constituted in and with the stimulated self-consciousness to the act of the individual, the distinctive element in Christian piety is that we are conscious of all turning-away-from-God [Abwendung von Gott] in ourselves as our own original act which we call sin. Conversely, whatever fellowship with God [Gemeinschaft mit Gott] we have, we are conscious of it as depending on a communication from the Redeemer which we call grace.[9]

Actual fellowship with God is dependent on a special communication from God mediated exclusively through the Redeemer. Consequently a consideration of generic religious consciousness alone would not reveal the full Christian God-consciousness or its distinctive features, nor would it disclose the divine causality:

> We call the power of the God-consciousness in our soul grace, because we are conscious of it as not our own act, and ascribe it to a special divine com-

munication independent of the general divine concursus without which even sin would not be possible. Conversely, we call a moment of time which lacks such determining activity of the God-consciousness sin, because we are conscious of such a moment as our own act, which is cut off from that special divine communication.[10]

Redemption illumines the actual situation of human freedom, and produces some modifications in the general regional ontology of man and world.

MODIFICATIONS OF THE REGIONAL ONTOLOGY
OF MAN AND WORLD BY REDEMPTION

Generically and abstractly considered, the basic features of the regional ontology are its polar contrasts and reciprocity between beings. Redemption involves and reflects this general structure. The relation between Redeemer and man is an instance of reciprocal interaction, and the Redeemer has something to do with man's turning towards God and fellowship with God. But this is very indefinite, and must be more precisely determined and further qualified. For, in the abstract, reciprocity between beings means that despite differences, they are homogeneous and fundamentally alike. Homogeneity in turn implies that no difference between beings is absolute, all differences are relative. From this it would appear to follow that no one person is unique except in the sense in which all are unique: no difference or uniqueness abrogates the homogeneity of the natural order. But this implies that any two persons are "more or less" interchangeable. However, Schleiermacher qualifies this general structure when he says that redemption is something which has been universally and completely accomplished by Jesus. There is something distinctive about Jesus; he is not unique simply in the sense in which all others are unique. Rather Jesus is the historical figure who, by virtue of his exclusive dignity and superiority to other men, is indispensable to the very meaning of redemption. Redemption is his work alone, such that without him, there could be no redemption. Redemption qualifies the natural order of reciprocity in two important respects: it involves a reciprocal relation between unequals, and no autonomous human striving or development can overcome or dispense with that inequality.

These points come out with force and clarity in the discussion of the natural heresies of Christianity.[11] The anthropological presuppositions of redemption are that man is both in need of redemption, and capable of receiving redemption or of being redeemed. In other words, the so-called human capacity for redemption and appropriation of grace is a passive potency, not an active potency. Man is capable of being redeemed, not capable of liberating or redeeming himself. At the same time however, redemption is something which man really needs, such that without it, he would not fulfill or realize his essential perfection, including his religious and spiritual capacities. On the other side of the polarity, the christological presuppositions of redemption are that the Redeemer is like all men in every respect save one, that is, he must not himself be in need of redemption, he must be sinless. If he were in need of redemption, then he too would be striving after some apparently unattainable ideal of perfection, and so could not accomplish redemption, either for himself or for others.[12] In contrast, the sinless perfection of the Redeemer signifies that a sinless human development is possible, and that measured against such actual perfection, all other men fall short of what they are essentially capable of, and thus are revealed to be in sin and in need of redemption. However, the sinless perfection and exclusive dignity of the Redeemer do not conflict with his genuine humanity; rather, he alone fully embodies genuine humanity in its religious potential.[13]

THE DECISIVE MODIFICATION:
TWO-STAGE CREATION COMPLETED BY REDEMPTION

The modifications of natural reciprocity noted above lead to a two-stage view of creation. God creates man initially imperfect and ontologically unstable in the sense that moral and spiritual perfection must be developed and achieved by man in time. God cannot create a being who is both free and morally perfect. This is not a restriction on divine omnipotence, but a reflection of impossibility of a ready made free being which is perfect in the sense of having learned and developed through experience. Man has to take command of himself and master himself,[14] and this requires time and a temporal career, which in turn presupposes that man is initially imperfect and thus capable of such moral development. Owing in part to this existential imperfection (despite essential perfection), free human development is accompanied by sin. Man is not only imperfect, he also succumbs to and is corrupted by sin, for which he is responsible. Man exists at cross-purposes with himself, that is, he has an unstable and unruly nature with an impotent and corrupted higher consciousness. Sin is thus a "disordering" of essential human nature, and an alienation of man from God.[15] Man acquiesces to the promptings of the flesh, even if he does not "want" to do so, and then he seeks to absolve himself of guilt and responsibility by scaling down the moral demand to make it coincide with what is actually done and achieved.[16] Such a reductive interpretation of the moral demand is closely linked with idolatry, for if the moral demand is merely mundane and finite, the "highest being" qua lawgiver must also be finite. Thus, not only is man weak and immature, he rejects God and refashions God in his own image and thereby passes into the bondage and corruption of sin.[17]

However, although sin is a rejection of God which comes into conflict with both God's law and essential human nature, sin is not an independent reality capable of resisting God. Despite the contingency of human freedom and the accompaniment of human development by sin, sin does not force God to change his plan: "For although in the first creation of the human race only the imperfect state of human nature was manifest, yet the appearance of the Redeemer was already eternally involved in creation."[18] The alternatives are either denying that sin has any basis and any reality at all—even proximately—in eternal divine causality, or finding some basis for it in the eternal causality of God.[19] To be sure, sin is that which God forbids and prohibits, but it is a virtually inevitable accompaniment of free human development. Rather than say that God "permits" it, Schleiermacher faces this issue more squarely by bluntly asserting that God ordains sin, but only relative to redemption, to be overcome only through redemption.[20] Schleiermacher's "theory is that sin was ordained only in view of redemption, and that accordingly, redemption is manifest as the gain bound up with sin, in comparison with which there can be no talk whatever of a loss owing to sin, since the merely gradual and imperfect development of the power of the God-consciousness is one of the necessary conditions of human existence."[21] Conversely, redemption is the completion of creation which brings human being to fulfillment, both in respect to its essential humanity, and in respect to its capacity for fellowship with God. Redemption discloses and actualizes the inner telos of creation:

> Everything in our world—that is, human nature in the first place and all other things in direct proportion to their proximity to it—would have been disposed otherwise and the entire course of events would have been different, if the divine purpose had not been the union of the divine being with human nature in the person of Christ, and as a consequence, the union of the divine being with the fellowship of believers through the Holy Spirit . . . We must mark off two periods in the divine government of the world: one before the union just mentioned was realized in time and space, when all was merely preparatory . . . the other subsequent to that union, a period of fulfillment and development.[22]

TWO STAGE CREATION IN CONTRAST WITH PLENITUDE

Schleiermacher both echoes and transforms the so-called principle of plenitude[23] in his contention that redemption is the completion of creation.

This sounds like Plato, who maintained that in creating God communicates being as far and as completely as possible.[24] Despite similarities, there are irreducible differences between Schleiermacher and Plato (plentitude). According to plenitude, God creates in order to fill up the lower visible realm so that it will be as complete as possible. Plenitude means that the more being there is, and the more diverse being is, the better and the more complete the world is. Note that this does not mean that the world is completed, but rather, completed as far as is possible. Perfection is actualized in varying degrees, and not absolutely.

On the theological side, plenitude implies that divine power is limited. According to Plato, the demiurge cannot make his creation conform fully to the ideal pattern; his power is limited by a recalcitrant preexistent matter. And there is always an element of contingency, if not chaos, introduced by the errant cause (necessity). Moreover, limits on divine power are also evident in the Neoplatonic emanation theory: divine power flows downward from above, and grows progressively weaker as it descends the hierarchy of being, finally exhausting itself in a lower limit. Lovejoy notes a pessimistic, even tragic motif in the supposedly optimistic logic of plenitude: "It was possible to hope that in the fullness of time the Devil might be put under foot, and believers in revealed religion were assured that he would be; but logical necessities are eternal, and the evil which arises from them must be perpetual,"[25] that is, structural. Thus in plenitude as in the tragic myths, God perpetually struggles against forces which oppose him, without being finally victorious.

We have noted that at the formal ontological level, Schleiermacher tends to agree with plenitude. Bracketing the distinctively Christian contrast between sin and grace, Schleiermacher's formal ontology shows that finite perfections are developed in degrees of more and less. There is no absolute or final actualization of human being, for no member of a species can exhaust the generic perfection; each member merely instantiates the generic perfection to a greater or lesser extent.[26] Moreover, the divine causality is abstractly compatible with and supportive of both good and evil, yet evil runs counter to the divine causality and its purpose. Although ambiguous and abstract, such contentions are reminiscent of plenitude.

However, at the concrete level, Schleiermacher breaks with plenitude. True, redemption is the completion of creation, but this means something fundamentally different from plenitude. As the completion of creation, redemption is the final stage of development of creation beyond which no further development is possible. Redemption means that all that is religiously possible for human being has been actualized, namely, that man is liberated from the universal bondage of sin and exists in uninterruptible fellowship with God, thanks to the mediation of the Redeemer. Further, the claim that all that is religiously possible for human being is actualized is a christological claim: "If we are to see everything that can develop out of the original perfection [of human nature] altogether in a single instance, it is not to be sought in Adam . . . but in Christ."[27] Moreover, in order to be certain that sin is not a necessary concomitant of free human development, a sinless human development must not only be possible, but actual.[28] The claim that redemption is the completion of creation is nothing less than the claim of "an historically given, real perfection, posited as original."[29] The distinctiveness of Jesus consists in his sinless perfection and perfect God-consciousness, which in him is not merely a union of God with man, but an incarnation, an existence of God in him.[30] The unsurpassability of redemption as the completion of creation is based on the distinctiveness and unsurpassability of the Redeemer, and the unsurpassability of the Redeemer in turn is based on the unsurpassability of God. This constitutes a radical departure from plenitude.

The departure from plenitude consists in Schleiermacher's thesis that God is *fully* manifest in the world. This controversial thesis assumes its distinctively Christian theological meaning in incarnation. The Redeemer is "the only other in which there is an existence of God," such that "he alone mediates all existence of God in the world and all revelation of God through the world, since he bears within himself the entire new creation and he develops and contains the full power of the God-consciousness."[31] Once again, Cusanus may clarify Schleiermacher's thought, since he has a similar christological conception, but makes it more explicit theologically, that is, in relation to the doctrine of God.[32] His argument is as follows: the power of God qua maximal being can terminate only in itself, because God has no opposite and there is nothing outside of God equal to him or opposed to him. However, God's infinite power can make any merely finite being more perfect. No finite being can exhaust God's power—since such a being is infinitely perfectible, yet falls short of the actual infinite—or be regarded as God's full self-disclosure.

However, the distinctiveness of the Redeemer consists in his perfect union with God, that is, incarnation. The Redeemer is a genuine human being, but one which subsists not merely in and for itself, but wholly in and through union with God. In such perfect union with God, God's power and causality go beyond God himself into another. However, God's power does not overflow and surpass this other because this other is not other than God himself. Owing to the perfect union between God and man constitutive of incarnation, God's power does not simply terminate in a creature as in plenitude, but rather returns to and terminates in God himself. But in such termination God is also fully manifest in man and to man, that is, in the finite: this is what the existence of God in the Redeemer means. Schleiermacher describes such final, perfect self-manifestation of God in incarnation "from below": the Redeemer is the only other in which there is an existence of God. But he shares fully Cusanus' view; he would agree that the Redeemer is the *maximum concretum,* the absolute maximum in concrete historical form. The Redeemer is the one finite being which is capable of the infinite, that is, equal to the absolute maximum. This contention has trinitarian presuppositions and implications, which shall be explored in chapter 6. However, it can be said in anticipation that this concrete "equality of unity" is an expression equivalent to the orthodox term *homoousios.*

The Redeemer is unsurpassable and irreplaceable by another human being, because the divine power in which and through which he exists is itself unsurpassable, and does not admit of degrees of more or less. The unsurpassable perfection of the Redeemer is based on the unsurpassable perfection of God: the Redeemer is all that man can be religiously because God is everything that can be absolutely. That which subsists in perfect union with God is likewise perfect and wholly actual. With this concept of divine power and perfection the principle of plenitude is fundamentally modified and transformed. Redemption is the completion of creation, beyond which no further development is possible because God is unsurpassable. Conversely, if God is unsurpassable and has no opposite, then in redemption divine power is both fully manifest in the finite and coincident with itself. Redemption is the triumphant actualization of God and God's purpose in all being other than himself. Incarnation is the specific way in which God wills to be with his creation; the telos of all being is God himself, reigning over his creation in incarnation.

IMPLICATIONS FOR THE DIVINE CAUSALITY

Thus far we have considered only the christological and anthropological presuppositions of the essence of Christianity. We learned that man must both be in need of redemption (against Pelagianism) and capable of receiving redemption (against Manicheanism). Conversely, the Redeemer must be both like all other men in order to communicate to them what they really need (against Docetism) and yet unlike all other men in respect to the need of redemption, he must not be in need of redemption himself, that is, sinless. In short, while the Redeemer is like all other men, he is not merely another man (against Ebionitism). Schleiermacher proceeds to indicate a correlation between these various types of heresies: a denial of the human need of redemption pairs with an ebionite view of the Redeemer; hence Pelagianism goes hand in hand with Ebionitism. Conversely, a denial of man's capacity for redemption pairs with a docetic view of the Redeemer.

However, the natural heresies of Christianity are not limited only to views of the Redeemer and man, they also have correlations and implications for the conception of the relation between God and world and the divine causality. The pairing of the docetic and manichean heresies tends to go hand in hand with supernaturalist presentations of the relation between God and world, whether these are dualist, or whether they stress miracle in the crude sense. On the other hand, the pairing of the ebionite and pelagian heresies tends to go hand in hand with rationalist presentations of the relations between God and world.[33] The natural heresies have definite implications for the conception of the divine causality, and so does the essence of Christianity. We are now in a position to develop these implications.

We have learned that Schleiermacher rejects supernaturalism because its contention about special divine interventions in the course of nature makes God out to be a bungler, and destroys the feeling of utter dependence. In light of this criticism, Schleiermacher contends that the generic religious consciousness requires that the divine causality be understood as everywhere the same, without any distinction of more or less: "Just as belief in the eternal omnipotence implies that the world is the complete revelation of it, so belief in the original perfection of the world implies that through the feeling of utter dependence the divine omnipotence in all its vitality reveals itself everywhere in the world as eternal, omnipresent, and omniscient, without any distinction between more or less."[34] If Manicheanism and Docetism are to be avoided, and supernaturalism is rejected, then the divine causality must be uniformly related to the entire world order and all of its parts.

However, the thesis that the divine causality is everywhere the same and uniformly related to all aspects of finite being is also the specific thesis of the pelagian heresy. Owing to its formal rationalism, Pelagianism "abolishes all distinction in the divine causality, which would thus be identical in both the activities of the flesh and in the vitality and dominion of the God-consciousness."[35] Pelagianism means that the divine causality is identically present in and related to human existence in all its aspects, including the specifically Christian contrast between sin and grace. God would therefore be equally related to both sin and grace; conversely both would be equally caused by God and have equal standing in the divine causality. The contrast between sin and grace would be a nonteleological one: God wills neither more than the other, and could not will sin as relative to grace. Moreover, this would imply that human freedom would have the same function in both: if sin is the act of man, so also is redemption. Therefore no less than sin, redemption would depend on human freedom, if not in a completely autonomous sense, then at least in the sense of a necessary human cooperation with grace in order to render it finally efficacious. Thus Pelagianism minimizes the meaning of sin and the need of man for redemption. Conversely, it also minimizes the requirements of the Redeemer for redemption; incarnation is tacitly denied, resulting in Ebionitism, and with that the essence of Christianity is undermined.

Schleiermacher's rejection of supernaturalism and his reconstruction of creation and preservation appear to have pelagian implications for his conception of the relation between God and world. For if God must be uniformly related to the whole of finite being (against supernaturalism) then the divine causality must apparently be the same everywhere, and indifferent to all polar contrasts and relative oppositions. This means that God must be the author of sin in the same sense in which he is the author of grace, and/or indifferent to both. It is apparent that rationalism, Pelagianism, and Ebionitism taken as a whole amount to generic formalism, and represent a substitution of the generic elements of religion for the specific and distinctively Christian elements and features. If Schleiermacher is guilty of generic formalism, then his account of Christianity must be pelagian. No less a figure than Karl Barth thinks that this is what happens in Schleiermacher's theology. However, Barth is mistaken, as I will show.[36] But before pressing on to this demonstration, let us note carefully Schleiermacher's apparent dilemma. If he rejects supernaturalism, then he apparently must adopt the pelagian interpretation of the divine causality as everywhere the same, and thus undermine the essence of Christianity. On the other hand, if there is something distinctive about the way in which the divine causality is related to redemption, then it would seem that Schleiermacher must fall into the very supernaturalism which he has rejected. It would appear that Schleiermacher must choose between two utterly unacceptable and disastrous theological alternatives: either a supernaturalism which destroys piety, or Pelagianism which undermines the essence of Christianity.

INCARNATION AND TWO-STAGE CREATION
AS A THIRD ALTERNATIVE

There is a third alternative to manichean-docetic-supernaturalism on the one hand, and pelagian-ebionite-rationalism on the other. This alternative is presented by the essence of Christianity, and in particular by the specific teleology derived from Christian faith. These specific elements have not been and cannot be simply "deduced" or inferred from the generic scheme. Rather, specifically Christian elements are derived from actual Christian religious experience. It is this specific teleology which distinguishes Christianity from Pelagianism, for rationalistic Pelagianism either amounts to a denial that the divine causality is teleologically oriented towards redemption, or simply substitutes another teleology, such as plenitude, for the specific teleology of redemption. Schleiermacher tends to present Pelagianism as a denial of a teleologically oriented and directed divine causality. God causes and orders all things, but with no purpose in mind.[37] Thus, according to Pelagianism, the divine causality is indifferent to all relative polar contrasts, including sin and grace. It is present in exactly the same way in both sin and grace, and this implies that any difference between these two is due solely to the activity of human freedom. An indeterminate nonteleological divine causality underlies and goes hand in hand with an indeterminate human freedom.[38]

In contrast to Pelagianism, the essence of Christianity and the two-stage theory of creation imply a teleological view of the divine causality and of human freedom. Redemption overcomes man's sin and elevates man to a superior condition of freedom; hence redemption completes creation by bringing it to fulfillment. On the other hand, if redemption completes creation, it also is the full disclosure of divine eternal-omnipotence and the latter is disclosed as having a specific telos and teleological orientation. God is not indifferent to sin and grace; redemption is both the means by which he moves creation to its completion, and the completion of creation.

There are several questions which arise. For given the above important differences between Schleiermacher and Pelagianism, how can Schleiermacher agree with pelagian rationalism that the divine causality is uniformly related to all finite being? His claims about the superiority of Jesus, and that God is not indifferent to sin and grace all appear to contradict the formal demand that the divine causality is uniform and uniformly related to all of finite being. Conversely, is not his interpretation of Christianity such that Christian faith is merely a determinate instance of the generic scheme? Does not this imply that no claim to finality can be advanced for Christian faith and its teleology, but that finality can only be claimed for the whole?

Schleiermacher seeks to move between the horns of this formal dilemma by means of his two-stage creation theory derived from his anthropology, and by means of Christian faith in divine incarnation. These are the basic elements in his account of the specifically Christian teleology. Therefore, he can agree with pelagian rationalism that the divine causality is uniformly related to the world, because the specific aim and telos of the divine causality is also the telos of created being. Redemption is not a mere restoration of the status quo, nor is it a heteronomous re-creation. Rather redemption is the inner telos, which when actualized, perfects and fulfills the creation. Creation is ordered for redemption through the specific form of God reigning over creation in incarnation. Although creation and redemption form a unified homogeneous order, this homogeneity is accessible only from the standpoint of redemption, because redemption is the final self-disclosure of the divine causality on which the created order—including its homogeneity—depends. Conversely, if creation and redemption form a unified homogeneous order, then the divine causality is uniformly related to that order as it orders and moves all things towards redemption. The uniformity of the divine causality towards creation is accessible only from the standpoint of redemption.

The second facet of the problem is dealt with in a similar way. Christianity is not merely a particular instantiation of the abstract generic structures of religion. Rather, since the actual is more than the merely abstract and cannot be derived from the merely abstract, Christianity is a particular instantiation which renders determinate and modifies the generic structures. The controversial thesis that divine causality is fully manifest in the world is meant not as the principle of plenitude, but as the principle of incarnation and final divine self-disclosure. The Redeemer is the first born of creation and the telos of creation: "The Christian faith that all things were created for the Redeemer implies . . . that by creation all things—whether as preparatory for redemption or as . . . making redemption necessary—were disposed with reference to the revelation of God in the flesh, and the most complete transference possible of the divine presence to the whole of humanity in order to form the kingdom of God."[39] Incarnation has important implications for the divine causality which further modify and transform the principle of plenitude:

> The conception of the divine preservation of the world derives its full meaning exclusively from the relation between the divine causality and that element in our consciousness which becomes the consciousness of grace. Hence we can say

with regard to two points previously made, that the essence of things in relation to each other, and the order of reciprocal interaction between them, exist through God as they do in relation to the redeeming revelation of God in Christ, which develops the human spirit to perfection. Therefore, everything in our world . . . would have been ordered and disposed otherwise . . . if the divine decree had not been for the union of the divine being with human nature in the person of Christ.[40]

Incarnation is the clue to the meaning of the whole and the divine causality ordering the whole, and it transforms the pelagian logic of plenitude. This has profound implications for the doctrine of God and divine attributes. Redemption is an expression of God's being and causality which transcend the abstract formal elements of the Transcendent as limit. In the consciousness of redemption there will be expressed divine attributes which could not be determined or deduced from the abstract generic nature of the divine. These will necessarily be essentially bound up with and expressive of God's actual self-disclosure in redemption. In the next two chapters we shall examine the implications of incarnation and redemption concerning the divine being and causality in respect to the divine attributes and trinity.

NOTES

1. *Gl*, § 64.2.
2. *Gl*, § 62.1
3. Ibid.; see § 11.2.
4. Ibid.
5. *Gl*, § 62.3.
6. Ibid.; see *Gl*, § 63.
7. *Gl*, § 11.2.
8. *Gl*, § 62.3.
9. *Gl*, § 63.
10. *Gl*, § 80.1.
11. *Gl*, § 22.
12. *Gl*, § 68.3.
13. *Gl*, § 94; 98.3.
14. *Gl*, § 67.2; 68; 81–83.
15. *Gl*, §68.
16. *Gl*, § 68.1.
17. Ibid. Schleiermacher himself makes the connection between idolatry and sin.
18. *Gl*, § 89.3.
19. *Gl*, § 81.1.
20. *Gl*, § 65.2.
21. *Gl*, § 81.4.

22. *G1*, § 164.2.

23. Arthur O. Lovejoy, *The Great Chain of Being* (New York: Harper Torchbook, 1960).

24. Plato, *Timaeus* 29d ff., translated in F.M. Cornford, *Plato's Cosmology* (New York: Bobbs Merrill, 1937), pp. 33 ff.

25. Lovejoy, *The Great Chain*, p. 209.

26. *G1*, § 72.3.

27. *G1*, § 61.5.

28. *G1*, § 68.3.

29. *G1*, § 57.1.

30. *G1*, § 94.

31. *G1*, § 94.2.

32. Cusanus, *De Docta Ignorantia*, 3.1–4 (Cusanus, *ET,* pp. 127–41).

33. *G1*, § 22, Postscript.

34. *G1*, § 57.1.

35. *G1*, § 80.

36. Karl Barth, *Church Dogmatics,* III/1, trans. G.W. Bromiley and R.J. Ehrlich (Edinburgh: T.&T. Clark, 1960), pp. 319 ff. Barth's interpretation of Schleiermacher is irresponsible and tendentious. He simply ignores Schleiermacher's careful distinctions in his analysis of the generic and determinate elements of Christian faith. Barth treats G1, # 65–85 as if this section represented all that Schleiermacher has to say about sin and grace. Barth ignores Schleiermacher's numerous and clear warnings that this entire section is an abstraction from the full Christian consciousness. Given such abstraction and Schleiermacher's contention that divine causality is full disclosed in redemption, Barth's portrayal of Schleiermacher is a caricature.

37. There appears to be no consensus in process theology concerning God's purposing and telos for creation. On the one hand, Hartshorne argues that God cannot guarantee any particular telos because it is contradictory for any one member of a social process to guarantee the outcome of the process; Lewis S. Ford argues that "there is no fixed, final end towards which God and world are moving." See his "Divine Persuasion and the Triumph of Good," *Process Philosophy and Christian Thought,* Delwin Brown et al., eds. (New York: Bobbs Merrill, 1971), p. 293. On the other hand, Daniel Day Williams is critical of the view that God creates and strives with no purpose and telos in mind. See his *The Spirit and the Forms of Love* (New York: Harper & Row, 1968). Schleiermacher would regard the former thesis as the plenitude-Pelagian motif in process theology.

38. For this interpretation of Pelagius, see Paul Lehmann, "The Anti-Pelagian Writings," *A Companion to the Study of St. Augustine,* ed. Roy Battenhouse (New York: Oxford University Press, 1955). See also Loraine Boettner, *The Reformed Doctrine of Predestination* (Grand Rapids: Eerdmans, 1954): "The Pelagian denies that God has a plan; the Arminian says that God has a general but not a specific plan; but the Calvinist says that God has a specific plan which embraces all events in all ages" (p. 22). Measured against this yardstick, Schleiermacher is a Calvinist (see *G1*, § 164) with minor qualifications (see *G1*, § 116–20).

39. *G1*, § 164.1.

40. *G1*, § 164.2.

5

Divine Attributes Expressed in
Sin and Grace

METHODOLOGICAL CONSIDERATIONS

The removal of the brackets of the first half of the *Glaubenslehre* opens up new thematic inquiries. The general principles and content of such inquiries have been discussed in the previous chapter. Here the focus will be on the particular problems of the explication and treatment of the attributes derived from the Christian consciousness of sin and grace.[1] The object here is the same object previously described in generic terms and in abstraction; what is new is that the specific modes of appearance of that object now enter into consideration and shape the actual meaning of the generic elements and scheme.

The God-consciousness has two general modes of temporal manifestation, that is, a turning-towards-God (*Hinwendung zu Gott*) and a turning-away-from-God (*Abwendung von Gott*). As initially presented, these two contrasting modes of appearance were in relative opposition, that is, more or less. However, Christian faith introduces a modification of these generic elements and possibilities which determines and qualifies their contrast. That element described as a turning-away-from-God is now specified as the act of man, called sin. That element described as a turning-toward-God is specified as the action of the Redeemer communicated to man, called grace. This qualification is very important both theologically and methodologically for it means that considered by himself apart from redemption through Christ, man is not only estranged from God, but also has rejected and turned away from God. There is consciousness of God, but not fellowship: "If we assume that fellowship with God is mediated by Christ, we presuppose that there is no fellowship with God except in connection with Christ; apart from redemption, man appears to us to be in

117

a state of separation [*Trennung*] from God and incapable of overcoming the separation."²

This description of the Christian God-consciousness shows that the concrete modes of its existence are not innocuous, but are meaning-determining. The apparent neutrality of the God-consciousness to all determinate, temporal phenomena was the result of the methodological abstraction practiced in the first half of the *Glaubenslehre*. Concretely considered, the God-consciousness appears either to be threatened with extinction owing to man's alienation from God, or animated by fellowship with Christ. The God-consciousness is not neutral or indifferent to its concrete appearance.

Sin creates serious difficulties for the discussion of the divine attributes of the second half of the argument. For if man is separated from God, there is some question whether there can be any divine attributes at all which express this estrangement: "As regards the divine attributes, it is . . . evident that statements concerning God cannot issue from a condition of alienation from God, but are possible only when a man is in some sense turned again towards God; for all statements concerning God presuppose a turning-towards-him."³ Given the situation of sin, man appears isolated from and cut off from God. Yet he is conscious that sin is sin *against God,* a turning away *from God.* The generic a priori God-consciousness is presupposed even in estrangement from God. Thus the divine attributes expressed in sin-consciousness are meant to express man's rejection of God. However, the estrangement of man from God is not the result of God's causality or willed by God, but rather is the result of man's turning away from God. Sin is not God's act, but the act of man. However, while sin is a disordering of human nature, it is not a destruction of it. God does not simply abandon man to sin, but effects his recognition of sin and his need of redemption. While there is a God-consciousness which is coconstitutive of sin-consciousness, this is far from a fellowship of man with God.

Nevertheless, if God coconstitutes the sin-consciousness, then "the divine causality must be determined in a special way with respect to sin's existence."⁴ This does not mean that God causes sin or that sin is God's purpose, but rather that God effects man's disavowal of sin as something contrary to God and to his own essential humanity.⁵ The God-consciousness qualified by sin expresses only alienation from God, and not a fellowship of man with God. Yet in such alienation there are expressed divine attributes which bear upon the disavowal of sin and the recognition of the need for redemption. These serve to prepare man for redemption, but no more; considered in themselves the attributes of holiness and justice are problematic or ambiguous.

Since all statements concerning God presuppose a turning towards God and fellowship with him, the attributes expressed in sin-consciousness receive their full sense and expression only in relation to redemption. This means that there is fellowship with God not as he forbids and condemns sin, but only as he overcomes sin and abolishes it in redemption. Christian fellowship with God is mediated exclusively through redemption, and thus all elements of the God-consciousness derive their final arrangement and ordering—and therefore their final meaning—from redemption. Schleiermacher issues an important warning that "in considering the consciousness of sin per se, we are moving in the region of the abstract, and should err therefore, were we to look for divine attributes bearing on sin purely by itself."[6] The decisive consciousness of sin derives from redemption. Consequently, in setting forth the divine attributes expressed in sin-consciousness: "We are dealing with elements of the religious consciousness which are provisionally abstracted from redemption . . . we must always presuppose redemption as that on which everything turns and as that to which everything is related."[7] Redemption is that central part of the *Glaubenslehre* which completes and fulfills the argument of the whole. Anthropologically, redemption provides the decisive illumination of the condition of sin even as sin is overcome. Christologically, redemption displays the being of God in Christ and also the full perfection of human nature. Theologically, redemption is the positive expression of the divine being and causality which underlies and modifies the generic elements affirmed concerning God in the first half of the argument. Redemption is both the completion of creation and the final divine self-disclosure.

It should be noted that in the second half of the *Glaubenslehre* the divine attributes are paired as in the first half. Holiness and justice express divine inwardness and vitality qualified by sin. Love and wisdom express the same as qualified by redemption. However, love is unique among the attributes, for love alone can stand as an equivalent expression for God.

DIVINE ATTRIBUTES EXPRESSED IN
SIN-CONSCIOUSNESS: HOLINESS AND JUSTICE

Sin presupposes the emergence of the highest grade of self-consciousness, or the God-consciousness, in order to be constituted as sin against God. There is no fellowship with God in sin, but only a sense of estrangement and alienation from God. God is the One who is rejected, from whom man has turned away. When divine causality is apprehended in this state of alienation, there is constituted a sense of one's being out of accord with the divine power and order. This is constitutive of conscience. Conscience arises out of the discord between man and God and is expressed in a general sense of guilt, which in turn mediates the consciousness of sin. This does not mean that sin is identified with a particular act or action; rather sin is mediated by the sense that one has fallen short of the moral demand of the divine causality: "We use the term 'conscience' to express the fact that all modes of activity issuing from our God-consciousness and subject to its prompting, confront us as moral demands, not theoretical demands; they validate themselves in our self-consciousness in such a way that any deviation or departure of our conduct from them is apprehended as a hindrance of life and therefore as sin."[8] The consciousness of sin is mediated by conscience; however, sin is not simply identified with finitude or with the guilt accompanying finitude. Rather the full consciousness of sin is based on and derives from redemption.[9]

Despite such categorical differences, it is clear that Schleiermacher thinks that the consciousness of sin is constituted by the moral divine attributes expressed in such consciousness. The divine causality is not merely a physical power, but actually appears as a moral command, and the corresponding image or representation of God is that of a lawgiver. Schleiermacher does not offer an explanation of this image of God or how it is that God has moral attributes; he simply states it as something obviously implied in his doctrine of God: "Divine attributes and modes of action which bear exclusively on the development of human states of mind, and this can be said of all so-called moral attributes of God, cannot be understood without a prior acquaintance with these states of mind."[10] Schleiermacher is contending that the sense of guilt and of sin are both coconstituted by the sense of God as the Holy One from which man has turned away.

The divine attribute coconstitutive of sin and guilt is holiness. Holiness signifies God as the giver of the moral law and the source of its demands upon conscience. It should be noted that holiness is not simply a function of an individual's private sense of estrangement from God. Schleiermacher indicates that the proper locus of conscience is human communities and social life: "A conscience manifesting itself solely in each individual by himself would be too variable to secure the certainty of its judgments and of their being attributable to the divine causality."[11] Conscience is not only a sense of being out of accord with the law, but also it is mediated by a social perception and recognition of that law. This does not identify the law with mere public opinion, for "the true conscience emerging in society as the same in all for all, is law, primarily the moral law, although it finds expression in civil law."[12] The formal demands of the law as such, namely, that it be the same in all for all, is derived from the uniform omnipresence of God to all finite being. God is present without distinction of more or less. Divine holiness qualifies the eternal-omnipotence: the "holiness of God is the divine causality that legislates in the corporate life of man."[13] Like the general formula for eternal-omnipotence, God's holiness is equal in scope to the moral law effective in the corporate life of humanity only insofar as it is also opposite in kind to any merely mundane purity. The former is constant and invariant, while the latter is subject to degrees of more or less.

Justice is the second divine attribute expressed in sin-consciousness. Justice refers to the connection between actual sin and evil in universal human experience apart from redemption. Since sin not only disorders human being but also disorders the original harmony between the world and man,[14] sin is accompanied by evil as its result and in part as its recompense. To be sure, Schleiermacher carefully qualifies this notion; divine punishment is not merely vengeful or retributive. Moreover, Schleiermacher observes that the connection between sin and its punishment is properly sought in social or corporate life. The distinguishing feature of Christian consciousness is that it recognizes no reward at all proceeding from divine justice to man, and that "anything that might possibly be called reward is for us something unmerited, and attributable only to divine grace."[15] Conversely "from our own religious consciousness we can know only of God's punitive justice."[16] The attribute of justice is constitutive of the religious consciousness of penal desert, that is, that as a member in the corporate life of sin, one merits only punishment. Man is thus not only convicted in his conscience by the divine moral law, he also recognizes that owing to sin, he deserves punishment.

Although holiness and justice have their foundation in God himself, in abstraction from redemption they do not express human fellowship with God. Holiness and justice reflect the divine condemnation which falls on humanity as a result of sin. However, they do not express the full divine causality, or reflect the totality of God's will for humanity. Both attributes express the divine causality as it "falls within the . . . antinomy in which we now live."[17] Such a statement appears to imply that holiness and justice are merely relative to the existence of sin; thus if sin is overcome in redemption, it would seem to follow that holiness and justice "are not divine attributes in the same sense as those dealt with in the first part of our system."[18] It appears that in redemption God would cease being holy and just.

There are several considerations which suggest that holiness and justice are genuine divine attributes and do not simply disappear in redemption. The first is simply that this analysis abstracts from redemption; consequently statements concerning God are problematic in light of human alienation and estrangement from him. All such statements are conditioned by the antinomy of sin, and thus all attributes present in such a self-consciousness do not exhibit God's full power and will for humanity. Second, in order to set forth the antinomy of sin, Schleiermacher makes use of a distinction between God's commanding will and God's productive will. This distinction is not simply included in or deducible from the religious a priori and the divine attributes expressed therein. In fact it is no more deducible from the religious a priori than is the fact that the world is the locus of evil included in or deducible from the a priori idea of the original perfection of the world.[19] In other words, such a distinction involves a modification and determination of the generic structures constitutive of the religious a priori. Such a distinction is derived from the biblical, and in particular, the Pauline understanding of the status of the law of God in relation to righteousness by faith alone. I. A. Dorner traces this particular formulation of the distinction to Luther and Calvin, and acknowledges that Schleiermacher also makes use of it.[20] According to Schleiermacher's discussion the divine omnipotence is not fully exhibited or expressed apart from redemption through Christ. Apart from redemption therefore, the law expressed in conscience is not sufficient to secure obedience to the divine will. Given sin, the law cannot perform its intended function; it can only convict man of sin. In and of itself, God's law is holy and just, but in fact it is ineffective. The commanding will of God, expressed in the law, does not secure obedience. The productive will of God, considered apart from redemption, is not fully exhibited in the first stage of creation, and this constitutes the antinomy in which man lives apart from redemption.

On the other hand, it is clear that God does not cease to be holy and just when the antinomy is annulled by redemption. On the contrary, "holiness is an essential element in our consciousness of God, for we can be conscious of the absolute power of the God-consciousness only as we are conscious of the annullment of the state of sin through redemption. The same is true of divine justice."[21] Finally, Schleiermacher's discussion of election also indicates that he thinks justice is an essential attribute of God mediated by redemption. He is critical of the Augustinian doctrine of double predestination, namely, "justice for the lost and mercy for the saved."[22] He observes that such an interpretation of God's full self-disclosure "does not cover the special case in which divine justice would also be completely manifested if all that is possible through redemption were completely realized, for then it would show itself as rewarding Christ, and as punitive toward all as long as they belonged to the common life of sin."[23] Schleiermacher follows Paul in his contention that "God has consigned all men to disobedience, that he may have mercy on all" (Romans 11:32). However one may evaluate the thesis of universal election, it is apparent that Schleiermacher thinks that it does exhibit divine justice; consequently, while justice is coconstitutive of sin consciousness, it is decisively expressed only in redemption.

DIVINE ATTRIBUTES EXPRESSED IN THE CONSCIOUSNESS OF REDEMPTION

The essence of Christianity signifies that the divine causality is teleologically ordered such that redemption is the completion of creation. Redemption through the incarnation of God in Christ is the means by which God brings his creation to completion and fulfillment. Accordingly, the divine causality is fully disclosed only as it brings creation to fulfillment in redemption. Only in redemption through Christ is there that "special divine impartation which gives the character of grace to every approximation to blessedness."[24] Consequently, only now do the divine attributes presented earlier in the *Glaubenslehre* receive their full content and significance: "Since we find ourselves for the first time in the sphere of the potent God-consciousness, all those moods of the feeling of utter dependence which were only indeterminately described in the first part must here receive their full content, for in Christianity there is no other consciousness of the divine eternal-omnipotence and the attributes attaching to it, except in relation to the kingdom of God."[25] The "potent" God-consciousness is the result of the special divine impartation to men mediated through Christ and redemption. The efficacious God-consciousness depends on the intervention of the Redeemer on behalf of man, and thus is a socially mediated one. The efficacy of the God-consciousness is based solely in the Redeemer, but it can be communicated to others because of the common human nature shared by the Redeemer and men.[26] Thus the fact that this efficacious God-consciousness constitutive of fellowship with God is mediated and depends on another, does not detract from its efficacy.

The divine attributes expressed in the consciousness of redemption are love and wisdom. These differ from the attributes discussed earlier because they express the God-consciousness in its full, efficacious form, such that all the other attributes come to their full, concrete expression only as paired with and mediated by redemption. Love and wisdom are the final, determinate forms assumed by the divine absolute inwardness and absolute vitality, respectively. Love is the determinate form of inwardness which is revealed in incarnation and redemption. It is the underlying motive disposing and ordering the divine causality in its full manifestation in the world.[27] Similarly, wisdom is the determinate form assumed by omniscience, and refers to the actual divine ordering of the world relative to redemption.

Despite its brevity, Schleiermacher's discussion of love and wisdom as divine attributes is very complex and dense, drawing upon many different aspects and motifs previously set forth in the doctrine of God, and at the same time it breaks new ground. The following topics can be distinguished and analyzed separately: (1) Love and wisdom are virtues, that is, moral concepts, and when applied to God they yield moral attributes and set forth God as an ethical subject. (2) Love and wisdom have certain distinctively Christian features, including their basis in God and their significance. (3) Love is unique among all the divine attributes, since it alone can be equated with God. (4) Wisdom is a teleological modification of omniscience.

LOVE AND WISDOM ARE MORAL ATTRIBUTES

In his discussion of love and wisdom, Schleiermacher makes use of a human analogy borrowed from his treatment of virtue. According to Schleiermacher, love is one of the four cardinal virtues; specifically, it is a representational and creative virtue.[28] It is representational because love expresses the inner being of the one who loves, and it is creative because love seeks to create and maintain fellowship: "There is no more ultimate and universal description of the striving to effect fellowship than love."[29] The *Glaubenslehre* is even more specific: "Love is the disposition to unite oneself with other and the desire to be in another."[30] Love therefore discloses the being of the lover and creates fellowship with the beloved. Consequently, the divine absolute inwardness is conceived by analogy with a human subject, and the divine absolute vitality is conceived by analogy with the execution of the motive. Love is God's motive in creation and redemption, and wisdom is the ordering of the world in preparation for redemption and the spread of redemption.

If Schleiermacher were reflecting traditional Neo-Aristotelian theism,

God's absolute inwardness would nullify and put an end to any divine self-disclosure to the world. God's love—if *actus purus* can love, as well as contemplate—would remain wholly inward. But divine love is manifest in the world as the motive of creation and redemption. Instead of being utterly inaccessible, God's love is manifest completely in the world in incarnation, and is thus accessible by all. Paradoxically, love *expresses* the absolute inwardness of God and makes it accessible. Schleiermacher is not far from Schelling when the latter writes: "God's self-revelation should be regarded not as an unconditioned, arbitrary act, but as an act morally necessary, in which love and goodness triumph over absolute inwardness."[31] Incarnation and redemption indicate that divine eternal-omnipotence is not blind, impersonal power, but power motivated by love: "If then the cardinal point of the divine world-rule is redemption and the foundation of the kingdom of God, which depend on the union of the divine being with human nature, the underlying disposition can only be regarded as love," says Schleiermacher.[32] He understands the union of the divine with human nature in traditional christological terms: "In his suffering unto death . . . there is exhibited to us an absolute, self-denying love; and in this self-denial there is represented and vividly conveyed to us the way in which God was in Christ to reconcile the world to himself . . . we see God in Christ, and we regard Christ as the most immediate partaker in the eternal love which sent him forth and endowed him for his task."[33] Divine love, the motive of God in creation and redemption, expresses God's absoluteness in relation to the world, that is, it is this specific sense in which God is absolute.

Wisdom is also one of the cardinal virtues; it is understood as the "right outlining of plans and purposes."[34] However, Schleiermacher does not follow his analysis of wisdom as a virtue strictly in application to the conception of God. In man wisdom is a contemplative rather than an active virtue. Such distinction is not applicable to God, because wisdom is a determinate mode of divine omniscience, which expresses the vitality of God. Thus, *divine* wisdom is "the art . . . of realizing the divine love perfectly."[35] Wisdom as a divine attribute is derivative from divine love: "Without ascribing any limitation to God, therefore, we may assert that the divine wisdom is not capable of producing any other order of things . . . than that in which the divine love is perfectly realized; and just as little is the divine love capable of leading to self-impartations other than those in which it finds perfect satisfaction, and in which it presents itself as absolute wisdom."[36] Although Schleiermacher does not apply the concept of personality to God because that concept is essentially finite, he does apply to God the moral and ethical attributes of love and wisdom. The justification for doing so lies in the concept of God as absolute coincidence of opposites and therefore as living and dynamic. Such attributes are required to designate those elements in the divine being and life itself which ground and support these predications. Schleiermacher's conception of God as living and spiritual omnipotence is an attempt to steer a middle course between a conception of God in crude anthropomorphic terms and a conception of God as impersonal, static substance and fate, as in Spinoza. Therefore, while God is not simply a finite person, it is not inappropriate to represent and think of the living God in terms appropriate to an ethical subjectivity.[37]

THE DISTINCTIVELY CHRISTIAN
FEATURES OF LOVE AND WISDOM

The distinctively Christian features of love and wisdom derive from incarnation and redemption. In particular, the divine love is apprehended exclusively in its decisive sense in redemption through Christ. Schleiermacher is aware that critics object to the apparent restriction which this places on the media and locus of divine love. His reply is that divine love is not unambiguously manifest in the general preservation of the world, because "apart from redemption and considered in the abstract, the divine love is always doubtful."[38] To be sure, in and of itself the divine love is neither doubtful nor ambiguous, but given the situation of sin, which is constituted by alienation from God, it appears doubtful to man. Moreover, if there is any recognition of divine love in such a situation, this recognition is qualified by the apparently conditional qualification of divine love, that is, man must be worthy of it and merit it. Since sin rules out the possibility of meriting divine favor, the love of God appears to be unattainable; thus the generic God-consciousness, "seen through Christian eyes, appears everywhere outside of redemption to be in a depressed condition."[39]

Apart from redemption there is no decisive and efficacious recognition of divine love. Schleiermacher makes this claim in a passage which surely recalls Augustine's comments about the "Platonists" who approximate the truth of Christian faith concerning God, but who fall short of the divine love manifest in incarnation and redemption:

For even though every form of God-consciousness, however imperfect, including its latent presence as something merely longed for, counts . . . as a divine communication to human nature, yet it is not one in which we can repose. . . . indeed all men, insofar as they are capable of God-consciousness, are objects of the divine love; but it does not "get through" to them. Starting from the fear of God—which is the predominant state of mind under the law— they at most succeed in attaining the negative consciousness that the highest being is not jealous, which is still very far from being a recognition of the divine love. That only comes from the actual efficacy of redemption, and it proceeds from Christ; conversely, it is only when they are in Christ that they recognize the divine love.[40]

The decisive recognition of divine love is not the result of human striving after God; rather it comes from the prior love of God for man which is exhibited in incarnation and redemption.

Schleiermacher continues and develops the Johannine theology of God as love, citing it in his dogmatic exposition. It might be useful to compare Schleiermacher's thought concerning divine love with some aspects of Nygren's analysis in *Agape and Eros*.[41] To be sure, Schleiermacher does not distinguish between *agape* and *eros,* much less adopt a sharp separation between the two as does Nygren. Schleiermacher would probably agree with Tillich that there are not two loves, but two different forms of love. Nevertheless, Nygren's analysis of Johannine theology of love is useful in understanding Schleiermacher. According to this theology, agape is spontaneous, not motivated by external forces, but has its basis exclusively in God himself. It is freely bestowed independent of any merit or lack of merit; it is creative, and thus creative of the value of its object; finally, agape as spontaneous, creative love signifies that God takes and retains the initiative in establishing fellowship with man.

Similar features are also exhibited in Schleiermacher's doctrine of divine love. Since the divine causality is apprehended through the medium of ontological moods such as joy in God, and since such moods can neither be produced nor nullified by human freedom (they are its a priori foundation), they appear as if by pure grace. Schleiermacher comments that "according to our general formula, divine grace is always prevenient."[42] What is true of the general relationship of utter dependence is a fortiori true of its instantiation in the consciousness of redemption. There too God has the initiative, and his exercise of such initiative manifests the divine love: "We have the divine love immediately in the consciousness of redemption, and since this is the basis on which we appropriate and express all other [elements of the] God-consciousness, it naturally represents for us the essence of God."[43] Divine love is the foundation and the ordering principle in the value-nucleus of the Christian God-consciousness; love is that with which and through which all other elements—including the full eternal-omnipotence—come to positive expression.

Such divine love, coming as the divine initiative to man, is something unmerited. As such, it can have its basis only in God himself. And since love is God's motive in redemption as the completion of creation, it follows that for Schleiermacher love is the ultimate motive of God in creation. Divine love is the creative source of the being and value in all creation. Schleiermacher has built divine love into the very structure of his theology, for creation and redemption form a single unified order which has its basis and arrangement in the divine love. God creates in order to love.

THE UNIQUENESS OF LOVE AS A
DIVINE ATTRIBUTE: GOD IS LOVE

Divine love is not merely an instantiation of general prevenient grace, nor is love merely one attribute among others. Although divine love appears in one particular historical event and figure, it is not a merely contingent expression of God. The central motif of Johannine theology is that love is not an attribute which God "has," rather love is what God *is:* "Its [Johannine agape-metaphysics] positive significance lies in its attempt to do full justice to the fact that God is in his very 'essence' Agape. When we speak of God's love we are not speaking of something contingently displayed by God, but of that which in every respect and in all circumstances characterises his mind and will toward us."[44] Schleiermacher follows the Johannine theology in identifying love with God, thereby qualifying, if not abandoning, negative theology and learned ignorance. It is at this point that he enters his objection to the traditional scheme of divine attributes and its distinction between divine essence and attributes: "In God there can be no distinction between essence and attributes and . . . just for that reason the concept 'attribute' is not particularly well suited to set forth the divine essence."[45]

It is clear that on the one hand, Schleiermacher is not objecting to the traditional Augustinian notion that God does not "have" attributes, but that God "is" his attributes. All divine attributes which are genuine are not mere contingent or accidental modifications of God's being, and therefore "it must be possible to form similar propositions, affirming of Him all other attributes if these have any right to be posited as divine attributes at all."[46] And yet no such proposition exists in Scripture or in church creeds; no creed flatly asserts that God is eternity, or is omnipotence, "and while we certainly might venture to say that God is loving-omnipotence or omnipotent love, yet we must admit that in either case, love alone is equated with the being or the essence of God . . . love is the only attribute which can be so equated and identified with God."[47] The assertion that God is love is an original, distinctive *Glaubenssatz,* or faith-assertion, concerning God. In the pretheoretical nucleus of value constitutive of the Christian God-consciousness, love is the chief or "first" value among equals. Love is first because it names the whole of God active in his redemptive and reconciling activity; to be sure, other attributes are present as essential aspects, but these derive their order and significance from divine love.

Given such a configuration of the value-nucleus of "god" in religious consciousness, the reflective theological task is to justify the exclusive form of the proposition "God is love," and to transform it from a *Glaubenssatz* into theological knowledge. Schleiermacher reflects on the genesis and meaning of all the divine attributes and seeks to distinguish between love as an essential divine attribute and all other essential divine attributes. The question is, what makes love "more essential" than the others? The original a priori attributes were arrived at by means of an abstraction from the full, determinate feeling-content of Christian God-consciousness. Taken as a whole, the four a priori attributes do not exhaust or fully constitute the God-consciousness. To be sure, these do express the divine inwardness and vitality, but they abstract from its motive. Although they are coconstitutive of divine essence and existence, nevertheless "belief in God as almighty and eternal is nothing but the shadow of faith which even the devils can have."[48] To believe that there is a God and that the world is created by him is not enough, for such belief still leaves "uncertainty concerning the divine will coposited in omnipotence."[49] The same uncertainty attaches to the other a priori attributes.

On the other hand, holiness and justice are not full, decisive manifestations of divine omnipotence. They are expressed in the consciousness of sin and do support the important condemnation of sin and sense of penal desert. But considered by themselves and even as taken together with the four a priori attributes, these are constitutive of a God-consciousness which exists in estrangement and alienation from God. Their positive expression occurs only when combined with the consciousness of redemption; for then they are perceived as preparatory expressions of the divine love.

Love and wisdom are distinct among the divine attributes because they derive from and express the special divine self-impartation in incarnation and redemption. They are mediated by redemption through Christ in the sense that apart from such redemption no human being could be conscious of himself as an object of divine good-pleasure and grace:

> For that is his action alone which completely corresponds to the divine will, and which gives complete and pure expression to the dominion of the God-consciousness in human nature—this is the basis of our relation to him; and on the recognition of this everything distinctively Christian depends. This implies that, apart from Christ, no individual man, nor any part of the common life of men, is at any time in and for itself, an object of the divine good-pleasure or righteous before God.[50]

The distinctive feature of such fellowship with God is the sense of being an object of divine good-pleasure and love.[51] Although it is true that no God-consciousness is a simple human possibility, this is true in the eminent sense of Christian fellowship with God, for its conditions of appearance and its significance are different from the conditions of all other divine attributes. The first six divine attributes can appear in human religious consciousness apart from redemption. To be sure, these are presupposed by and also appear in redemption, but they are not restricted to this specific, determinate form. However, love and wisdom appear in the God-consciousness only on the basis of incarnation and redemption, and therefore they are mediated exclusively through redemption. Consequently, these attributes cannot be deduced or derived from the God-consciousness a priori for they are not based on it, although they do include it and transform it. Similarly, these attributes do not accompany or express God as the object of human striving; such striving has led to human alienation and separation from God. Love and wisdom are the divine attributes which are expressed in God's self-impartation to man through redemption through Christ. Love and wisdom therefore express God's concrete historical actuality in incarnation, and cannot be derived or deduced from the religious a priori. They are the final and decisive expressions of God's initiative toward man.

Divine love is directly and immediately expressed in religious consciousness as it is shaped and conditioned by redemption. This is the reason why love is equated with God, for it expresses both God's supreme and his concrete actuality. This means that there is nothing more ultimate in God than his love. God is not simply eternal-omnipotence as such, or holiness and justice as such; he is all of these to be sure, but only as these elements are paired with and decisively expressed and ordered by his love: "Both of these attributes [holiness and justice], like the others, are attached to and merged with the divine love as it is considered solely in its preparatory expressions. Conversely, the divine love is holy and just since it begins essentially with these preparatory works; in the same way it is almighty and eternal love."[52] Love is God's concrete and supreme actuality which not only orders God's own being, but also directs and orders God's creative activity towards the world.

Isaac August Dorner has given eloquent expression to Schleiermacher's point, which summarizes succinctly the argument of Schleiermacher's doctrine of God:

All so-called proofs for the existence of God are, rightly apprehended, only preludes to the ontological, which attains its truth, however, only by the ethical. And the ethical does not have merely physical or cosmological or logical necessity; rather it must be conceived . . . as existing because it is the *absolutely valuable* in itself, which alone has its basis and goal within itself, and alone is absolute end in itself. Only in the ethical concept of God . . . does even aseity achieve its true meaning and absolute foundation . . . as love, he eternally takes up what is in the highest sense the necessary, the ethical, into his will so completely that his freedom is wholly identified with the ethical. And *everything else that is or may be conceived in God exists for this his love,* is willed by God for it, and as it requires. Thus not merely (to speak with Plato) does everything outside of God have the guarantee of existence and harmony in God's goodness; rather *the love of God also contains the supreme absolute guarantee for everything which may be designated a divine attribute.* The so-called physical attributes do not exist for themselves, as if they had in themselves the absolute necessity of being and actuality; rather *there is in God the subordinate and the superordinate, and the physical attributes serve the ethical essence of God, which is the power over them.* . . . In a word, all the divine powers and attributes do not in the last analysis exist for themselves, as if they were themselves absolutely valuable and necessary; they exist for absolute love.[53]

Religious experience is the source of the idea of God which comes to explicit expression in the ontological argument. It yields an important and essential aspect of God, but it is by no means a complete statement of God's actual qualities and attributes. However, any attribute which God "is" must be consistent with and a determinate mode of God's being as the Most High, the "Absolutely Valuable." What is supremely valuable is God's love, and this can be understood only as a moral or ethical attribute of God. Therefore, God must be conceived as moral or ethical subjectivity, even if personality *qua* finite cannot be ascribed to him without qualification. But if God is love, and such love is both preceded by and codetermined by divine existence, holiness, and justice, this is tantamount to conceiving God as living and dynamic coincidence of opposites. Such a fundamental conception underlies and is presupposed by Dorner's and Schleiermacher's distinction between superordinate and subordinate elements—that is, value-qualities—in God. Although God's being is one, within that unity not all aspects are equally valuable; love alone is supremely valuable such that all other essential attributes of God serve his love. Thus does the ontological approach find completion and final explication in the ethical. It is God's love, and not simply his existence or power as such, which is the very "essence" of deity, or the most valuable element within the essential attributes which God is.

WISDOM: THE DETERMINATE FORM OF DIVINE OMNISCIENCE

Wisdom is the second attribute expressed in the consciousness of redemption. Although it is paired with divine love, it is not as directly expressed in immediate religious consciousness as is love. The reason for this is that while love is directly given in redemption, divine wisdom comes to expression in the extension of the self-consciousness to include the world as the "theater" of redemption. Thus wisdom is less directly expressed in the consciousness of redemption, and statements concerning it are not as certain as the assertion that God is love:

> But of the two [namely, love and wisdom] love is more direct, for the forgiven man is conscious of himself as the object of the divine disposition [namely, good-pleasure] since he is the recipient of divine self-impartation. However, the consciousness of the perfect agreement and harmony of all things is just as true, but not as immediate and direct. For not everyone is as certain as he is of redemption, either that he co-conditions the production of good in his contemporary situation, or that everything else has co-conditioned and still conditions his regeneration and growth in grace.[54]

With such qualifications, Schleiermacher defines wisdom as the "principle ordering and determining the world for the divine self-communication in redemption."[55] As a result of incarnation and redemption, the world-historical order is different than it might otherwise have been: "The entire course of human and natural events would have been otherwise if the divine purpose had not been the union of the divine being with human nature in the person of Christ."[56] As was indicated earlier, wisdom is the concrete form assumed by divine omniscience relative to redemption.[57] But there are problems in stating this. Wisdom and omniscience are not two different attributes, for that would imply that divine omniscience—and thus divine omnipotence—were not completely expressed in the world. But neither are they simply the same, for wisdom is identifiable with omniscience only from a special point of view. This suggests that they are both identical and yet different. However, such difference too creates problems, for "it will always indicate an imperfection if the latter cognition of the artist of the whole of his work contains something besides what was in his purpose."[58] If God's plans in creation are changed as a result of some alien power invading his creation and working mischief in it, this implies that God is a bungler, and limited either in knowledge (he was unsure of his plans) or in power, or in both.

Schleiermacher understands wisdom as the attribute which orders the world for the final divine self-disclosure in redemption: it is expressed in the order and mode in which election is carried out. Wisdom is the fore-ordaining, predestining decree of God in election; as such it is the logical foundation of creation and the exhibition of both divine omniscience and omnipotence. Thus when the inner telos of creation is apprehended and seen to be redemption, the apparent discrepancy disappears. The two are identical with respect to their actual content when seen from the special point of view in redemption. Thus, it is wisdom which includes omniscience and not vice versa. For it is only from the standpoint of redemption and its spread that one learns the motive of God in creation, namely, that all being should be "posited in God as mediated by his love."[59] Wisdom is the attribute which orders the world for this final theophany, such that "when, through us, the world has become ready for us, it will be clearly shown that nothing can really *be* except as an object of the divine love."[60] God does not change his plan, but his plan can be seen and grasped as a unity only from the standpoint of redemption as the completion and fulfillment of creation.

In light of the identity between wisdom and omniscience as divine attributes, we can appreciate why Schleiermacher changed his formulations concerning the status of the world understood as the theater of redemption. In the first edition of the *Glaubenslehre* he wrote: "The world, as the theater of redemption, is the perfect and complete revelation of the divine wisdom, or the best world."[61] In the second edition he writes: "The divine wisdom is the reason by virtue of which the world, as the theater of redemption, is also the absolute revelation of the highest being, and therefore good."[62] The reason for the change in wording is that "we must stop at the affirmation that the world is good, and can make no use of the formulation that it is the best, because the former assertion signifies far more than the latter."[63] Schleiermacher continues to dissociate himself from Leibniz. To say with the latter that this world is the best world means that it is the best among possible worlds, and therefore good by comparison with other alternatives. In Schleiermacher's view, God is the source of possibility, and given his supreme perfection, there is but one possible world, and it is good. The world is good because it is the revelation of God, who is the Good itself.[64] Since the world is the theater of redemption by which the creation is completed, it is not merely good in comparison with other alternatives, but actually good in itself, for the world is the scene of the actualization of God's purposes for all being. Such actualization is the final world-constitution.

Such a contention stands in tension with Schleiermacher's earlier assertion that the consummation of the church founders on the indefinite propagation of the species, since that consummation apparently requires that the propagation of the species cease.[65] However, the two may not be irreconcilable; Schleiermacher approaches eschatology and theology of history—topics which lie beyond experience—on the presupposition of redemption as the completion of creation. The preparation of man for redemption and redemption itself both require a temporal process. If such a process is gradual, even asymptotic, it is not entirely open-ended. Incarnation is God's specific telos, and through the redemption of man creation is being completed. To be sure, such assertions lie on the boundary of religious experience, but that is the reason why neither personal religious experience nor collective experience can settle the question of the consummation of history. Such a question can be treated, if at all, only on the basis of incarnation and redemption. Incarnation means the fullness of time,[66] and provides a clue to future possibility. On the basis of divine incarnation Schleiermacher proceeds to construct eschatological doctrines by postulating an analogy between the incarnation of God in Christ and the regeneration of man. Incarnation is to the species what regeneration is to the individual.[67] Incarnation guarantees and gives full and final expression to the meaning of humanity.[68] Thus incarnation and redemption are the theological norms for interpreting the doctrine of the church and its consummation; they are paradigmatic for interpreting how God deals with human being, and for determining the telos of human being.

Such theological norms cannot be simply subordinated to the previously noted biological and social facts such as a potentially infinite propagation of the species. Thus if at any particular time not all men can be assumed into the kingdom of God owing to the ongoing propagation of the species, this does not mean that all men cannot be so assumed. It may be necessary to postulate a conditional immortality, however difficult this is to conceive, in order that the elect shall equal the original creation. Such a postulate is not knowledge, but it is necessary to avoid the absurd contention that biological nature, which after all is created by God, sets limits to divine power and sovereignty, such that biological death is the termination of divine gracious activity.[69] Schleiermacher does postulate such a conditional immortality, and affirms a universal election and single predestination. Calvin's double predestination is revised in order to affirm the all-inclusive divine good-pleasure, which is "to make human affairs perfect through Christ."[70] It is in this sense that Schleiermacher affirms that the world is good, rather than the best. There is but one telos of the divine good-pleasure. If Schleiermacher has not "solved" the problems which accompany his assertions, he is acutely aware of this and also of the fact that it is the nature of such "problems" that they are never finally solved. But he has not contradicted himself in his assertions concerning the historical and transhistorical aspects of Christian faith. For biological truths are phenomenal and apply to one part of life, whereas theological assertions are expressions of man's fellowship with and participation in the life of God, in whom all contrasts, including life and death, are overcome. All of this analysis merely serves to confirm Schleiermacher's thesis that Christian consciousness is less certain and less expressive of divine wisdom than it is concerning divine love.

Divine love therefore is the central and unifying element in deity, and this must be reflected in the doctrine of God. The identity of God with love signifies that the Creator and Redeemer are one and the same. "God is love" implies the ontological unity of creation and redemption—a unity which is not reversible. Schleiermacher is clearly not saying that love is divine, but that God is love. That identity and unity are accessible only from redemption, and it is on this same basis that the Christian faith-community hopes that all existence will finally be posited in God as an object of his love, such that nothing *is* save as object of God's love.

NOTES

1. *G1*, § 50.4 It should be noted here that the contrast between sin and grace is Schleiermacher's shorthand expression for the full essence of Christianity. The contrast between sin and grace has anthropological implications and dimensions, but it cannot be reduced to merely anthropological dimensions and considered as a relative contrast within the genus humanity, or as a mere contrast immanent in religious consciousness. If such a reduction occurs, the result is a truncated and reductive account of Christianity. Barth interprets Schleiermacher in such a reductive way, and does to Schleiermacher the very thing that he accuses Schleiermacher of doing, reducing theology to anthropology. Barth is blinded to Schleiermacher's actual meaning by Feuerbach. (Cf. Karl Barth, *Church Dogmatics*, III/3, trans. G.W. Bromiley and R.J. Ehrlich [Edinburgh: T. & T. Clark, 1960] pp. 330 ff.) Schleiermacher clearly indicates that the contrast between sin and grace essentially involves a relation of man to the Redeemer, and therefore has both an anthropological dimension and a christological dimension. He pursues this point in his later dogmatic elaboration (CF. *G1*, § 63, 87). While it is true that the church mediates redemption in some sense, Schleiermacher carefully qualifies this assertion: "This proposition [*G1*, § 87] is not meant to be a complete statement of specifically Christian piety, since no mention is made in it of the fact that every approximation to the state of blessedness essentially includes a relation to Christ" (*G1*, § 87.1). The importance of this qualification is evident from the following: "In the case of sin there is lacking that specific divine impartation which gives the character of grace to every approximation to salvation" (*G1*, § 80.1). It is the relation to the Redeemer which determines the fluctuations and approximations to salvation and blessedness, and not, as Barth would have it, the other way around.

2. Schleiermacher, *Die christliche Sitte nach den Grundsätzen der evangelischen Kirche*, ed. Ludwig Jonas (Berlin: G. Reimer, 1884), pp. 35–36.

3. *G1*, § 64.2; no original state of innocence which is lost in a temporal fall is involved in this conception. Cf. *G1*, § 72.6.

4. *G1*, § 79.1.

5. *G1*, § 83.3.

6. *G1*, § 79.1.

7. *G1*, § 84.4.

8. *G1*, § 83.

9. *G1*, § 68–69.

10. *GI*, § 31.2.

11. *GI*, § 83.2.

12. Ibid.

13. Ibid.

14. *GI*, § 75.1.

15. *GI*, § 84.1.

16. Ibid.

17. *GI*, § 83.1.

18. *GI*, § 84.4.

19. *GI*, § 75.1.

20. Isaac August Dorner, "On the Proper Version of the Dogmatic Concept of the Immutability of God, with Special Reference to the Interrelation between God's Transhistorical and Historical Life," *God and Incarnation in Mid-Nineteenth Century German Theology*, trans. Claude Welch (New York: Oxford University Press, 1965), p. 133.

21. *GI*, § 84.4.

22. *GI*, § 118.2.

23. Ibid.

24. *GI*, § 80.1.

25. *GI*, § 90.2.

26. *GI*, § 60.

27. *GI*, § 165.1.

28. Schleiermacher, "Ueber die wissenschaftliche Behandlung des Tugendbegriffes," *Saemmtliche Werke* III/3 (Berlin: G. Reimer, 1839), pp. 350 ff.

29. Ibid., p. 375. Schleiermacher also indicates that love is a representational and creative virtue, and that it expresses the inner being of the lover. It is clear that Schleiermacher does not regard love as a mere emotion or sentiment. It is a moral virtue or excellence, and it discloses the inner being or the moral character of the one who loves.

30. *GI*, § 165.1.

31. F.W.J. Schelling, *Of Human Freedom*, trans. James Gutmann (Chicago: Open Court, 1936), pp. 76 ff. Schleiermacher may have borrowed this terminology from Schelling.

32. *GI*, § 165.1.

33. *GI*, § 104.4.

34. *GI*, § 165.1.

35. Ibid.

36. *GI*, § 165.2.

37. The question whether God is personal, or whether this is merely an anthropomorphic representation, is a perennial one. Commenting on German idealism, F.C. Copleston argues that "to attribute to the infinite a process of becoming self-conscious is an evident expression of anthropomorphic thinking." See his *A History of Philosophy,* 8 vols., pt. 1 (New York: Image Books, 1963), 7:41 ff. Measured against this statement, Schleiermacher is not an idealist, nor is his attribution of moral attributes to God anthropomorphic in the above sense. Such "anthropomorphisms" in the *Glaubenslehre* are not the result of speculative fancy, but depend upon a given: "Instead of a first principle [*Grundsatz*], dogmatics has merely a given state of affairs [*Grundtatsache*]" (*GI,* § 28.2). The anthropomorphisms of the *Glaubenslehre* are not simply at the disposal of the theologian; rather they are inevitable and necessary expressions of piety: "Everyone must recognize it as an almost absolute necessity for the highest stage of piety to acquire the conception of a personal God, and . . . he will recognize

the essential imperfection in the conception of a personality of the Highest Being . . . The conception is necessary whenever one would interpret to himself or to others the immediate religious emotions, or whenever the heart has immediate intercourse with the Highest Being.'' See Schleiermacher, *On Religion: Speeches to Its Cultured Despisers,* trans. John Oman (New York: Harper & Row, 1958), p. 116. Schleiermacher is not far from Barth when the latter contends that owing to its sources, theology has no stake in the concept of personality or the attribution of such a concept to God. According to Barth, "Everything depends on the statement that God is the One who loves. But nothing at all depends on the statement that he is or he has personality." See Barth, *Church Dogmatics,* II/1, p. 296. To be sure, this does not settle the issue.

38. *Gl,* § 166.1.

39. Ibid.

40. *Gl,* § 166.2.

41. Anders Nygren, *Agape and Eros,* trans. Philip Watson (New York: Harper & Row, 1969), pp. 176–77.

42. *Gl,* § 108.2n; see *Der christliche Glaube,* ed. Martin Redeker (Berlin: Walter de Gruyter & Co., 1960), 2:159 (*The Christian Faith,* trans. H.R. Mackintosh [Philadelphia: Fortress Press, 1976], p. 485).

43. *Gl,* § 167.2.

44. Nygren, *Agape and Eros,* p. 153.

45. *Gl,* § 167.1.

46. Ibid.

47. Ibid.

48. *Gl,* § 167.2.

49. Ibid.

50. *Gl,* § 104.3.

51. Ibid., § 166.2.

52. *Gl,* § 167.2.

53. Dorner, "The Immutability of God," pp. 159-60, italics by R.R.W. This important essay has received little attention in recent discussions of divine immutability. Barth admits indebtedness to Dorner and praises this work as a "great essay" (See Barth, *Church dogmatics,* II/I, p. 439). Since Dorner was influenced by Schleiermacher, there is a theological lineage here. What Barth has to say about divine love is virtually identical with Schleiermacher (Barth, *Church Dogmatics,* II/I, pp. 272-87).

54. *Gl,* 1st ed., § 183.3; cited in Redeker ed., 2:451.

55. *Gl,* § 168.

56. *Gl,* § 164.2.

57. *Gl,* § 55.1; 168.1.

58. *Gl,* § 55.1.

59. *Gl,* § 168.1.

60. *Gl,* § 169.2, italics by R.R.W.

61. *Gl,* 1st ed., § 185, Redeker ed., 2:562.

62. *Gl,* § 169.

63. *Gl,* § 59.3.

64. *Gl,* § 83.1.

65. *Gl,* § 114.1.

66. *Gl*, § 118.1.

67. *Gl*, § 113.4; 116.2; 118.1; 120.2; 97.4.

68. *Gl*, § 118.1.

69. *Gl*, § 119.3.

70. *Gl*, § 120.3. For immortality as a christological postulate, cf. *Gl*, § 158.2. Schleiermacher clearly indicates that the topic of immortality is a concern for Christian faith only as it bears on and attaches to the central event of redemption. In this limited and qualified sense, it can be affirmed that the Redeemer is the mediator of eternal life to the human species. Admittedly Schleiermacher's statement is not as clear or unambiguous as one would like.

6

God Hidden and Revealed:
Schleiermacher on Trinity

INTRODUCTION: THE PROBLEMATIC STATUS OF TRINITY

As is well known, the doctrine of trinity is problematic for Schleiermacher, partly because it is not an immediate utterance of Christian religious consciousness, but only a combination of such utterances. This gives the impression that the doctrine is at best secondary, and at worst superfluous, to the argument of the *Glaubenslehre*. Despite such an appearance, I shall attempt to show that, far from being dispensable, trinity is, as Schleiermacher says, the very cornerstone of Christian doctrine, including the doctrine of God. However, if the doctrine itself is problematic, Schleiermacher's treatment of it has also been problematic and puzzling to his students and interpreters. To some extent, Schleiermacher himself is to blame for this because his treatment is incomplete and fragmentary. His most explicit study of trinity is not to be found in his *Glaubenslehre* but in a separate publication, an historical-critical comparison of the Athanasian and the Sabellian versions of trinity.[1] Moreover, neither discussion makes much sense apart from the other: Schleiermacher's "historical account" of Sabellianism sheds more light on his own doctrine of God than it does on Sabellianism. Conversely, the leading contentions concerning the doctrine of God in the *Glaubenslehre* receive support and logical foundation in the "Sabellian" account of trinity which Schleiermacher approves. Therefore, only by taking the two accounts together can something approaching a complete picture of Schleiermacher's thought result.

On the other hand, despite problems surrounding trinity and Schleiermacher's views on the subject, he has suffered excessively at the hand of both friend and critic alike. Many discussions critical of Schleiermacher presuppose the validity of the assumptions which Schleiermacher is out to demolish, namely, that the doctrine of God can be taken piecemeal, and that it presupposes the speculative distinction between the essence and attributes of God. A relatively recent study of trinity in contemporary theological thought includes a section on Schleiermacher. It follows a procedure of pursuing and analyzing Schleiermacher's account of trinity independently of his doctrine of God and divine attributes.[2] The critic assumes the validity of the speculative distinction between divine essence and attributes. Not surprisingly, Schleiermacher is censured for a reductive, economic interpretation of trinity. This reductive interpretation is traced to Schleiermacher's "subjectivism," that is, that religious doctrines are merely accounts of human emotions. His theology is interpreted as noncognitive and antimetaphysical: the consciousness of redemption neither presupposes nor requires any assertions concerning God's being; the doctrines of trinity and divine attributes do not express God's being, but only the different ways in which the religious consciousness is related to the pure, undifferentiated divine unity. The result is a merely economic or Sabellian interpretation of trinity, and a nominalist interpretation of divine attributes. Influential and pervasive as this view of Schleiermacher is, it is a mere caricature.

It is axiomatic for Schleiermacher that the doctrine of God should form a unified, systematic whole. As integral elements of the doctrine, trinity and attributes must be treated in accordance with the same principles. The doctrine of trinity is of central importance in determining the relation of the generic elements and the historically determinate elements constitutive of the Christian doctrine of God. In Schleiermacher's view, the theological tradition has been methodologically inconsistent in its development of the doctrine of God. It derives the doctrine of divine essence and attributes largely from natural theology and the doctrine of trinity from Scripture or historical revelation. The result is a problematic conglomerate of disparate elements whose integral relation has not been shown. This point is not simply methodological; such an eclectic procedure has influenced and shaped the substantive understanding of faith itself. In deriving the doctrine of divine attributes from natural theology, the tradition has also taken over and accepted the speculative distinction between essence and attributes. The result is a separation between God's being and God's act, and a subordination of the historically determinate elements of Christianity to general speculative principles.

Not only has this speculative apparatus affected the doctrine of divine attributes, it has affected also the understanding of the doctrine of trinity.

The theological tradition has been Origenist in its practical interpretation and understanding of trinity, if not in its explicit doctrinal formulations. God as Father stands in a different relation to the divine essence than does God the Son, which implies a subordination.[3] Even more important, God the Father is identified with the utterly transcendent, abstract unity and eternity which has dominated classical philosophical and theological thought from Aristotle through Origen to Plotinus. Schleiermacher's reading of the classical understanding of the orthodox creeds is similar to Harnack's. According to the latter, the post-Nicene interpretation of the term *homoousious* really amounts to a new Origenism.[4] The result is a tension in trinitarian thought between the God who stands beyond history, that is, the "God beyond God," and the God who manifests himself in history. The fundamental idea is that there is more in God than is revealed or manifest in history, and that "genuine deity," so to speak, is not found at the historical level, but only at the transcendent level. Thus, although God has manifested himself in incarnation and redemption, there remains more in God which is hidden; while God loves the world, yet there is more in God than love, namely, his power, understood as abstract omnipotence, *potentia dei absoluta*. Here lies the theological foundation of the "horrible decree" of double predestination: mercy for the saved, justice for the damned.

Schleiermacher is critical of this theological position. His alternative is to develop the entire doctrine of God, including attributes and trinity, as the objective correlate of religious experience qualified by redemption. He seeks to put the entire doctrine on a single, nonspeculative footing, namely, as a description and analysis of the historically positive and determinate Christian consciousness of redemption. He separates his *Glaubenslehre* from speculative or rational theology, including the distinction between divine essence and attributes. In setting forth the doctrine of God as the correlate of religious consciousness, Schleiermacher seeks to overcome the speculative separation between God's being and God's act, not only in the treatment of divine attributes, but also in the doctrine of trinity.

Accordingly, there are three distinct but related theses taken up and advanced in this chapter: (1) Schleiermacher's critique and reconstruction of the doctrine of trinity, (2) his leaning towards Sabellianism in this reconstruction, and (3) what distinguishes Schleiermacher from both orthodoxy and historical Sabellianism, his proposal that God is coincidence of opposites and that trinity is the central and crucial element in the very idea of God as coincidence of opposites.

SCHLEIERMACHER ON TRINITY

THE FUNDAMENTAL INTENTION OF THE DOCTRINE

Schleiermacher subscribes to the fundamental intention of trinity, which is to make as complete an identification as is possible between the being of God incarnate in the Redeemer, and the being of God in itself.[5] So understood, trinity is not a secondary or dispensable theological doctrine, rather it is "the cornerstone of Christian doctrine," such that with it "the whole view of Christianity set forth in our church teaching either stands or falls."[6] However, the orthodox formulations have failed to realize this intention because they presuppose the speculative background of classical thought, particularly its abstract conception of divine transcendence, omnipotence, and eternity. Specifically, in its formulation of the classical doctrine, the tradition took "the intermediate step . . . of *eternalizing in separation* the being of God in itself, and the being of God which makes union with human nature possible."[7] This is not a criticism of the intellectual, reflective task of determining the theological conditions of redemption; it is a criticism of the precritical, speculative mode of thought reflected in the classical formulations. The step of "eternalizing in separation" God in himself and God in relation to the world paves the way for the Origenist, subordinationist interpretation of the classical doctrine previously noted.

The problem of the trinity is to find an acceptable way of both distinguishing and identifying God incarnate with God himself. In his essay on trinity Schleiermacher formulates the matter in the following way: Christian theology is a third alternative to strict monotheism and to polytheism.[8] The former rejects all distinctions in God and asserts his sole supremacy and unity of rule. Christianity is distinguished from such monotheism by its claim that God in his supreme unity does not remain apart from or external to man, but rather incarnates himself in the Redeemer. Thus what sets Christianity apart from strict monotheism is its view of the economy or history of salvation which has its focal point in incarnation and redemption through Christ.

On the other hand, this claim implies that God does not have merely one, essentially negative, mode of existence, but at least two (and three, if the Spirit is included). This appears to be polytheistic, that is, it appears to posit a plurality of divine beings and/or principles. Schleiermacher observes that such a concept of a plurality of divine beings amounts to a deification of natural powers which are universally accessible, that is, they are not bound up with an economy or history of redemption. Against the polytheistic view, Schleiermacher indicates that Christianity is still a monotheism, insisting on the sole supremacy and unity of rule of God, or the divine monarchy. Divine unity and supremacy are asserted to exclude the proliferation of divine beings and principles of polytheism, but they are not meant as an exclusion of all distinctions in God whatsoever. Therefore Christian thought has the task of maintaining both the divine monarchy and the economy of redemption. Both elements are essential to the Christian concept of God. The problem is to show how the transmundane, trans-historical *monarchia* of God is united with the historical economy of redemption, and in particular, its self-disclosure in incarnation. Note that this formulation of the trinitarian problem is not the anti-Arian formulation of an Athanasius, but rather a formulation of the problem as it arises out of the historical essence of Christianity itself. How to unite the monarchy with the economy in a nonreductive, nonsubordinationist way? The trinitarian problem is transposed by Schleiermacher from classical ontology and metaphysics (that is, the logos doctrine) to the historical and transhistorical categories appropriate to the historical essence of Christianity.

THE FUNDAMENTAL INTENTION IN RELATION
TO THE ESSENCE OF CHRISTIANITY

Given this transposition and reformulation of the trinitarian problem, there are ways in which the identification of God incarnate with God himself can be distorted, which parallel the natural heresies of Christianity. As distortions, these are distinct from simple denials or rejections of Christianity, since they purport to be accounts of Christianity. Hence these distortions are distortions of the trinitarian formulations themselves. Basically, the distortions occur through a maximizing of one of the essential elements of God while minimizing the other, for example, monarchy over economy and vice versa. A maximizing of the economy of redemption and minimizing or suppression of the monarchy leads to a merely economic interpretation of trinity in which the manifestations of God lack foundation in God himself, but are mere relations between God and world. This view can also go hand in hand with a strict view of monotheism in which divine monarchy or unity is conceived as excluding all distinctions, as in Origenism. This view, that is, the economic interpretation of the trinity, has been charged to Schleiermacher himself, but he would reject it as an unacceptable distortion of the essence of Christianity and of his own thought as well. Although God is one, his unity does not simply exclude all distinctions. Hence a merely economic trinity is unacceptable.

The second way in which trinitarian theology can be distorted is to maximize the ontological element and minimize the historical element. Curious as it may sound, this is the danger Schleiermacher senses in the orthodox doctrine of the immanent trinity: "The dominant symbols of the church maintained that there is in God a trinity which is *purely internal;* that there is something that was originally distinct and separate *independent of all operations of the deity;* that the deity was Father, Son and Holy Spirit in itself, from eternity, and would have been such even if there had been no union with human nature, and no indwelling in the community of faith."[9] Schleiermacher thinks that the ontological mode in which immanent trinity is asserted is both speculative and precritical; it bypasses the historical and cultural shaping of the specific Christian terminology for the ontological distinctions in God. But the terms "Father," "Son," and "Spirit" are not simply universal ontological structures or potencies generally accessible to reflection, rather they are historically and culturally shaped elements of the divine self-disclosure constitutive of the economy of redemption. To render these elements as an immanent ontological trinity in the above sense is to begin the speculative enterprise of transforming them into general ontological principles. Schleiermacher is acutely conscious of the development of speculative trinities in German idealism; in reference to such trinities he writes that even though these may be superior conceptually to the church doctrine as accounts of the inner divine life and self-differentiation, they are unusable in a *Glaubenslehre* because they are neither based on nor explications of the fundamental fact of Christianity, redemption through Christ.[10] A purely immanent ontological trinity in itself is no guarantee of a genuine theological account of the possibility of redemption, but must be itself grounded and exhibited in the economy of redemption.

The problem of trinitarian construction is not merely to strike a balance between the ontological monarchy and historical economy, but to *conceive* this synthesis. This is not to assert that all representatives of the tradition failed to do so, but simply to bring out the fundamental problem and its ramifications. To be sure, Schleiermacher thinks that the Sabellian version of trinity is comparable to and perhaps even superior to the traditional. It is now time to turn to his essay on Sabellianism to understand this judgment.

THE ATTRACTION OF THE SABELLIAN ACCOUNT OF TRINITY

Harnack has observed that an interest common to the Monarchians and Sabellians is the elaboration of "the conception of the person of Christ founded on the history of salvation, as against one based on the history of his nature."[11] Since Schleiermacher too is concerned with emphasizing the historical as well as the ontological elements of Christian faith, he is attracted to Sabellianism as a more historical, less speculative account of Christian faith. This does not mean that Schleiermacher wholly or simply embraces Sabellianism, only that there are reasons for his attraction to it. In Sabellianism the problem of God is formulated in a way congenial to Schleiermacher, namely, both the divine monarchy and economy of redemption must be asserted and balanced.

It is interesting to note that Monarchianism was critical, if not rejecting of the logos doctrine, particularly the idea of preexistence. Moreover, when the logos is distinguished from God as such, the suspicion remains that this represents a continuation of polytheism, and the three divine hypostases of Neoplatonism in particular. Not only are such hypostases incompatible with strict monotheism and divine monarchy, they are not derived from the economy of redemption, but from independent philosophical speculation. Thus the formulation of the doctrine of trinity as one substance and three persons (hypostases) suggests the Neoplatonic trinity. Even if such hypostases are coequal, to declare them eternal elements in God is to constitute them independently of the economy of redemption. Sabellianism rejects this terminology and the consequences which appear to follow from it. The economy of redemption and incarnation of God in human nature in the Redeemer do not divide or partition the divine being. God is indivisible, and this excludes hypostatic distinctions in God. Schleiermacher puts the issue in the following way:

> Now according to this mode of representation, *hypostasis* in the divine must be something necessarily existent and independent of all *oikonomia.* Such a view of the subject Sabellius felt himself bound to oppose, in order to preserve a proper balance between the *monarchia,* i.e., the doctrine of the essential unity of deity, and the *oikonomia,* i.e., the doctrine of those distinctions in God which refer to the world and the order of salvation . . . This opposition he could not have expressed more sharply than by contending that the special *perigraphe* [circumscription] of deity which occurred in incarnation had such an utter and intimate relation to men that if men should cease to exist, it too would cease to exist.[12]

According to Schleiermacher, this is the background of the Sabellian denial of distinctions in God. Note that it is not a denial of all distinctions whatsoever, but only a denial of hypostatic distinctions. Schleiermacher takes this denial as having positive implications, namely, it represents a resistance to the reduction of the historical persons of the economy of redemption to general ontological structures. Such speculation not only separates God from the world, it also reifies this distinction and projects it into God himself. This is foreign to Christianity: "Who of us would venture to say that the impression made by the divine in Christ obliges us to conceive such an eternal distinction as its basis?"[13] The evidence of Christian consciousness points the other way, namely, to a positive relation between God and world such that the latter, particularly history, functions as the medium and vehicle of divine self-disclosure. Specifically, God in his revelation is identical with God himself.

To be sure, the exact nature of the distinctions in God which are allowed after the rejection of hypostatic or genus-species distinctions is not clear. Scholars following Origen have tended to regard Sabellianism as holding a merely economic view of trinity. All economic distinctions are excluded from the being of God in itself and thus fall within and are relative to the religious consciousness. Still, the matter is far from clear. For example, Bethune-Baker notes that on the one hand Praxeas and Noetus deny real distinctions in God, but on the other hand they make and insist upon an important distinction between God invisible and God visible, or revealed in the world, particularly the theophanies of the Old Testament, culminating in the self-manifestation of God in Christ.[14] The target of the denial of real distinctions in God seems to have been the Neoplatonic trinities and the proliferation of divine principles or hypostases. The economic distinctions retained are reflective of God's actual historical self-manifestation. God is both visible and invisible, both revealed and hidden. This is less than a positing of real hypostatic distinctions in God, but more than a merely economic trinity.

This impression is strengthened from Schleiermacher's own account of Sabellianism cited above which speaks of distinctions in God expressed in the order of salvation. To anticipate, the Sabellianism with which Schleiermacher is familiar is a special sophisticated post-Nicene variety stemming from Marcellus of Ancyra. Kelly points out that Marcellus held a logos doctrine and thus distinguished between God and his logos, while at the same time maintaining their ontological identity or consubstantiality.[15] Not only are there ontological distinctions in God, these distinctions become developed and made explicit in God's historical economy of redemption. This information prepares the way for Schleiermacher's challenge to the traditional interpretation of Sabellianism as teaching only an economic trinity of revelation without basis in the divine being itself. What Schleiermacher finds especially attractive here is the thesis that the divine monarchy or unity, and divine economy or trinity, are conceived as opposites which coincide.

GOD HIDDEN AND REVEALED

At the conclusion of his discussion of trinity in the first edition of his *Glaubenslehre,* Schleiermacher calls for a reconsideration of the doctrine, and that in any reconstruction of it "We should attentively examine the distinction between God hidden and revealed."[16] This remark has been ignored by most discussions of Schleiermacher, yet it is of crucial, fundamental significance. For as the foregoing study has shown, his entire discussion of God makes use of a unique procedure of pairing positive and negative attributes, for example, eternal-omnipotence, holiness and justice, and so forth. The justification for such a procedure is that God is conceived as coincidence of opposites, namely, absolute inwardness and absolute vitality. It is no exaggeration to say that Schleiermacher's doctrine of God and divine attributes is structured by the fundamental contrast between God hidden and revealed. The above-quoted remark from the first edition of the *Glaubenslehre* merely serves to bring his actual meaning into focus.

To be sure, this terminology of God hidden and God revealed does not originate with Schleiermacher. Behind him stands Luther, and behind Luther stands Cusanus, who wrote an entire essay on the theme *"De Deo Abscondito"* and used it to illustrate his point that theology is not absolute knowledge, but learned ignorance. If the terminology is not new or original with Schleiermacher, what is novel and original is his making it the central operative concept in the entire doctrine of God. Further, it is the central structuring theological principle because hiddenness and revealedness are the general phenomenological features of divine self-disclosure constitutive of actual religious experience. As such, these concepts continue to have central, even foundational significance in contemporary phenomenology of religion, from Otto to Eliade. However, neither his predecessors nor his successors have made such explicit, systematic theological use of these categories as has Schleiermacher.

He proposes to use such phenomenological categories in lieu of the whole speculative apparatus and distinction between divine essence and attributes. Such use is the clue to the merely apparent "subjectivism" of Schleiermacher concerning divine attributes and trinity. Theological language describes and sets forth God as the correlate of religious experience qualified by redemption. This appears subjective in comparison with natural theology, because the theological language of the *Glaubenslehre* sets forth God as the intentional object of historically determinate Christian consciousness. However, such language is not merely subjective, but reflects a genuinely empirical approach to theology through the medium of religious experience. It is no exaggeration to contend that in rejecting the traditional speculative apparatus of natural theology, Schleiermacher is seeking to avoid the contention that there is nothing in God (that is, God's essence speculatively viewed) to support theological predication (that is, divine attributes fall "outside" God's *nuda essentia*).

The restriction of theological language to the explication of the correlate of religious experience is only an apparent one. It does not mean or imply that something less than genuine deity is manifest in such historical self-disclosure. *That* assumption *is* part of the speculative tradition deriving from Origen, according to which the deity manifest in the economy of redemption is something less than the transcendent God himself. Such a speculative downgrading of religious experience occurs when it is said with Plato and Plotinus that the Supreme is beyond both being and essence, or when it is said with Thomas that the divine essence is not known through itself, but only through its effects from the standpoint of the creation, or when it is said with Tillich that when the historical symbols of God collapse, the God beyond God remains. In rejecting the speculative apparatus and replacing it with the phenomenological contrast between God hidden and revealed, Schleiermacher is rejecting the contention that there is more in God than his actual self-manifestation discloses, or that the historical disclosure is somewhat less than the transhistorical being of God itself.[17] Rather, God is one with his self-disclosure: he is absolute as related, and related as absolute. The speculative distinction between essence and attributes is not well suited to a *Glaubenslehre* or phenomenological theology because it tends to obscure if not actually undermine the point that whatever is said about God on the basis of his actual self-manifestation truly expresses God, for example, God is love.[18]

It is this distinction between God hidden and revealed which is drawn by the Monarchians and Sabellians which attracts Schleiermacher to the Sabellian account of trinity. In this ancient theological tradition, the divine *monarchia* is God invisible or hidden, and economy of redemption, including incarnation, is God revealed or visible. This distinction between God hidden and revealed is the one crucial distinction retained by the Sabellian tradition, and deserves to be refined and developed further. Schleiermacher writes: "The contrast between God as hidden and God as revealed has never been carried out more completely and with greater rigor in connection with the idea of the trinity than by Sabellius. In his interpretation, both [i.e., God hidden and God revealed] *completely coincide,* with the result that the whole trinity is God revealed, and the divine being considered in itself in its unity is God concealed."[19] This is an extremely important passage and claim. The doctrine of trinity is being interpreted as signifying not just *a* coincidence of opposites, but rather *the complete* coincidence of opposites in God. Let us begin our analysis of this claim with some historical observations and reservations, and then proceed to the systematic theological issues and implications of this assertion.

It is far from evident that historical Sabellianism did assert the complete identity between God incarnate and God himself. It is questionable whether it succeeded in overcoming the Origenist tendency to subordinate the visible God to the transcendent invisible divine monarchy. This tendency seems apparent in modalistic Monarchianism as traditionally interpreted. Moreover, Schleiermacher's own exposition of Sabellius' predecessors preserves this subordinationist tendency. For example, the revealed trinity is not really essential to God himself, but merely relative to the world and man.[20] Further, the circumscription of the Godhead is interpreted as the addition to its simple unity of an external, secondary, differentiating element. In himself God· is undifferentiated, but becomes differentiated through union with something else. Thus the *prosopon* "Father" is distinguished from other *prosopa* of trinity and from the simple unity by its union with the world and its unified rule over the world. However, "before" the creation of the world, deity is not Father, but merely unity as yet undifferentiated.[21] Similarly, the second person of trinity is a differentiation of the divine unity through its union with a human being in the *prosopon* of the Redeemer.[22] In both cases, differentiation seems to be external to deity as such, and therefore not a feature of God in himself.

However, the case against Sabellianism is not clear-cut. Schleiermacher rejects the adoptionist interpretation of the Sabellian Christology, and by extension he rejects the implication of the above remarks that God creates the world and thereby becomes Father by a simple imposition of order and form on a preexisting, uncreated chaos:

No one however must here admit the idea that Sabellius regarded the world as preexisting in its chaotic elements (as Anaxagoras supposed that it did before the *Nous* acted upon it), and that afterwards the Godhead arranged and adapted it for its use. . . . Sabellius did not hold that the person of the Redeemer first existed, and then the Godhead united itself with it; but that the person itself sprung from this union. In like manner, he did not view the church as first having existence, and then the Spirit as uniting with it; but the church itself took its rise, and the peculiar *perigraphe* of the Spirit was developed by his union to it. In this way every development of personality [*prosopon*] in the Godhead, even the second and third, must be regarded as creative in nature.[23]

Schleiermacher's remarks make it seem that that which differentiates deity and finitizes it is itself created by the deity. This suggests that deity is self-differentiating, and that it includes a finite element in itself. This moves in the direction of a panentheism rather close to that of the idealists. Further, it moves in the direction of trinitarian orthodoxy because the distinctions in the divine self-disclosure are intrinsic to and inherent in God himself. What kind of Sabellianism is this?

The Sabellianism which Schleiermacher admires is that of Marcellus of Ancyra, a post-Nicene version put forth by a defender of the Nicene term *homoousios*. Harnack and others mention him as an interesting if odd and historically unimportant figure on the fringes of orthodox theology. A contemporary of Athanasius, it is significant that he was never condemned by Athanasius, who was apparently requested to do so. Athanasius was satisfied with Marcellus' orthodoxy on the central issue of the consubstantiality of God's logos with God himself.[24] Marcellus taught a version of the logos doctrine together with the important trinitarian qualification that the logos is *homoousios* with God himself. Thus he in effect taught an immanent trinity or logos doctrine, coeternal and coequal with God himself.

Schleiermacher is not simply mistaken or wrong in representing Marcellus' Sabellianism as teaching that God hidden and God revealed completely coincide, for this is the meaning of the term *homoousios* within the Sabellian framework. In historical terms, *homoousios* means the ontological identity between the divine monarchy and economy of redemption, of God's logos with God himself. As such it negates the subordinationism of pre-Nicene theology from Origen through Arius, and is the ontological equivalent of the anti-Arian Athanasian formulas. For Marcellus, the trinitarian persons are not merely transitory theophanies as in Noetus and Praxeas, rather they are abiding elements in God himself which are made explicit in his self-disclosure in the economy of redemption. Although there remain substantial problems in Marcellus' formulations,[25] he may not be legitimately accused of teaching a merely economic trinity in which the economic distinctions are excluded from God's being itself. Since it is this version of Sabellianism which Schleiermacher is attracted to because it asserts the complete coincidence (*homoousios*) of God hidden and revealed, neither may Schleiermacher be accused of a merely economic trinity. This conclusion may be accepted on no less an authority on trinity than Athanasius himself!

A CRITICAL ESTIMATE OF
SCHLEIERMACHER'S "SABELLIANISM"

Schleiermacher never formulated constructively his own views on trinity; his remarks in the *Glaubenslehre* are very tentative and do not express much satisfaction with orthodoxy on the one hand, or much confidence in the viability of the Sabellian version of trinity on the other. Granted this fragmentary character of the text and evidence, neither a construction of Schleiermacher's own complete views of trinity, nor a critical estimate of such are possible. We have only some clues concerning how Schleiermacher would likely have proceeded if he had completed the doctrine of God. Thus a critical estimate can be offered only in light of the evidence, fragmentary as it is. The following remarks are intended merely as my own brief sketch of the potential in Schleiermacher's remarks; they are not intended as solution of the problems involved in a Sabellian version of trinity, but only as the most plausible interpretation of Schleiermacher.

THE AMBIGUITY IN GOD HIDDEN AND REVEALED

Schleiermacher makes this concept of God much more central to the doctrine of God than does the ancient tradition or even Cusanus. Divine hiddenness is the *terminus a quo,* revealedness the *terminus ad quem* of the divine self-disclosure. This means that hiddenness is not antithetical to revelation, but rather is an essential feature of it, namely, that from which or out of which revelation proceeds and makes manifest. Conversely, revealedness is not simply revelation made unmysterious or rational, but rather the self-disclosure of the Most High, that beyond which nothing greater can be conceived. This makes it evident that Schleiermacher appropriates the biblical concept of theophany and construes it as the experiential religious a priori, the pretheoretical foundation of speculative natural theology. Religious experience itself is a source of theological knowledge independent of and irreducible to speculative theology; the latter derives from the former as a second order, reflective discipline.

However, the concept of theophany, and particularly the dialectical interplay of hiddenness and revealedness, are not free from ambiguity. If hiddenness is an essential feature of divine revelation, is God really disclosed and made known? Or is there more in God than is disclosed (and how is that ascertained)? If one answers in the affirmative, the result is a return to the subordinationism of historical theology to speculative theology which derives from Origen. The problem can be seen in Cusanus.

It belongs to God to disclose himself in an infinite variety of ways, none of which exhausts his being or self-disclosure. In effect Cusanus combines the notion of theophany with the principle of plenitude: divine infinity is manifest completely not in any particular historical religion, but only in the totality of all religions, each of which represents something true, but is only a partial, one-sided grasp of the infinite. The result is a subordination of positive historical theology to the speculatively determined comprehension of the whole.

SCHLEIERMACHER'S CORRECTIVE

Although Schleiermacher may have held similar views (compare his Fifth Address on Religion), his flat assertion that God is love represents a significant departure from negative theology and learned ignorance. This comes to the fore in his novel and original interpretation of the Nicene term *homoousios* to mean a *complete* coincidence of opposites between God hidden and revealed. What is disclosed through incarnation and redemption is not merely *a* coincidence of opposites, or a relative coincidence as in the case of a theophany, but rather *the complete* coincidence of opposites: God hidden is *homoousios* with God revealed. There is nothing held back in incarnation: God and Redeemer are one and the same, in two modes of existence. The term *homoousios* "gives" as it were, the ultimate coincidence of opposites in God which is the foundation of the doctrine of divine attributes, particularly the assertion that God is love.

Not only does this thesis concerning the identity of opposites in God exclude subordinationism in all forms, it also establishes that the Redeemer is identical with God himself and therefore immanent in God's being. But it does so in such a way that the actual historical divine self-disclosure in incarnation is the foundation of this ontological immanence, and not merely a speculatively derived deduction or inference concerning God's inner life. The *homoousios* principle cannot be deduced from a priori speculative structures of God without the attendant subordination of the historical which occurs from Origen to Cusanus. Schleiermacher's novel interpretation of the *homoousios* as complete coincidence or identity of opposites amounts to a corrective of this subordinationist, formal tendency.

THE STATUS OF THE DISTINCTIONS IN GOD

It is clear that Schleiermacher cannot be responsibly regarded as teaching a merely economic trinity of revelation. It is equally clear that he stops short of the traditional version of immanent trinity because he considers that to concede too much to speculation and to run the danger of transforming the historical persons of redemption into ontological structures or principles universally accessible to reason, bypassing the historical. Once the theologian gets into the business of offering an account of God's inner life prior to the creation of the world, his theology has ceased to be governed by the principle of positivity and the fundamental fact of Christianity, namely, redemption through Christ.

What then can be said concerning Schleiermacher's version of trinity? If it is not economic or immanent, then what is it? Claude Welch has observed that this classification of alternatives is not exhaustive or clear. He proposes the following scheme of classification of alternatives: economic trinity, essential trinity, and immanent trinity.[26] The economic trinity means simply the threefoldness of God in his historical manifestation, which is not grounded in God himself, but only in the relation between God and world. This is theologically unacceptable since it fails to show how redemption is grounded in God himself. The essential trinity includes the doctrines of *homoousios,* coeternity, and coequality, including terms to express the essential nature of such distinctions in God. Finally, there is the immanent trinity, which adds to the essential trinity the doctrines of internal relations (generation and procession) and perichoresis or coinherence.

Given such distinctions, it is fair and accurate to say that Schleiermacher teaches an essential trinity. Like Marcellus, he goes as far as the doctrine of *homoousios* between monarchy and economy, together with its implications of the abiding character of the trinitarian persons in God. But Schleiermacher does not teach an immanent trinity in the traditional sense. Both he and Marcellus can see only ontological subordination in the idea of an eternal generation of the Son, and he reserves his sharpest criticism and attack for Origen's concept of eternal begetting. Such a process is never completed, and therefore deity is never really Son or Father, but only on the way to becoming such.[27] The question is, given his rejection of immanent trinity, does Schleiermacher seriously and detrimentally part company with the theological, that is, Athanasian tradition? I think not. Athanasius' refusal to condemn Marcellus is significant historical information concerning this Sabellianism, and I submit that there is little cognitive difference between Schleiermacher and the tradition in their claims concerning the inner being of God.

Schleiermacher sees the tradition as preparing the way for speculative mischief in offering its account of immanent trinity. Why stop merely with the immanent trinity? Theology is tempted to go a step further and transform the Augustinian program of faith seeking understanding into an Hegelian quest for absolute knowledge. Clearly the latter is not the sort of cognitive claim advanced by the classical tradition with its doctrine of internal relations in God. It qualified the doctrine of internal relations with the doctrine of perichoresis or coinherence, thereby calling attention to the element of depth and mystery in God as trinity. I submit therefore, that there is no significant *cognitive* difference between Schleiermacher's essential trinity and the immanent trinity of the tradition when properly qualified by coinherence. However, Schleiermacher's view of the limitations of theological knowledge has the virtue of focusing on the mystery of God's self-disclosure as a constitutive, phenomenological feature of such, and not an afterthought added at the level of theoretical and doctrinal formulation. Schleiermacher avoids the fallacy of misplaced concreteness, for the mystery is not located simply in the terminology, but in the thing itself—the divine self-disclosure in redemption—and this is the reason the problem remains despite changes in metaphysical schemes and frameworks.

IS SCHLEIERMACHER'S THEOLOGY BINITARIAN OR TRINITARIAN?

Granted that there are immanent distinctions in God, the question remains, what kind of distinctions are these? Are these genuine trinitarian distinctions, or do they fall short and imply only a binitarian distinction between God and his logos? This question is difficult to answer given the incomplete, fragmentary character of Schleiermacher's discussion. However, while Marcellus did not develop an account of the third person of trinity, the fact that Athanasius did not think this deserving of condemnation indicates a certain flexibility even within orthodoxy. Nevertheless, the most likely interpretation of Sabellianism, including Marcellus, is that the logos is the generic term for the divine self-disclosure, comprehending and including all Persons of trinity. God the Father is not simply identified with divine unity, but is one of the revealed persons.

If this interpretation of Sabellianism is correct, then some serious problems arise which indicate that Sabellianism exhibits an unacceptable binitarian scheme, and does not overcome the formalism of the speculative tradition. If the logos is the generic term for revelation, and if it is identified with God incarnate in the Redeemer, this says far too much, for it implies that revelation is essentially (that is, generically) incarnation. But in Christianity only the second person, the Son, is said to be incarnate; not every revelation of God is an incarnation or can be such without emptying that term of its distinctive, historical meaning. On the other hand, if generic divine revelation means only that God manifests himself through a potentially infinite series of theophanies, this says far too little. For in this interpretation there can be no essential difference between the Redeemer and an inspired man, in short, no genuine doctrine of incarnation. This fails to account for the specific incarnation of God in the particular historical Redeemer, Jesus of Nazareth. In either case, the result is an unacceptable formalism which implies either that all men are christs, or that no man is. Both implications contradict the essence of Christianity.

May such Sabellian views be attributed to Schleiermacher? Is his theology ultimately bipolar in structure? This is a difficult question. Although hiddenness and revealedness are not themselves bipolar structures in God himself, absolute inwardness and absolute vitality appear to be such. But is this fundamentally a bipolar conception? One can so argue only by ignoring Schleiermacher's thesis that God is a coincidence of opposites. God is bipolar by transcending such contrast and opposition; hence bipolarity is one element in God, and coincidence of opposites is another. Still, this observation is not decisive.

It is true that Schleiermacher's account of the Sabellian version of trinity develops it in bipolar, binitarian fashion: God hidden is correlated with divine unity, and God revealed is correlated with trinity. But this is a rather crude way of developing trinity, and Schleiermacher need not be so interpreted. Specifically, hiddenness and revealedness can be detached from a bipolar framework, and there are indications in Schleiermacher how this can be done. It is clear from his argument in the doctrine of divine attributes that hiddenness and revealedness structures that entire account. This means that Schleiermacher need not identify the content of God's self-manifestation simply or wholly with trinity. For it is clear from his treatment of divine attributes that the contrast runs throughout the entire doctrine of God and is exhibited in each pair of attributes, for example, eternal-omnipotence. This pairing of positive and negative elements sets him apart from crude Sabellianism. Further, the doctrine of divine attributes is one stratum in the apprehension of God as trinity.

Thus it seems that the phenomenological features of divine hiddenness and revealedness are not simply imbedded in a bipolar or binitarian theological scheme. Schleiermacher has demonstrated that hiddenness and revealedness apply not only collectively to the doctrine of God as a whole, but also apply to each pair of attributes distributively. If this contrast may apply distributively to the attributes of God, I see no reason in principle why it may not also apply distributively to each of the trinitarian persons. It seems possible and appropriate to speak of the hiddenness and revealedness of the Father, the Son, and the Spirit. But if each person of trinity exhibits the phenomenological features of hiddenness and revealedness, then trinity as a collective whole ceases to be identified with merely one element of God's bipolar structure, namely, God revealed. If hiddenness and revealedness apply distributively to the trinitarian persons, then Schleiermacher can be read as approximating Barth's reconstruction in which revealer, revelation, and revealedness designate moments of the divine self-disclosure. His Sabellianism can keep good trinitarian company!

It cannot be denied or overlooked that Schleiermacher did not complete his doctrine of God, or develop constructively and systematically the possibilities inherent in his theology. But neither is his incomplete treatment of the trinity the unmitigated theological disaster claimed by his critics. Schleiermacher's original accomplishment is his thinking through of trinity in relation to the phenomenological features of revelation—hiddenness and revealedness—and in relation to the concept of God as coincidence of opposites. He has put the entire doctrine of God—including divine attributes and trinity—on a single, nonspeculative, phenomenological footing. Few theologies approach his systematic organization and his integration of the doctrines of trinity and divine attributes. Schleiermacher is aware of the ground-breaking implications of his formulations. After noting that the *homoousios* "gives" the complete coincidence and identity of God hidden with God revealed, he points out its implications for the doctrine of the divine attributes:

> It needs only be mentioned in order to be plain to everyone that such views would have had a decisive influence on the further construction of the doctrine of divine attributes if only it had been settled that deity as such is an inexpressible, simple nature of which it could never be said that it consists in a duality of essence and attributes . . . But all of this must have remained in a perpetual state of confusion, since deity as such was simply identified with God the Father, and conversely.[28]

Thus, the doctrine of God should form a coherent, systematic whole.

For this reason the doctrine of trinity is not a superfluous appendix to the doctrine of God, rather it is the ultimate foundation of the doctrine, because it sets forth the fundamental identity between God and his revelation. It gives the ultimate identity of opposites in God himself, and thus is the presupposition of the doctrine of divine attributes, particularly the assertion that God is love. At the same time it serves as the corrective to the formalizing, speculative tendency of subordinationism. The principle of the *homoousios* or consubstantiality of God incarnate with God himself, and the proposition that God is love, represent correctives and modifications to the view of theology as simply learned ignorance.

Finally, the doctrine of trinity appears last, even as an appendix to the discussion of the *Glaubenslehre,* not simply because it is more than an immediate utterance of religious consciousness, but rather because it sets forth the condition of possibility of redemption. Therefore, it cannot be set forth until redemption itself has been set forth, including its anthropological and ecclesial dimensions. In his account of the conditions of possibility of redemption, Schleiermacher does not regard trinity as superfluous and dispensable to the doctrines of incarnation and redemption. Neither does he play it down by offering a merely economic interpretation. It is simply not true, as Welch contends, that according to Schleiermacher the consciousness of redemption requires only Christology and incarnation, "but nothing was to be asserted about the being of God."[29] Schleiermacher's essential trinity *is* an assertion about the being of God, and one which is very close to Athanasian orthodoxy.

NOTES

1. Friedrich Schleiermacher, "Ueber die Gegensatz zwischen der Sabellianischen und der Athanasianischen Vorstellung von Trinitaet," reprinted in *Friedrich Schleiermacher und die Trinitaetslehre,* ed. Martin Tetz [*Texte zur Kirchen und Theologiegeschichte,* ed. Gerhard Rubach] (Gütersloh: Gutersloher Verlagshaus, Gerd Mohn, 1969). This essay has also been translated: "On the Discrepancy between the Sabellian and Athanasian Method of Representing the Doctrine of Trinity," trans. Moses Stuart, in the *Biblical Repository and Quarterly Observer* 5(1835):265–353; and 6(1835): 1–116. As is apparent in the translation of the title, the translation is not always reliable. Stuart warns the reader that "I have given a free, in some cases even a paraphrastic version, because I felt that the matter would not be intelligible to the religious public of our country" (6:59). His paraphrases sometimes omit significant phrases and terminology. Hereafter I shall abbreviate this work simply as *Trinity,* and will cite first the German text and then, in parentheses, the translation. I am citing from a reprint of the *Biblical Repository* article, and the pagination may not correspond to that of the Journal itself.

2. Claude Welch, *In This Name: The Doctrine of Trinity in Contemporary Theology* (New York: Charles Scribners Sons, 1952), pp. 3–10. Welch has subsequently modified his view of Schleiermacher; see below, n. 29, and also his *Protestant Thought in the Nineteenth Century,* vol. 1 (New Haven: Yale Univ. Press, 1972).

3. *Gl,* § 171.5.

4. Adolf von Harnack, *History of Dogma,* 7 vols., trans. E.B. Speirs and James Millar (London: William & Norgate, 1898), 4:82.

5. *Gl,* § 170.1.

6. Ibid.

7. *Gl,* § 170.3.

8. *Trinity,* p. 38 (p. 67).

9. *Trinity,* p. 88 (p. 158), italics by R.R.W.

10. *Gl*, § 170, Postscript.

11. Von Harnack, *Dogma,* 3:62.

12. *Trinity,* p.76 (p. 140).

13. *Gl*, § 170.3.

14. J. F. Bethune-Baker, *An Introduction to the Early History of Christian Doctrine* (London: Methuen, 1903), p. 103.

15. J.N.D. Kelly, *Early Christian Doctrines* (New York: Harper & Row, 1960), pp. 117 ff.

16. *Gl*, 1st ed., § 190.2 (also cited in Tetz' edition, *Friedrich Schleiermacher und die Trinitätslehre*).

17. For a similar analysis, cf. von Harnack, *Dogma,* the appendix on the concept of preexistence, 1:318–31.

18. *Gl*, § 167.1.

19. *Trinity,* p. 82 (p. 149), italics by R.R.W.

20. *Trinity,* p. 76 (p. 140).

21. *Trinity,* pp. 80–81 (pp. 147–48).

22. Ibid.

23. *Trinity,* p. 76 (p. 140).

24. Von Harnack provides the following information concerning Marcellus: "Marcellus is an extremely interesting phenomenon in the history of theology: he did not however, succeed in effecting any change in the history of dogma or in creating any noteworthy number of followers. At the Council of Nicea he belonged to the few who zealously championed the *Homoousios.* After the council he was, besides Eustathius, at first the sole literary representative of orthodoxy, since he wrote a comprehensive treatise *peri hypotages* by way of reply to the work of the Arian Asterius. This work, in which he defends the unity of substance of the Logos, drew upon him from the dominant party the accusation of Sabellianism . . . His case was dealt with at the councils of Tyre, Jerusalem, and Constantinople, since he also personally defended Athanasius and opposed the restoration of Arius. In spite of his appeal to the Emperor he was . . . deprived of his office as a teacher of erroneous doctrine . . . Eusebius of Caesarea endeavored in two works to refute him. These works are for us the source for the teaching of Marcellus. . . . the Logos is the indwelling *power* in God, which has manifested itself in the creation of the world as *dynamis drastike,* in order then . . . to become personal with the view of saving and perfecting the human race. Thus the Logos is in and for itself, in its essential nature, the *unbegotten* reason of God indwelling in God from all eternity and absolutely inseparable from him; it begins its actuality in the creation of the world, but it first becomes a personal manifestation distinct from God in the incarnation, through which the Logos as the image of the invisible God becomes visible. In Christ consequently the Logos has become a person and Son of God—a person who is as surely *homoousios* with God as he is the active working of God himself. . . . what is of . . . importance is that Athanasius and consequently also the Council of Sardica did not abandon Marcellus . . . That Athanasius [in] spite of all remonstrances should have pronounced Marcellus orthodox is a proof that his interest in the matter was confined to one point, and centered in the godhead of the historical Jesus as resting upon the unity of substance with God. Where he saw that this was recognized, he allowed freedom of thought on other points" (von Harnack, *Dogma,* 4:65–66).

25. Von Harnack mentions the following problems: (1) Marcellus called only the Incarnate One "Son of God"; (2) he taught no real preexistence; (3) he assumed that the kingdom of Christ would have an end in which the Son subordinates himself to God the Father such that God is all in all and the hypostatic form (circumscription) of the logos ceases (Marcellus acknowledged that he did not know what became of the humanity of Christ); (4) he spoke of an extension of the indivisible monad, not unlike the Stoic concept. (Ibid.)

26. Welch, *In This Name,* pp. 293–94.

27. *Trinity,* pp. 60 ff., especially 62; (pp. 111 ff., 114).

28. *Trinity*, p. 82 (pp. 149–50).

29. Welch, *In This Name*, p. 9. Welch's account and estimate of Schleiermacher in this book is inconsistent. He correctly identifies Schleiermacher with the essential trinity (293–94), yet this judgment is conveniently absent from the earlier polemical chapter from which this quotation is taken (see p. 9). In correspondence with the author, Welch acknowledges this implicit contradiction and sides with the correct interpretation he presents in his appendix against the polemics of the opening chapter. He also indicates that he is persuaded by the argument and interpretation of Schleiermacher on trinity set forth in this chapter. I am indebted to Welch for his helpful appendix on the economic, essential, and immanent trinities.

7

The Accomplishment
of Schleiermacher

It is time now to draw together the various strata of our study and exposition of Schleiermacher. If the foregoing interpretation of Schleiermacher is correct, what has he accomplished? While we attempt to sort out these questions, it may also be useful to consider Schleiermacher's accomplishment in light of two standard criticisms made of his theology, namely, that he is guilty of a reductive interpretation of theology in general and Christian theology in particular, and that he is under the domination of classical theology, particularly its monopolar concept of God as immutable.

Concerning the first question, we have already noted that the question of a reductive interpretation of Christian faith is a question posed by Schleiermacher's two-step phenomenological procedure or method of correlation. As a phenomenologist, he performs eidetic analyses in the first part of his *Glaubenslehre,* namely, analyses of the generic God-consciousness, the relation between God and world, and the first set of divine attributes. As a Christian theologian, in the second part of the *Glaubenslehre* Schleiermacher removes the brackets of the initial abstraction and considers the theological eidetics in concrete, determinate modified form. Thus the question of generic formalism is a question posed by Schleiermacher's very method; it is not simply a question generated externally by criticism. To be sure, the contemporary theological mind is conditioned to see Feuerbach as Schleiermacher's fate. And this pervasive judgment is reason enough to raise and pursue the question. However, if Schleiermacher has done his job satisfactorily as a phenomenological theologian, that will also constitute a reply to Feuerbach. At least, it will be so argued.

Concerning the second question, it should be borne in mind that

Schleiermacher has warned us that while he makes use of some traditional theological language, he does so in his own way and with his own sense and meaning.[1] Although he borrows such terminology, he is not necessarily committed to classical theology. That is, he intends to speak of the Transcendent as limit not in metaphysical abstraction from the world, time, relation, and so forth, but rather in methodological abstraction from its actual occurrence in Christianity. This methodological abstraction renders metaphysically ambiguous and indeterminate virtually all the metaphysical language concerning God in the first part of the *Glaubenslehre*. Does Schleiermacher intend any of this to be taken in a metaphysical sense? Or is it not rather the case that the metaphysical sense of his descriptions and abstract language is left open pending the full exposition of the doctrine of God? Our thesis is that the metaphysical sense of Schleiermacher's theology cannot be determined from the prolegomena or even from the first half of the *Glaubenslehre*, but must be developed and interpreted from the standpoint of the whole. When we do so, we shall find that Schleiermacher moves away from classical theology in some important respects, and that an immanent extension of his argument points in the direction of process theology on the question of divine immutability.

PHENOMENOLOGICAL THEOLOGY AND THE QUESTION OF GENERIC FORMALISM

THE PROBLEM OF THE FOUNDATION OF THE DOCTRINE OF GOD

The question of generic formalism can be pursued fruitfully only if the entire argument of the *Glaubenslehre* is taken into account. The question of generic formalism in the doctrine of God can be determined only from the standpoint of the whole because the doctrine is only completed with the full elaboration of the argument, and is the key to the unity of the argument. The question cannot be determined from the standpoint of the first half of the *Glaubenslehre*, because the religious a priori and the divine attributes based on it are not constitutive of fellowship with God, but are merely indirect and formal schema of the Transcendent. They do not add up to the living image of deity expressed in actual religious experience. In addition, Schleiermacher's principle of positivity means that the generic schema of transcendence does not appear unchanged in its determinate state of actualization. The question of generic formalism can be addressed only if the actual, fully determinate God-consciousness is attended to.

On the other hand, a consideration of the distinctive Christian attributes of the second half of the *Glaubenslehre* by itself cannot decide the question of generic formalism either. These features gain their distinctiveness as religious representations of God only when they emerge with and fill the generic schema of monotheism. The latter schema serves to delineate the transcendence of God and prevent idolatry. Consequently, the question of generic formalism can be pursued only at the level of the concrete interrelation of the formal schema of the Transcendent and the consciousness of redemption, that is, God hidden and God revealed. The expository problem of the doctrine of God is to set forth this interrelation of the generic and the historically determinate divine attributes and to allow this determinacy to transform the abstract generic schema of the Transcendent. Schleiermacher agonized over this task, and at least considered presenting the distinctively Christian divine attributes first in his order of exposition.[2]

The question is not what should come first in the order of exposition, and what should be last, but rather what is the logical foundation of the doctrine of God? What is prior logically, and what is derivative? If Schleiermacher starts the exposition of the doctrine of God from the standpoint of the religious a priori, this gives the appearance that the foundation of the doctrine of God is a natural theology, whether this is derived from resources other than Christian religious consciousness or from the existential version of the ontological argument. The historically determinate elements of Christian faith tend to be regarded merely as particular instantiations of the abstract generic scheme. This violates Schleiermacher's principle of positivity. On the other hand, if Schleiermacher begins with the attributes based exclusively on redemption, this gives the appearance of a merely intraecclesiastical fideism which has no cognitive significance and no potentially universal significance for humanity as such. The meaning of redemption is lost in either case: redemption is not simply something present in generic religion as such, because it is essentially bound up with a historical Redeemer. On the other hand, redemption is not merely something for Christians only; rather it is the completion and fulfillment of creation. Both the historical element and the universal element of redemption must be present in the doctrine of God, otherwise generic formalism and a reductive interpretation of Christianity are not avoided.

Schleiermacher decided to expound the doctrine of God in a way that proceeds from the generic to the determinate strata. This study too has followed this order of exposition. Schleiermacher begins his doctrine of God with an existential-phenomenological description of the feeling of utter dependence, which is related to the ontological argument, and then proceeds to fill this scheme of transcendence with ontological and historical elements, the latter as expressed in the consciousness of redemption. The crucial question is whether this order of exposition is also the logical and founding order of the doctrine of God, that is, whether the formal-generic elements found and permit the deduction of the concrete determinate elements. I think not. The Christian Platonism related to Anselm's ontological proof is not the foundation of the doctrine, although it is present in and coconstitutive of Christian experience. Rather the foundation, the bedrock stratum, is the thesis that God is love. This is the full, concrete reality that funds and modifies the abstract generic scheme of the Transcendent. This is not to deny that the latter is presupposed logically in the God-consciousness mediated by redemption. It is to claim that while it is a necessary condition of that concrete God-consciousness, the latter is the full, concrete actuality, and thus the sufficient condition of human fellowship with God. God is decisively—Schleiermacher claims fully— manifest in his redemptive and reconciling activity in incarnation. This has important implications, therefore, for the actualization of the God-consciousness: "The original feeling of utter dependence which coposits the highest being, does not come to actual consciousness in Christianity except in relation to Christ . . . Therefore, in the whole region of Christian piety, relation to God and relation to Christ are inseparable."[3]

If the generic God-consciousness is the necessary condition of redemption, the consciousness of God as love is the sufficient condition. Hence the proposition "God is love" is foundational for Christian God-consciousness: "We have the divine love immediately in the consciousness of redemption, and since this is the basis on which we appropriate and express all other [elements of the] God-consciousness, it naturally represents for us the essence of God."[4] The way in which the generic God-consciousness comes to full, concrete expression in Christianity is meaning-determining. The proposition "God is love" together with the trinitarian affirmation that God is identical with his self-expression in incarnation, are the ultimate constitutive principles of Christian theology. Neither is simply deducible from the generic God-consciousness. With this discussion in mind, we can turn to the question of generic formalism and the question of a reductive interpretation of Christianity.

GENERIC FORMALISM?

Formalism occurs whenever the concrete distinguishing features of an entity are either replaced by or subordinated to its generic structures and features. However, the question raised by formalism in phenomenological theology is also a theological question, for it presupposes an account of the concrete distinguishing features of Christianity, that is, the essence of Christianity. I submit that there is no greater clarity concerning such essential distinguishing features today than there was in Schleiermacher's time, and that to the extent that there exists a consensus on such matters, the contemporary consensus is indebted to Schleiermacher's pioneering work. Therefore I doubt if much of importance will be omitted if I assume Schleiermacher's own account of the essence of Christianity, and proceed with an immanent criticism and analysis.

Granted Schlerimacher's account of the essence of Christianity, the question of generic formalism amounts to the question whether his account of the doctrine of God reduces Christianity to any of the natural heresies. I have already pointed out that the "natural heresy" which is equivalent to generic formalism is the pelagian-ebionite-rationalist heresy. In this distortion of the essence of Christianity, the Redeemer is merely an exemplary human being which other men are to emulate and thereby work out their own salvation. This minimizes the corruption and bondage of man in sin on the one hand, and on the other minimizes the requirements that the Redeemer must meet in order to effect redemption. Most important of all for our considerations is the rationalist-formalist thesis that the divine causality is effective in the same way in all existence as apprehended from the generic standpoint. This simply bypasses and overlooks God's specific redemptive activity and the telos of creation in redemption. It overlooks or distorts the specific way that God is Christ, and the irreplaceable role of the Redeemer in redemption.

I believe that enough has been said about Schleiermacher's doctrine of God to support my judgment that his presentation of Christianity is not reducible to the above dimensions. Rather his theology is a deliberate, self-conscious effort to correct such formalism in Christian thought. Although Christianity does reflect universal structures of human existence and its relation to the world, it renders such concrete and determinate, and modifies their actual sense. This is the reason why Schleiermacher has sought to erect his doctrine of God on the basis of the historically determinate Christian consciousness of redemption, and why he seeks and presents an alternative view of theological method and substance. His original and novel treatment of this concrete determinate synthesis of historical and generic elements in the doctrine of God and throughout the argument of the *Glaubenslehre* makes it the first and perhaps the greatest Protestant systematic theology. According to Schleiermacher, the foundation stratum of the Christian God-consciousness is God as Redeemer and as love. Such is the way that the generic God-consciousness is concretely emergent and present in Christian faith. This determinate God-consciousness means that God's love is unambiguously apprehended only in redemption through Christ, and that God wills to be with his creation in incarnation and in its continuation in the kingdom of God. Redemption is both the telos of creation and means whereby creation is brought by God to its final telos. Generic formalism is avoided, at least in the doctrine of God.

A REDUCTION OF THEOLOGY TO ANTHROPOLOGY?

A *Glaubenslehre* is an account of faith for the religious community which shares and is constituted by the common element of redemption. As such, a *Glaubenslehre* does not need to demonstrate or prove the truth of faith as is attempted in natural theology or philosophical theology. In a preliminary and tentative sense it can be said that the *Glaubenslehre* is relative to the faith-community whose current faith and whose tradition of faith it sets forth. However, it does not follow that what faith believes is merely subject-relative in a psychological or sociological sense. Faith has an intelligible content which can be reflected on, and made intelligible and explicit. When this is done, it becomes readily apparent that Feuerbach is not Schleiermacher's nemesis or fate.

Let us consider the religious a priori. It should be recalled that for Schleiermacher the religious a priori is not merely a transcendental structure of human existence comparable to Kant's transcendental aesthetic or analytic. Kant's transcendental subjectivity or transcendental unity of apperception from whose structure the categories of understanding can be transcendentally deduced is a purely formal and abstract structure. Schleiermacher's religious a priori is not abstract in Kant's sense. It implies that its object, the Transcendent, exists somehow, and that human being is related to the Transcendent in utter dependence. In other words, the religious a priori is indeterminate, but not purely formal. It is never without some particular concrete instantiation, whether as filled or unfilled. In short, the religious a priori presupposes, and in one aspect is synonymous with, the life-world a priori of determinate religious consciousness.

Anselm's ontological proof is a reflective expression of the religious a priori, and it forms the basis of a reply to Feuerbach. Religious consciousness has a radically different intentional structure that the contrast between the human individual and the species. The Transcendent as limit, as made explicit conceptually in Anselm's formula, contradicts Feuerbach's basic thesis that all truth is relative to the human species such that the object of any subject is nothing but the nature of the (human) subject taken objectively.[5] Feuerbach apparently allows that the ontological argument is successful. If it is, it cannot deliver a being which has merely possible existence and/or possible nonexistence. Possible existence is a modality of existence excluded a priori from Anselm's concept of God. If God is possible, then he necessarily exists, and it is impossible that God not exist. The ontological proof cannot mean a being which is identical with or relative to the human species. For it is possible that the human species might cease to exist. If it is true that all truth is relative to the human species, then if the human species ceased to exist, it would be true that there is no truth. Feuerbach's relativism is self-contradictory because it makes truth depend on a contingent fact, namely, the existence of the human species. On the other hand, as Anselm's formula makes clear, the object intended by religious consciousness is necessary being, and such being is transcendent to the contingent human species. In short, the Transcendent is not relative to or a mere projection of religious consciousness. Feuerbach's so-called transformative method of reversing human predicates and theological subject cannot be successfully employed against Schleiermacher or Anselm because the latter reject the absolute identity principle which the transformative method presupposes.[6] Since the Transcendent is not identical with man, Schleiermacher and Anselm can refuse Feuerbach's reduction of theology to anthropology.

There is another sense in which a Feuerbach-style reduction of theology to anthropology might be charged against Schleiermacher. Are not the distinctively Christian beliefs in redemption, the divine attributes expressed in redemption, and so forth, relative to the Christian faith-community? Does it not follow that such beliefs are valid only within the existential and theological circle formed by that community? How does the church set forth truths about something other than and transcendent to itself? Schleiermacher is not free from ambiguity on this point. On the one hand, he indicates that systematic theology exists primarily for the purpose of church guidance, and that it articulates the beliefs currently valid in the church at a given time. Moreover, he does not think that Christianity should relate itself to other faith-communions by means of the dogmatic distinction between true and false religion (idolatry). Such contentions have been taken as support for the standard caricature of Schleiermacher as a romantic and subjectivist. According to the caricature, Schleiermacher simply surrenders all interest in the truth of Christian faith and sets forth a noncognitive, antimetaphysical theology. Such a theology, in surrendering all truth-claims, reduces itself to anthropology.

If the above caricature were true, Schleiermacher would have to set forth redemption without making any claims about the being of God, or without bringing God in at all. When the issue is formulated in this somewhat more explicit fashion, it becomes apparent that Schleiermacher is making truth-claims about Christian faith and redemption, and not simply giving phenomenalistic reports on Christian religious experience. That Schleiermacher thinks Christian faith is true in some sense is evident from his observations (1) that it requires metaphysical elaboration in the third form of proposition, and (2) that not *any* metaphysics will do for purposes of such elaboration. Because redemption is the case, and because redemption presupposes and is based *in God,* only those metaphysical schemes are theologically acceptable which distinguish God from the world, good from evil, and the higher from the lower self-consciousness in man. That is, if redemption is true, some metaphysical schemes, for example, materialism, cannot be true. To be sure, the *Glaubenslehre* is not a full-blown metaphysics. Nevertheless, to claim that Christian faith is true is to make a public claim about something transcending human subjectivity. Since objectivity, generality, and transcendence of consciousness are ideal goals of the metaphysical enterprise, Schleiermacher does not think it possible for theology to dispense with metaphysics altogether. That Schleiermacher is far from surrendering all truth-claims in theology is evident from the following passage:

> The Christian doctrines of God and redemption cannot possibly recognize . . . a distinction between ecclesiastical doctrines [as mere subjective opinions] and the essential truths of religion. . . . Therefore, if anyone is disposed to say that the ecclesiastical doctrine of any given time and place is mere opinion . . . it must be replied that there is nothing superior to it in the realm of Christian knowledge, except the purer and more perfect ecclesiastical doctrine which may be found in some other period and in other presentations.[7]

Schleiermacher clearly thinks that the Christian doctrines of God and redemption are true, and not merely subjective, private opinions. Moreover, there can be no ultimate separation or dualism between what is true in Christianity and what is true in religion in general, even though the distinctive, positive Christian elements cannot be deduced or proved by universal reason. Schleiermacher's declarations are by no means beyond criticism or without problems. Nevertheless Schleiermacher is no more guilty of a noncognitive interpretation of theology, or of reducing theology to anthropology, than are Augustine, Calvin, or Tillich.

SCHLEIERMACHER'S REVISION OF CLASSICAL THEOLOGY

A full treatment of the issues raised by Schleiermacher's theological reconstruction, its criticism and defense, would require another book. In the limited space remaining, we select and distinguish two central issues: first, Schleiermacher's treatment of the divine attributes. We shall discuss briefly his departure from and revision of classical natural theology, namely, his attempt to dispense with the distinction between essence and attributes. Then we shall discuss the issue raised by his own ontological approach, namely, the question whether all theological language is symbolic. Finally we shall examine the question of the unity and compatibility of divine attributes, namely love and omnipotence. The second central issue raises the possibility of extending his argument and of developing its implications for the question of divine immutability. Here we shall focus on his two-stage theory of creation and its theological implications, namely, the sense in which God may be mutable.

SCHLEIERMACHER ON DIVINE ATTRIBUTES

The Ontological Approach to the Divine Attributes

Traditional natural theology, for example, Thomas Aquinas, maintains that God is not known through his essence, but is rather apprehended indirectly from the standpoint of the creation, that is, God is known, but known through his effects in and upon the world. Thomas denies that the knowledge of God is self-evident, and insists that human knowledge of God comprehends only his existence, not his essence. One of the central problems, therefore, is to justify in what sense, if at all, God is truly known from the standpoint of the creation. To be sure, Thomas affirms that substantial theological predication of God is possible.[8] He even utilizes the Augustinian dictum that God is his essence and is his attributes. Nevertheless, Thomas qualifies all affirmative theological predication by denying that the divine essence is known or comprehended. Thus, even though Thomas allows substantial theological predication about God (for example, God is good, wise), such a knowledge falls short of a full grasp of God in and through his essence. I am not sure whether Thomas is entirely consistent or whether he is finally prey to Feuerbach's charge that he posits an infinite being with finite predicates. The point is rather that, consistent or not, Thomas makes use of the distinction between divine essence and attributes, and that Schleiermacher rejects this distinction as employed by Thomas.

Schleiermacher's approach to the divine attributes differs from the cosmological approach to God; he takes an ontological approach deriving from and rooted in actual religious experience. To be sure, Schleiermacher is not the first to do so, or even the only one. He shares the ontological approach with such diverse figures as Augustine, Anselm, Cusanus, Tillich, and Hartshorne. The distinctiveness of Schleiermacher lies in his attempt to construct a doctrine of God and divine attributes on the basis of religious experience. Schleiermacher is unique in this group in his willingness to allow the general structures of existence to undergo transformation in their determinate, concrete actualization. Before spelling this out, let us note the general features of this approach. According to Anselm, divine unsurpassability is the definitive feature of deity. As such, it is the essential structure present in all aspects of divine being. Therefore, each divine attribute must exhibit the general sense of God established by the ontological principle: each attribute is the maximal, unsurpassable instance, the archetype of its property or quality. Now if each attribute is unsurpassable, it is infinite; that is, each attribute is formally identical with and equivalent to the divine essence. Conversely since the divine essence is the common formal principle in all the divine attributes, namely, unsurpassability, to know God's attributes is equivalent to knowing God himself. Despite the inevitable qualifications, the Augustinian approach involves a stronger, more daring claim about theological knowledge than does the Thomist.

Given the ontological approach, God is not an infinite being with finite predicates, rather, all attributes of the infinite are infinite and unsurpassable. The distinction between infinite essence and finite predicates is abolished as Schleiermacher observes: "If it be generally conceded that the difference between attributes is nothing real in God, each attribute is only another expression for the whole being of God, which is self-identical."[9] What is thus truly predicated of God as a divine attribute is truly predicated of God himself; it is not a merely phenomenal report on human religious experience.[10] This is Schleiermacher's version of the Augustinian dictum that God does not "have" attributes (and is more than his attributes), but rather, God *is* his attributes. Thus, to know God's attributes is not to know something less than God, but to know God himself. With this identification, the negative separation between God's essence and attributes is overcome.

Some Related Contrasts

Within the ontological approach to God, there are some important differences, namely, some interpret God in a monopolar sense and others, including Cusanus and Schleiermacher, interpret God in a bipolar sense. Unlike Anselm and with Cusanus, Schleiermacher believes that God is bipolar coincidence of opposites. That is, he understands divine perfection as modal coincidence; in God the greatest and the least, the maximum and minimum coincide. However, unlike Hartshorne and with Cusanus, he would contend that all aspects (attributes) of the infinite are infinite. Modal coincidence is precisely the claim that in God's infinity relative or finite contrasts are transcended and overcome. In Hegelian language, God's genuine or true infinity overcomes and reconciles the oppositions of the bad or spurious infinites (namely, the greatest and the least). Thus Schleiermacher (and Hegel) would probably reject Hartshorne's theses that all actuality is finite and that God is best conceived as an enduring society of actual occasions. These concepts might be viewed as too anthropomorphic and as tending to undermine the divine unity and perfection as modal coincidence. God's infinity and perfection mean that God eternally overcomes elements which are relatively opposed and noncoincident in finite being. Relative noncoincidence, therefore, is a sign of imperfection, and implies the potential threat of internal dissolution. Hence finite being is constantly involved in a struggle against opposing forces and against its own noncoincidence. But since God has no opposite, since he is maximal, unlimited actualization of being, he is free from the struggle for survival. Since he is perfectly coincident with himself, he is beyond the threat of dissolution, and has no ontological indigence.

The Critical Issue: Are the Attributes Symbolic?

We have said that Schleiermacher shares the general ontological approach to God, according to which it belongs to God to manifest himself, and all elements of his manifestation are equal to himself. He thus stands close to Cusanus. However, it must be noted that according to this speculative philosophical theology, theology is learned ignorance. Although the infinite must be understood as bipolar coincidence of opposites, the critical norm governing all theological assertions is that there is no proportion between finite and infinite. Thus, the infinite is not commensurable with finite knowledge. From this it follows that the truest knowledge of God is negative, that is, it consists in knowing what God is not, rather than in knowing what he is. Since God transcends the finite, it appears to follow that all knowledge of God and its constitutive assertions are symbolic, that is, nonliteral. According to the general speculative philosophical theology shared by Schleiermacher, Cusanus, and Tillich, no literal assertion about God is possible. On the other hand, Schleiermacher does make one nonsymbolic assertion about God, namely, that God is love. But surely this assertion (1) is inconsistent with his general philosophical theology, and (2) if true, amounts to a Barthian fideism, a positivism of revelation. Further, it can be maintained only at the price of inconsistency with the critical norm. I shall argue that it is neither inconsistent nor Barthian fideism.

As is well known, Tillich faced the question of symbolic theological language. If we say that all language about the Transcendent is symbolic, we must have some nonsymbolic grounds for affirming the symbolic character of theological predication. Tillich's grounds derive from his speculative metaphysics according to which God is determined as the power of being. This implies that every assertion about God is symbolic except the assertion that he is Being itself, or the power of Being itself. Tillich thus has the following problem: his ontological vision of God, if true, makes all assertions about God symbolic, and thus seems to undermine itself. For if God does transcend all determinate structures (attributes), Tillich's ontological theory cannot be both literal and articulate God in his transcendence of all literal, determinate distinctions. Consequently, as Neville has persuasively argued, Tillich's position must be defended and justified by a constitutive ontological dialectic.[11] In my opinion Tillich never does justify his position by such means, but rather remains within a formal, methodological dialectic. This implies that he in effect absolutizes his speculative ontology, and uses it to measure the theological assertions of Christian faith, for example, God as Father and Son, as symbolic. Thus, the speculative "God beyond the God" of Christian theism remains when the latter "symbol" ceases to mediate reality and disappears into the void. Tillich's theological method of correlation fails to work out a justifying constitutive dialectic of Christian theology, in which the formal ontology undergoes modification by the given. In short, Tillich suspends the principle of positivity in his method of correlation and doctrine of God.[12]

On the other hand, Barth makes it appear as if theological affirmations spring fully determinate from the positivity of revelation. To be sure, Barth actually performs the inevitable theological task of showing the constitutive dialectic of Christian theology in his doctrine of God, but this is not done explicitly in relation to the critical norms supplied by an independent speculative ontology. At the level of announced procedure, Barth simply refuses to be drawn into the enterprise of correlation and constitutive dialectic. He takes his stand in the positivity of Christian revelation and lets the ontological and justification problems fall where they may.

Schleiermacher presents an alternative to both Barth and Tillich on this question, which comes out clearly in his discussion of the proposition that God is love. This is the one literal assertion that can be made about God. Note that unlike Tillich, Schleiermacher does not absolutize his speculative philosophy and theology. Instead, he brings it into relation to the theological given, and allows it to undergo modification in its state of determinate actualization. It is true that finite and infinite are incommensurable, and that all theological affirmations are therefore symbolic. But that does not make God a prisoner of his own aseity, or prevent God from fully disclosing himself in and through the finite. Such is the historical claim of Christian faith mediated by incarnation and redemption. In short, the formal-critical norm is not absolute, but undergoes determinate modifications by the given: God is fully manifest only in the act of reconciliation and redemption. Schleiermacher allows the formal, indeterminate scheme of the Transcendent to undergo modification and he recapitulates the constitutive dialectic of Christian theology. That constitutive dialectic issues in the concrete identity: "God is love," and in the basic trinitarian affirmation that God is identical with himself (*homoousios*) in his self-disclosure.[13]

On the other hand, it is clear that Schleiermacher is not engaging in a Barthian positivism of revelation. The subject term of the proposition "God is love" is not simply derived from Christian positivity; rather it is derived from the antecedent God-consciousness. The historically given, distinctively Christian features of the Transcendent as God render determinate and modify the abstract schematism of the Transcendent as limit. Such historically positive elements do not supply, but logically presuppose the subject term of the proposition; conversely, such elements provide the determinate, concrete content of that subject. Moreover, they constitute and give the *homoousios,* the identity between God and his self-manifestation. This identity of subject and predicate is not, however, an immediate faith-utterance, nor is it simply read off the face of the positively given. The identification of love with God is the product of theological reflection on the immediate faith-utterance. The articulation of the proposition "God is love" in the third form of proposition amounts to an exhibition of the constitutive dialectic of Christian theology. Thus Schleiermacher measures this proposition against all other affirmations concerning the divine attributes and elicits its distinctiveness. This measurement involves the method of correlation and the modification of such by the principle of positivity. Apart from redemption, there can be no genuine certainty or knowledge of God.

In his recapitulation of the constitutive dialectic of Christian theology,

Schleiermacher differs significantly from his contemporary Hegel. According to Schleiermacher, Christian positivity authorizes only one literal, nonsymbolic utterance concerning God, namely, that God is love. In the case of all other divine attributes, the critical principle holds: we can make no literal identification of any other attribute with God himself (for example, omnipotence, omniscience) without exceeding the strictures of negative theology and without exceeding the theological given. In short, there is no theological basis for the identification of God with omnipotence. There is a theological basis in Christian positivity, God incarnate, for identifying God with love. As a speculative philosopher, Hegel would want to go beyond the theological given. He would argue quite reasonably that what is true of divine love must in principle be true of all other divine attributes. They too must be identical with God's essence. Although Schleiermacher would agree in principle, he observes that in fact no such proposition is identifiable as a faith-utterance.[14] Consequently, Schleiermacher rejects Hegel's attempt to formalize the theological given and translate it into the universal terms of his dialectical logic. Such formalization involves an illicit inversion of the principle of positivity. This inversion is seen in Hegel's use of his "speculative Good Friday" to gain his basic ontological vision and absolute standpoint, and in his subsequent derivation of the positive, given elements from his basic ontological principle that being determines itself.[15] Schleiermacher refuses to join in this enterprise. It is impossible to reach the concrete and particular by means of concepts alone. God incarnate is not simply deducible from the formal-ontological requirements of speculative ontology; it is the theological given, apprehended in its concrete particularity by faith. It cannot be converted into absolute knowledge save by illicit formalization.

Is the proposition "God is love" symbolic? I have answered that the answer cannot be simply yes without ignoring the constitutive dialectic of Christian theology and absolutizing some formal-critical norm and its underlying speculative ontology. Tillich tends to run this danger but Schleiermacher does not, since he maintains that the speculative scheme provides only an abstract, indirect schematism of the Transcendent as limit. Moreover, Schleiermacher is not affirming a Barthian rejection of metaphysics in favor of a positivism of revelation; he does not simply absolutize the theological given or dogmatic norm. Rather, the justifying constitutive dialectic of Christian theology takes place in correlation with speculative metaphysics and involves a transformation of that metaphysics by the principle of positivity, by the distinctive Christian theological given, namely, God incarnate for redemption. Thus theological reflection begins with the immediate faith-utterance, "God is love." However, this proposition cannot be simply declared symbolic or antimetaphysical as measured by some external, "adequate" criterion of language about the Transcendent. Schleiermacher maintains that *no* speculative language about the Transcendent is adequate; it is all abstract and indeterminate. On the other hand, the proposition "God is love" is the theological given. It renders the abstract schematism of the Transcendent determinate and concrete. Taken as the result of theological reflection, the proposition "God is love" affirms the identity of God revealed with God hidden, the identity of God *qua* Redeemer with God *qua* Creator. It articulates the theological unity and foundation of the whole argument of the *Glaubenslehre*. As such, the proposition is the result of reflection and is measured against the various theological, scriptural, and philosophical norms. It involves the claim of full and final divine self-disclosure: nothing is held back.

Consequently, the proposition "God is love" is neither simply symbolic nor simply literal. There are senses in which it is both literal and nonliteral, that is, symbolic; these senses are determined from the various perspectives of the justifying constitutive dialectic of Christian theology. Viewed as an immediate faith-utterance, the proposition "God is love" articulates the presence of God in his reconciling and redemptive activity, that is, his union with and affirmation of humanity despite sin. This is expressed in the concrete language and images of faith. However overdetermined or anthropomorphic these images are, they are not meant noncognitively or antimetaphysically. When reflected upon, they point to the underlying motive of God's redemptive activity, and thus articulate the being of God himself. Viewed from the perspective of the whole system of doctrine, the proposition is the ultimate criterion against which all other theological affirmations are measured. As such, the proposition has ceased being symbolic, and its nonsymbolic character can in turn be appreciated only from the standpoint of the entire system of faith-utterances. However, it would be an exaggeration to say that the proposition is simply literal, as if its literal truth could simply be read off the face of religious experience in general. If the proposition is taken literally (as criterion) it is no longer an immediate faith-utterance; it is theological truth in reflective form, the third form of proposition. The proposition "God is love" is funded by Christian religious experience, and purified by theological-critical reflection. As such it is a truth-claim, a meta-metaphysical principle, which is not derived from, but rather brought to the enterprise of speculative metaphysics.

The Coherence of the Divine Attributes

Recent discussions of Schleiermacher have raised the question whether his doctrine of God and divine attributes is internally self-consistent.[16] The contention that his doctrine of God does not form a coherent whole presupposes that Schleiermacher is under the domination of classical monopolar theology. This suggests that Schleiermacher conceives of God as absolute, apart from time and relation to the world, at least in the first part of his doctrine of God. On the other hand, he also inconsistently conceives of God as related to the world in redemption. Like the classical tradition, Schleiermacher has been pilloried for conceiving of God as metaphysically absolute, and failing to give adequate metaphysical expression to God's relation to the world. Thus it is alleged that his doctrine of God juxtaposes two incompatible concepts, namely, God as absolute, self-subsisting power, and God as love.

This reading and criticism of Schleiermacher can be sustained only if it can be shown that he speaks of God as actual in the full metaphysical sense outside of time and apart from the world. If our interpretation is correct, Schleiermacher's use of classical metaphysical language is not meant in the same sense as the tradition. That is, he speaks of God apart from time and relation to the world not in metaphysical abstraction, but only in methodological abstraction. He is not committed metaphysically to the abstract concept of God as *actus purus,* or to the metaphysics of *actus purus.* In fact, Schleiermacher cannot embrace such a speculative metaphysics, since all divine attributes are meant as expressions of the correlation between God and world constitutive of the feeling of utter dependence. To put this point in other terms, the range of interpretive possibilities appears to be: either Schleiermacher's language is ambiguous given the indeterminacy resulting from the methodological abstraction from the concrete, determinate Christian God-consciousness, or it points in a different direction metaphysically from the classical tradition. If the former possibility is chosen, much more work is required to convict Schleiermacher of the charge of inconsistency, particularly in view of his repeated warnings that the initial set of divine attributes is abstract and indeterminate, and can be fully understood only as coinherent with other concrete attributes. In our view, these warnings and other evidence presented in the foregoing study favor the second possibility. Schleiermacher's theology is bipolar, with an abstract and a concrete, a transcendent and an immanent, polar structure. It is quite possible to read Schleiermacher as saying that

God's abstract immutable nature is but one aspect of God's full reality, and that it exists concretely in coinherence with other concrete elements.

It must be conceded that Schleiermacher has not fully articulated the concept of God as coincidence of opposites, particularly at the level of explicit metaphysics. This concept is relevant to the question whether the divine attributes are compatible. For if divine perfection and unity are to be understood as modal coincidence, that is, overcoming of all contrasts and opposition in genuine infinity, then divine love and divine power would likewise be unified in modal coincidence. As Cusanus and Hegel have observed, God as a genuine infinite stands beyond the law of contradiction and the axioms of finite Aristotelian logic. Attractive as this suggestion is for the problem of compatibility of divine attributes, Schleiermacher cannot avail himself of it, at least not without important qualifications. For the concept of coincidence of opposites implies that all divine attributes are equal, on the same level. That is, their differences are overcome in modal coincidence. As a phenomenologist and theologian, Schleiermacher cannot allow such formal equality: his principle of positivity dictates that the way in which the God-consciousness comes to full, concrete expression is meaning-determining. That element in God which specially favors his presence in religious consciousness must be specially affirmed of God. Thus Scheiermacher maintains that love is the only divine attribute which can be fully identified with God.

As we found in our examination of trinity, it is the distinctively Christian elements which give the absolute coincidence of opposites in God. The term *homoousios* expresses the identity of God with his self-manifestation in redemption, and love as a divine attribute is another expression of this identity. The principle of positivity therefore requires a modification of the general dialectic or coincidence of opposites. It suggests that there are distinctions within God which must be preserved. To say that love is the only attribute which can be identified with God suggests that it is superior to the other attributes, and this suggests that there are levels in God. To be sure, there are problems with such an assertion: does it violate modal coincidence? Or does it rather, as Schleiermacher insists, decisively express such modal coincidence? For our purposes the point that needs to be made is that love and omnipotence are compatible divine attributes because each designates a different level or aspect of divine being. Omnipotence does not contradict divine love because it is subordinate to and directed by the latter. This contention requires a revision of the traditional concept of omnipotence, and raises the issue of divine immutability.

DIVINE IMMUTABILITY

In order to discuss the revision of the concept of omnipotence and divine immutability we need to review Schleiermacher's argument concerning two-stage creation. If redemption is the completion of creation, creation has two different stages. But such stages of creation in turn have theological implications; God is not related to the world in the same way in redemption as he is in creation. This implies a change in God's relation to the world, and suggests a change in God. Thus we begin with Schleiermacher's two-stage or developmental creation.

The Principle of Positivity and Two-Stage Creation

That creation has two stages, an imperfect first stage brought to fulfillment through redemption *qua* completion of creation, is not deducible from Schleiermacher's abstract, generic scheme. Yet two-stage creation has important implications for understanding divine omnipotence and its compatibility with divine love. Let us examine first the concept of two-stage creation to discern why the first stage must be imperfect, and then the implications for divine causality.

If redemption is the completion of creation, then apart from or independent of redemption, creation is incomplete, imperfect. This challenges the traditional assumption that creation is perfect from the outset. Instead, it means that man is not created perfect, but rather perfectible. If man were created perfect in all respects, then no sin and rejection of God could have occurred.[17] Sin and evil have their proximate conditions of possibility in a human existence created imperfect and ontologically unstable. Man is created imperfect, but perfectible.

Why must man be created imperfect? Because the ethicoreligious perfection cannot be ready-made and "built into" human being at the outset since it is essentially a perfection which can only be gradually acquired and developed through the exercise of freedom. It is absurd and self-contradictory to posit such perfection as ready-made, as actual prior to and apart from the temporal conditions under which and through which alone it can be achieved. Therefore, in creating human being and willing that man attain the ethicoreligious perfection appropriate to a free autonomous being, God must also necessarily create and sustain the conditions under which such perfection is attainable.

Schleiermacher's view is similar to that of Irenaeus, as John Hick has observed. One commentator on the Irenaean view of the necessary imperfection of creation observes that "God cannot will to create a human being who possesses both freedom and perfection, unless he simultaneously wills the process or career of development through which the perfection is freely attained."[18] Schleiermacher continues this view: "We must infer that . . . sin can be overcome even by divine grace only in a time-process."[19] The necessary imperfection of creation is required in view of the necessity of acquiring ethicoreligious perfection through a temporal career. This necessary imperfection could not be deduced from the abstract generic scheme or from pure description. It is a new thematic inquiry introduced by the removal of the brackets of the first half of the *Glaubenslehre*.

The Theological Implications of Two-Stage Creation

We have argued that God cannot make a human being both free and perfect; in order for the requisite ethical perfection to be achieved man must be initially less than perfect, and he must strive to achieve ethical-religious perfection within a temporal career. Thus, if God cannot create a human being both free and already perfect, this raises a question whether the necessary imperfection of creation does not imply a limited divine omnipotence. Two observations are relevant here. The first is that we might argue following much of traditional theology that it is no imperfection or limitation on God's part not to be able to do something which is self-contradictory. The creation of a free human being with ready-made ethical and religious perfection is self-contradictory. Therefore, not even God can make a free human being complete with ethical perfection unless he also creates and guides the temporal career through which such perfection is attained. However, this inability is not a real one, because there is no real inability involved in being unable to do something which is self-contradictory. I see no reason to challenge this argument. However, it does imply that God respects the law of contradiction in his dealings with creation. And that suggests a qualification, if not a limitation or inability, on the part of divine omnipotence; namely, it is ethically ordered power. If we say that creation is initially imperfect, this means that omnipotence is not fully displayed or exhibited in the first stage.

The second observation is that if we were not speaking of two stages of creation an imperfect creation would imply that God is limited and imperfect. However, Schleiermacher's contention is that redemption is the completion of creation such that in redemption human being is brought to ethical-religious perfection. This suggests that in the second stage of creation (redemption) God does accomplish his goal in creation. God does not merely create the conditions for redemption, he accomplishes redemption. If this is the case, it implies that God's power is not limited in any theologically relevant sense, because in perfecting creation through redemption, God overcomes the initial imperfection. In Augustinian language, redemption is more than mere re-creation. This observation implies that God is not related to the creation in the same way in both stages of creation. In incarnating himself for the redemption of humanity, God changes his mode of relation to the world, and the efficacy of his power. This in turn implies that God is not absolutely immutable, and that his aseity does not preclude him from concrete relation to his creation.

If we say that there must be two stages of exercise of divine omnipotence correlative to the two stages of creation, does this mean that in redemption God's power is experienced as sheer coercive necessity? That would seem to follow from Schleiermacher's deterministic sounding statements about omnipotence and omniscience, and from his claim that these are decisively and fully manifest in the world relative to redemption. Contemporary process theology has sought to put distance between itself and all views of God's power as coercive, that is, as a monopoly. It is metaphysically impossible for God to monopolize power and to create free creatures. Instead of thinking of God's power as coercive, it is claimed that we must think of it as persuasive. There is no monopoly of power on God's part; rather power is shared, albeit in varying degrees, by both God and the world. God's power therefore should be conceived not as coercive efficient causality, but as the power to persuade those who have power.

Schleiermacher might respond to this discussion in the following ways. First, he might agree that God's power cannot be understood as sheer efficient causality, for that is equivalent to dead, mechanical necessity, and that amounts to atheism. Besides, to say that God is efficient causality and to think of him as coercive is to place God within the world, that is, to render him finite. However, he would probably add that the same objections apply to the concept of persuasive power, because persuasion and coercion appear to be relative, finite opposites. Coercion is power lacking persuasion, and persuasion may lack efficacy. The latter deficiency is exhibited in the following statement of Lewis Ford: "God is continuously directing, that is, persuading the creation toward good, but his persuasive power is effective only insofar as the creatures themselves affirm that good."[20] In this view, God appears to work only through persuading others to accomplish a common goal, and then must wait upon the others to do the work. To be sure, Ford's formulation appears in the context of a theodicy argument and is an attempt to reconcile God's power and perfection with the existence of evil. However, the theological problem with Ford's statement is that it will not do as an account of God's causality in accomplishing redemption.

If Ford's view of divine power were taken without further qualification as an account of God's action in redemption, the result would be a Pelagian distortion of Christianity, and generic formalism. Schleiermacher's thesis in his account of the essence of Christianity is precisely that, owing to human sin and evil, God does have a monopoly on *redemptive* power, that is, man's redemption is by God's grace alone, and not the result of human effort or cooperation with grace. Accordingly, Ford's metaphysical scheme requires further qualification and modification to express this distinctively Christian theological affirmation. On the other hand, I do not pretend that Schleiermacher has an adequate theodicy, or an explicit philosophical argument about the compatibility of gracious divine causality and human freedom. His point is that, whatever metaphysical stance the theologian adopts, the theologian will not be faithful to the historical essence of Christianity unless he allows his general scheme to undergo qualification and modification by the contrast between sin and grace. Furthermore, he would ask whether it is possible to develop an "adequate" theodicy (whatever that might be) if one ignores the central features of positive Christian existence, namely, sin and grace.

Schleiermacher himself might not draw the contrast between persuasive power and efficacious power so sharply; in idealist fashion he would probably want to say that God cannot persuade without also being effective, and that God's power efficacious in redemption includes persuasion. He would insist on two central theses: (1) God does not just create the conditions for redemption, he actually effects the redemption of men, and (2) redemption does not mean an annihilation of human freedom, but the liberation and fulfillment of humanity. Consequently, Schleiermacher's apparently determinist sounding language about divine omnipotence and omniscience must be subject to further qualification. Such qualifications are to be made in light of (1) the methodological abstraction in terms of which omnipotence is set forth, (2) the two-stage or developmental concept of creation, and (3) the bipolar concept of God as coincidence of opposites. If omnipotence expresses necessity, it must be qualified by its opposite, namely, divine freedom or inwardness. Such a qualification is suggested by the locution that God's omnipotence is power directed and motivated by love. The intention here is to distinguish God's power manifest in redemption from mere blind fate. In other words, it would be a serious mistake to think of the full manifestation of God's power in redemption as merely an extension of a theological determinism. An omnipotence which is held back and restricted in the first stage of creation in order that man might develop his ethical freedom and perfection cannot be more fully exhibited in a deterministic annihilation of man. That would be a bad infinite! On such assumptions the second stage of creation would not be the ethical perfecting and completing of man, but rather his ethical undoing! John Hick offers the following proposal as a possible interpretation: "But the second state of creative process is of a different kind altogether. It cannot be performed by omnipotent power as such. For personal life is essentially free and self-directing. It cannot be perfected by divine fiat, but only through the uncompelled responses and willing cooperation of human individuals."[21] Hick correctly notes that redemption as the second stage of creation consists in the ethical-religious perfecting of free human beings. Such free beings cannot be perfected by simple divine fiat; hence the work of redemption cannot be the work of omnipotence as such. Man is not redeemed or liberated by sheer omnipotence as such, but by divine love, which motivates and directs omnipotence.

However, Hick overstates his case when he says that the second stage of creation (redemption) differs *altogether* from the first, and that redemption depends on human cooperation. The first assertion tends to undermine the unity of creation, and with it, the unity of God. It appears as if omnipotence is active only in the first stage, and love active only in the second. Not only does this sound somewhat like Marcion, it is an admission that divine love and divine omnipotence are incompatible, and that human freedom and divine causality are likewise incompatible. In contrast, Schleiermacher's point seems to be that not only are the divine causality and human freedom compatible, they are directly proportional, such that the full divine self-disclosure in redemption results in the fulfillment and completion of human freedom and ethical-religious personality. Whether Schleiermacher has "solved" the metaphysical problems accompanying such an assertion is another matter. His discussions of conversion, justification, and universal election are relevant reading.

To summarize the argument of this section: (1) Schleiermacher's concept of two-stage creation involves some revision of the traditional concept of divine omnipotence, for an imperfect creation (that is, the first stage) implies a restriction of omnipotence, that is, it is not fully employed or manifest. (2) In identifying redemption as the completion of creation which is not simply derivable or attainable from the first stage, Schleiermacher seeks to avoid a pelagian distortion of Christianity. This too had implications for the divine causality. In neither case is it the nemesis of human freedom.

Love, Power, and Immutability

Classical theism, whether Augustinian-Platonic or Thomist-Aristotelian, lacks a concept of two-stage, developmental creation. The goodness and perfection of creation must derive immediately from the goodness and unlimited power of God, otherwise God is limited, or a bungler. Furthermore, classical theism denies that creation in time implies change or temporality in God; God knows and wills timelessly what emerges temporally.[22] God is conceived as abstract eternity, and is conceived as actual apart from the world and apart from time. According to the foregoing study, Schleiermacher is revising classical theology. As we have found, the *Glaubenslehre* deals with the actual correlation between God and world as immediately apprehended in religious consciousness, and thus differs from the speculative tradition of natural theology. According to the critical experiential principle, God cannot be separated from the world, and a *Glaubenslehre* has no basis for speaking about God beyond or in separation from his actual relation to the world. God's being is not to be separated from his act. Consequently, while Schleiermacher repeatedly states that God is not in time and that change must not be ascribed to God, it is by no means obvious that these assertions are to be interpreted in the same metaphysical sense as classical theism.

Schleiermacher's actual meaning can be clarified, if at all, by attending the actual correlation between God and world constitutive of religious experience as modified and qualified by redemption. That is, the theological sense of divine eternity and immutability is to be derived from God's actual self-manifestation. The correlation between God and world takes the concrete determinate form of two-stage creation completed in redemption. This concept constitutes a departure from classical theology. For, if classical theism would allow two stage creation at all, it would argue that the two stages of creation mean only that creation itself is mutable, but not that God is mutable. In short, the temporal order of creation and its completion have no implications for divine immutability. God's aseity transcends all relation. However, Schleiermacher cannot follow classical theism here. The second stage of creation—redemption—cannot be deduced or derived from the first. Incarnation and redemption represent something new, not fully foreseeable from the old, or capable of being produced from or by the old. In short, redemption as the completion of creation cannot be known in its determinacy in advance of its actualization.

That is why a temporal career and therefore time itself are necessary for the ethicoreligious perfecting of man, even for divine grace and causality.[23] If, as Schleiermacher says, love creates fellowship and is the desire to be in and with others, then divine love cannot be fully in and with man until man is capable of receiving it. Thus man must be developed through two-stage creation so that God, who is love, can be with him. This implies that time is real, even for God, and that God therefore must be positively related to time. Schleiermacher indicates that the propositions that God is love, and that God is Father are not derivable from the abstract schematism of the Transcendent set forth in the first half of the *Glaubenslehre.* [24] They represent something new and decisive about God, not fully determinable in advance of his historical self-manifestation, or in abstraction from this.

These considerations suggest the following interpretation of Schleiermacher, which is but a theological extension of his overall argument. There are two elements in God, which are called his inwardness and his vitality. We have seen that love and omnipotence are the chief divine attributes expressive of these two elements. The next step in the argument is to identify these two elements as immutable and mutable respectively. That is, divine love is the immutable element of God, his motive in creation and redemption. This remains constant. On the other hand, omnipotence is the mutable element of God, which changes in its exercise relative to the stages of creation. Omnipotence is only partially deployed in the first stage of creation (imperfect creation) so that man might freely develop; similarly, it is fully deployed in redemption such that redemption is finally accomplished and cannot be undone or nullified. This proposal means that Schleiermacher's declarations that God is not in time and that there is no change in God should be interpreted as applying to the immutable element in God (love) but not to the mutable element (power). Love alone is completely identified with God, but divine power is subordinated to and directed by love. Read in this way, Schleiermacher anticipates Dorner's argument concerning divine immutability:

> The ethical concept of God leaves room for livingness and movement in God—yes, it may well permit change and alteration to be reflected into God (to be sure, this must always be only ethically motivated), if only one thing continues to be preserved: the ethical self-identity and immutability of God. This must remain inviolate; according to the argument above, it must also be eternal actuality in God; it cannot in God himself be at any time merely or even partly potentiality; the inner personal reality of the ethical, which is God himself, can have no intermittent existence, but only one which is constant and self-identical. God in himself can never be the mere potence of love, nor become that, nor reduce himself to it.[25]

Dorner's argument is an extension of Schleiermacher's, particularly from the latter's exclusive identification of love with God himself. It is in the ethical concept of God as love that the dogmatic stake in divine immutability lies. God's love does not change and is not subject to time; God's love is unconditional.

This proposal amounts to saying that God's immutability is to be understood not in classical terms of self-sufficient power and being, but as eternal love. This transforms the classical concept of immutability. For love is the guarantee that God's power is exercised in correlation with the world. If love is God's immutable element, this means that God does not simply actualize himself in eternal separation from the world, but rather incarnates himself in the world, and reigns over his creation in incarnation. In incarnating himself for redemption, God binds humanity permanently to himself in a person-forming union, and in this way redemption is the completion of creation. Further, if God's immutability consists in eternal love, then God is not a prisoner of his aseity as in the case of *actus purus*. For love seeks not its own, but the good of another. Love orders omnipotence, holding it back in the first stage of creation, but also deploying omnipotence relative to redemption so that God's purpose may be actualized despite sin. In short, divine immutability conceived as love relates God positively to the world and to time.

This means that for ethical purposes God takes account of the world, and thus change and alteration are reflected into God. The immutability of divine love *requires* the mutability of divine power. Love establishes an order of reciprocity between God and world, that is, an order of developmental creation in which man is perfected through redemption, in a temporal career. This is the reason why God cannot be identified with blind power or fate, and why the concept of God as *actus purus* must be revised or replaced. God cannot love the world if he cannot take it into account, and his taking account of the world and man's need of redemption cannot mean an utter objectification of them. Love requires both mutability in God and reciprocity between God and world; it requires that mundane contingency, mutability, and potentiality be reflected into God. Hence, to this extent and for these reasons, change and mutability, even potentiality must be ascribed to God. However, such reciprocity between God and world is itself theologically grounded, that is, it has its basis in God himself. Reciprocity is founded on the unconditional, absolute element in God, namely, his eternal love. This cannot change or be regarded as potential. For while God's power is contingently deployed towards man in two-stage creation (and such contingency is dependent on man's need of and relative capacity for redemption), it is not contingent that God's power is so directed. Rather, such a contingent direction of God's power toward the world and man is itself ethically necessary given the nature of God as love. This ethical necessity presupposes and is grounded in the immutability of God as love itself.

In summary, Schleiermacher's account of the essence of Christianity, including two-stage, developmental creation, requires that God be both mutable and immutable. God must be mutable in order to enter into concrete relation with man, and because sin can be overcome even by divine grace and causality only in a temporal career and time-process. On the other hand, God must be immutable. To be sure, such immutability is not the same as a divine self-actualization in abstraction from or apart from the world. The content and concrete expression of divine immutability is divine love, manifest in redemption. This love remains constant throughout all of God's modes of relatedness—as Creator, Judge and Redeemer—because it is God's very nature. Consequently, although God enters into relation to the world, this does not contradict his absoluteness, rather, it is an expression of his absoluteness. In entering such a relationship, God does not simply become one member of a two-term relation. He is not subject to relation as something imposed on him from without. God is not subjected to relation, rather he relates himself to the world because he loves it, and because love is his very nature. God thus remains God even in relation, and this divine self-identity is the focus of systematic theological interest in divine immutability.

Furthermore, both divine mutability and immutability are required in order to prevent a reductive interpretation of Christianity. If God is simply immutable as in the classical theological tradition, he cannot take account of or enter into concrete relation to the world. He cannot manifest himself fully in the world; either his absoluteness or the finitude of the world is a barrier. This view stands in tension with, if not in contradiction to, redemption, and is ultimately docetic. On the other hand, God does not cease to be God in his relation to the world. He does not simply become finite (or a finite-infinite), or enter into a simple, reciprocal correlation with the world. He does not become dependent on the world. That view would lead to an anthropomorphic concept of deity, and a pelagian distortion of Christian faith. Schleiermacher's doctrine of God, like his entire theology, seeks to occupy the middle ground between these theologically unacceptable extremes.

Conclusion

It might be objected that the above reading of Schleiermacher goes so far beyond what he actually says that it amounts to a new theological construction. I admit that I have had to tug and pull a bit to coax a concept of divine mutability out of Schleiermacher, and that this conclusion moves beyond his explicit statements. However, I think that it is not ruled out but is indeed required by his overall argument. His bipolar concept of God, which lays equal stress on divine immanence and divine transcendence, and his concept of developmental creation point in the direction that Dorner and I have outlined. This judgment implies that Schleiermacher's doctrine of God is incomplete as it stands. For example, if the divine attributes are to be taken as mutually delimiting and qualifying pairs, some discussion of that mutual qualification is called for. It is misleading and ultimately insufficient to discuss the divine attributes singly and in relative isolation from each other. Schleiermacher needs to indicate precisely what modifications and qualifications are required in each case when the attributes are paired. He hints at this, namely, divine eternity is not pure timelessness. But surely more needs to be said. Furthermore, if the initial set of divine attributes are indeterminate pending further elaboration in part two of the *Glaubenslehre,* some additional discussion of them in their state of determinate actualization seems required. Schleiermacher does this only with omniscience and wisdom. I have tried to suggest the way in which his argument can and should be extended in respect to the question of divine immutability. Schleiermacher's apparently uncompromising language about God and time, the exclusion of potentiality, and so forth, requires further qualification in light of his actual argument. But Dorner and I have been led to make such qualifications by following and taking seriously Schleiermacher's own statements concerning the full, concrete, determinate actuality of the doctrine of God. This is not so much a going beyond Schleiermacher as an extension and further explication of his own argument. Obviously, much work remains to be done.

NOTES

1. *Gl,* § 50.4.

2. Friedrich Schleiermacher, *Sendschreiben an Luecke,* ed. Hermann Mulert (Giessen: Toepelmann, 1908).

3. *Gl,* 1st ed., § 39. Schleiermacher explains further that the initial description of the feeling of utter dependence is "a description not of an actual, determinate consciousness, but only the inner foundations of such." Therefore, "no one should imagine that there could be actual experiences in which Christ is absent." Consequently, "there must be an actual reference to Christ throughout Christian experience." Cf. *Gl,* 2nd ed., § 62.3.

4. *Gl,* § 167.2.

5. Ludwig Feuerbach, *The Essence of Christianity,* trans. George Eliot (New York: Harper & Row, 1957), pp. 3–14.

6. *Gl,* 1st ed., § 79; see also Anselm, *Proslogion,* chaps. 14–16, trans. M.J. Charlesworth (Oxford: Clarendon Press, 1965). Schleiermacher defends only a relative, not an absolute identity between man and God. "The union between our sensibly stimulated being and the co-posited being of God given in feeling is not absolute, but only relative. This relative unity means that disunion is also always present" (n. "c"). Schleiermacher is saying that although there is *epistemic identity* between man and God, that is, man does know God, there is no *ontological identity.* Feuerbach's transformative method of inverting subject and predicate of theological predication presupposes the latter ontological identity between divine and human. Schleiermacher's claim of only relative identity, and his explanation that disunion is present within identity, amounts to a rejection of Hegelian absolute identity, and with it, Feuerbach's reductive inversion.

7. *Gl,* § 19, Postscript.

8. Thomas Aquinas, *Summa Theologiae,* trans. The Fathers of the English Dominican Province (New York: Benziger Brothers Inc., 1947), vol. 1, § 13.2; 3.3.

9. *Gl,* § 50.3.

10. *Gl,* § 167.2.

11. Robert Neville (*God the Creator: On the Transcendence and Presence of God* [Chicago: University of Chicago Press, 1968], p. 148) has nicely formulated the distinction between methodological dialectic and constitutive dialectic: "Constitutive dialectic, in contrast to methodological dialectic, can be characterized generally by two points. First, it is connected with reality in a way that methodological dialectic is not. As denoting a method of philosophical inquiry, the latter is relatively neutral with respect to the alternative conclusions to which it is prejudicially committed by its very form. Of course, no method is completely externally related to its conclusions about the subject matter . . . But insofar as it is a method and not identical with the conclusions themselves, methodological dialectic is compatible in form with many possible conceptions of its subject matter. Constitutive dialectic, however, refers to a dialectical character in the subject matter of the inquiry, and hence is identical with the conclusions of the inquiry when those conclusions are adequate to the subject matter . . . To speak of constitutive dialectic is to speak both of the dialectical structure of reality and of the dialectical structure of our philosophy that exhibits reality's structure. Second, constitutive dialectic is characterized by the shift in the significance of its terms from one level to another. The significance of subject matter on one level forces us to a new level where the significance is different."

Neville argues correctly that Tillich does not develop a justifying constitutive dialectic to support his methodological assertion that all language about God is symbolic. I am claiming that Schleiermacher does present a justifying constitutive dialectic in his move from the first to the second and third forms of proposition. His account of God as love, both as an immediate faith-utterance, and as the identity between love and God which overcomes the abstract separation between divine essence and divine attributes, is a recapitulation of the constitutive dialectic of classical Christian theology. This recapitulation culminates in the doctrine that God is *homoousios* with his self-manifestation in incarnation and redemption. In short, part 2 of the *Glaubenslehre* is the constitutive dialectic of reality which justifies and makes explicit the formal-abstract methodological dialectic of part 1.

12. I believe this is a fair statement about Tillich's argument in his *Systematic Theology,* vols. 1, 2; however, cf. his remarks about reopening the trinitarian problem in vol. 3 (Chicago: University of Chicago Press, 1963), pp. 291 ff.

13. Neville, *God the Creator,* p. 167. Neville writes: "We know the indeterminateness, the absolute transcendence, the independence, the aseity, of God in himself only insofar as it gets incarnated in the created determination of being creator." This is very close to Schleiermacher's point that we know God's transcendence only on the basis of God's immanence. Schleiermacher would add to Neville's statement the idea that we grasp fully the "created determinations of God's being creator" only in and through the Incarnation and through redemption. The basis of constitutive dialectic lies not merely in formal ontology, but in the *given* with which theology deals.

14. *G1,* § 167.

15. Emil L. Fackenheim's study of the *Religious Dimension in Hegel's Thought* (Indiana: Indiana University Press, 1967) makes it clear that Hegel resembles Schleiermacher in seeing divine love as the central, unifying affirmation of Christian faith concerning God, that which unites God's inwardness with his self-manifestation and self-expression. Fackenheim shows that in Hegel's understanding of Christianity, love is the union between the immanent ontological trinity and the economic trinity of revelation: God who needs nothing, nevertheless freely incarnates himself for the salvation of man. Schleiermacher would agree with this statement. The critical issue, however, is whether Hegel's speculative comprehension and transfiguration of this *Grundtatsache* of Christian faith is compatible with it, much less a preservation of its meaning. Fackenheim states the substantive dilemma: For Christian faith divine love is a free gift to man, which God does not need or otherwise "have" to give. For speculative philosophy, divine love is an act of self-love, needed by a divinity incomplete without it (p. 204). Fackenheim argues that divine love is accepted by Hegelian philosophy as fact, a given, and that it remains unchanged in one respect by its philosophical-speculative transfiguration: "For philosophic thought divine Love remains such a gift, even though it is a divine self-othering" (p. 205). I am unable to see any justification for this claim. Charles Taylor likewise parts company with Fackenheim on this issue (*Hegel,* p. 494). Hegel's philosophical-speculative transfiguration of Christian faith involves a translation of it fully into the universal terms of his dialectical ontology, where it serves as the principle of synthesis and mediation. As a formal-ontological principle, love is the principle of divine self-othering in general, that is, the world as such becomes the son of God. Taylor is surely correct in saying that "Hegel's philosophy is an extraordinary transposition which "saves the phenomena" [that is, the dogmas] of Christianity, while abandoning its essence" (ibid.).

16. See Carl E. Krieg, "Schleiermacher: On the Divine Nature," *Religion in Life* 42 (Winter 1973), n. 4.; Van A. Harvey, "A Word in Defense of Schleiermacher's Theological Method," *Journal of Religion* 42 (July 1962), no. 3; Gerhard Spiegler, *The Eternal Covenant* (New York: Harper & Row, 1962); Nelson Pike, *God and Timelessness* (New York: Schocken, 1970).

17. *G1,* § 72.

18. Robert F. Brown, "On the Necessary Imperfection of Creation: Irenaeus' Adversus Haereses IV. 38," *Scottish Journal of Theology* 28 (1975), no. 1.

19. *G1,* § 80.3.

20. Lewis S. Ford, "Divine Persuasion and the Triumph of Good," *Process Philosophy and Christian Thought,* Delwin Brown et al., eds. (New York: Bobbs Merrill, 1971). See also John

B. Cobb, Jr., *God and the World* (Philadelphia: Westminster Press, 1969), chap 4.; and Charles Hartshorne, "The Dipolar Concept of Deity," *Review of Metaphysics* 22(1967): 273 ff.

21. John Hick, *Evil and the God of Love* (New York: Harper & Row, 1966), p. 291.

22. See Aquinas *Summa Theologiae* 1.14.15.

23. *Gl,* § 80.3.

24. *Gl,* 1st ed., § 39; cited in Schleiermacher, *Der Christliche Glaube,* ed. Martin Redeker (Berlin: Walter de Gruyter & Co., 1960), § 166–67. It is true that Schleiermacher speaks of the unity of creation and redemption as a single divine decree (*Gl,* § 94.3; 88.4; 164.3). Moreover, he speaks of the divine decree ordering the development of the human race by means of redemption in terms reminiscent of preestablished harmony (*Gl,* § 61.4). These statements appear to take Schleiermacher in the direction of orthodox classical theism. However, this interpretation is not free from problems. Schleiermacher offers an infralapsarian interpretation of the decree of election: "We have the certainty that from the beginning the whole disposition of nature *would have been different had it not been* that, after sin, redemption through Christ was determined for the human race" (*Gl,* § 164.1). Moreover, Schleiermacher's account of election involves the claim that free human actions "contribute something to the further course of the divine government of the world" (*Gl,* § 120.1). These passages are more consistent with Schleiermacher's developmental concept of creation. However, it should be noted that Schleiermacher never integrated the reformation concept of divine decrees into his doctrine of God; he tells us that he has provided no systematic place or schematism for the divine decrees (*Gl,* 1st ed., § 111.1). This is not a serious deficiency, since he intends to develop the entire doctrine of God—attributes, decrees, and trinity—on the basis of a description of the correlation between God and world given in immediate self-consciousness. And since the latter embraces and includes the results effected by divine grace in the world, the difference between the divine decrees and divine attributes is merely a difference of the mode and form of expression, not a difference of actual content (*Gl,* 1st ed., § 111.1). Therefore, Schleiermacher's mention of divine decrees need not be interpreted as evidence that he accepts the traditional concept of God as abstract eternity. The actual content of the divine decrees is developed from the actual correlation between God and world constitutive of religious experience.

25. Isaac August Dorner, "On the Proper Version of the Dogmatic Concept of the Immutability of God, with Special Reference to the Interrelation between God's Transhistorical and Historical Life," *God and Incarnation in Mid-Nineteenth Century German Theology,* trans. Claude Welch (New York: Oxford University Press, 1965), pp. 160-61.

Index

Actuality, 12; not deducible from abstract essence, 12, 78-80, 114, 122, 130

Anselm, 5, 24, 39-40, 49-50, 58, 64, 165-66, 169, 170

Apprehension: and belief, 48-52; as notional, 42-43; as real, 42-43

Aquinas, Thomas, 168, 188, 190

Arius, 150

Athanasius, 150, 153, 154, 158

Attributes of God: and divine essence, 80-82, 128, 168-70; coherence, 175-76; determinate, 117-23, 123-35; eternity. *See* Eternity of God; expressed in grace-consciousness, 123-35; expressed in sin-consciousness, 117-23; holiness. *See* Holiness of God; indeterminate (generic-abstract), 79-80, 88-98, 175-76; justice. *See* Justice of God; love. *See* Love (God's); omnipotence. *See* Omnipotence of God; omnipresence. *See* Omnipresence of God; omniscience. *See* Omniscience of God; pairing of, 70, 85-86, 123-24;

presuppose turning-towards-God, 117-19; symbolic, 170-74; wisdom. *See* Wisdom of God

Augustine, 38, 48, 58, 167

Augustinian tradition, 57-59, 169; Schleiermacher's criticism of, 58-60

Barth, Karl, vii-ix, 17, 92-94, 98, 100, 112, 116, 135, 137, 171

Beck, Lewis W., 14, 18, 53, 72

Beisser, Friedrich, 16

Belief: and feeling, 28, 30; and life-world, 30-32; and knowledge, 30, 42-43, 48-52; as real apprehension, 48-51; transcendental foundation of knowledge, 28-30

Berger, Gaston, 17

Bethune-Baker, J.F., 146, 158

Boettner, Loraine, 116

Bracketing, method of, 7-12, 77-80, 99, 117-19, 178

Brown, Robert F., 189

Cassirer, Ernst, 71, 72

Classical Theology, ix, 15, 59, 66, 68, 93-94, 124, 161, 170, 175, 184

Cobb, John B., Jr., 190